Entrepreneurship in the Informal Sector

How many business start-ups conduct some or all of their trade 'off the books'? And how many enterprises continue to do some of their work off the books once they are more established? What should be done about them? Should governments adopt ever more punitive measures to eradicate them? Or should we recognise this hidden enterprise culture and attempt to harness it? If so, how can this be done? What measures can be taken to ensure that businesses start up in a proper manner? And what can be done to help those enterprises and entrepreneurs currently working off the books to legitimise their businesses?

The aim of this book is to advance a new way of answering these questions. Drawing inspiration from institutional theory, informal sector entrepreneurship is explained as resulting from the asymmetry between the codified laws and regulations of a society's formal institutions and the norms, values and beliefs that comprise a society's informal institutions. The argument is that if the norms, values and beliefs of entrepreneurs (i.e., their individual morality) were wholly aligned with the codified laws and regulations (i.e., state morality), there would be no informal sector entrepreneurship. However, because the individual morality of entrepreneurs differs from state morality, for example, due to their lack of trust in government and the rule of law, the result is the prevalence of informal sector entrepreneurship.

The greater the degree of institutional asymmetry, the higher is the propensity to engage in informal sector entrepreneurship. This book provides evidence to show that this is the case both at the individual and country level and then discusses how this can be overcome.

Colin C. Williams is Professor of Public Policy at Sheffield University Management School, UK.

Routledge Studies in Entrepreneurship
Edited by Susan Marlow and Janine Swail
University of Nottingham, UK

This series extends the meaning and scope of entrepreneurship by capturing new research and enquiry on economic, social, cultural and personal value creation. Entrepreneurship as value creation represents the endeavours of innovative people and organisations in creative environments that open up opportunities for developing new products, new services, new firms and new forms of policy making in different environments seeking sustainable economic growth and social development. In setting this objective the series includes books which cover a diverse range of conceptual, empirical and scholarly topics that both inform the field and push the boundaries of entrepreneurship.

Entrepreneurship in the Informal Sector

An Institutional Perspective

Colin C. Williams

Routledge
Taylor & Francis Group

LONDON AND NEW YORK

First published 2018
by Routledge

2 Park Square, Milton Park, Abingdon, Oxfordshire OX14 4RN
52 Vanderbilt Avenue, New York, NY 10017

Routledge is an imprint of the Taylor & Francis Group, an informa business

First issued in paperback 2019

Library of Congress Cataloging-in-Publication Data
A catalog record for this book has been requested

ISBN: 978-1-138-92556-4 (hbk)
ISBN: 978-0-367-87372-1 (pbk)

Typeset in Sabon
by Apex CoVantage, LLC

Contents

Tables and Figures

Tables

Figures

Acknowledgements

Writing a book is a time-consuming endeavour. As such, I owe a debt of gratitude to my employer, the University of Sheffield, for making the time available to do so. Without such support, this book would not have been possible. I am also grateful for the financial support provided by the European Commission's Framework 7 Industry-Academia Partnerships Programme (IAPP) grant no. 611259, which released further time and resources to enable this book to be written.

I am also indebted to numerous individuals who have freely given their time in helping me formulate my ideas on entrepreneurship and the informal economy over the years. In this regard and in alphabetical order, I would like to express my thanks to Kwame Adom, Marijana Baric, Slavko Bezeredi, Pauline Dibben, Rositsa Dzhekova, Josip Franic, Anjula Gurtoo, Jason Heyes, Ioana (Alexandra) Horodnic, Abbi Kedir, Besnik Krasniki, Usman Ladan, Mark Lansky, Enrico Marcelli, Alvaro Martinez-Perez, Ged McElwee, Lyubo Mishkov, Sara Nadin, Olga Onoshchenko, Marina Polak, Monder Ram, Peter Rodgers, John Round, Abdoulie Sallah, Friedrich Schneider, Muhammad Shehryar Shahid, Rob Smith, Ruslan Stefanov, Tim Vorley, Richard White, Nick Williams, Jan Windebank, Lorraine Warren and Youssef. All have collaborated with me in recent years and helped formulate my ideas. I am particularly indebted in relation to this book to Alvaro Martinez-Perez and Abbi Kedir for their assistance with the World Bank Enterprise Survey (WBES). My sincere apologies to anybody I have forgotten. As always, however, the usual disclaimers apply.

1 Introduction

Introduction

What share of all enterprises start up on an unregistered basis, and how many continue to operate in the informal sector once they become more established? Does the tendency of entrepreneurs to start up and operate in the informal sector vary across countries? If so, how can one explain these variations? What, moreover, should be done to tackle entrepreneurship in the informal sector? Should governments adopt ever more punitive measures to eradicate such entrepreneurship? Should a laissez-faire approach be adopted? Or should governments recognise that this is a hidden enterprise culture and seek to facilitate its formalisation? If so, what policy approaches are required? Are these entrepreneurs purely rational economic actors whose behaviour can be changed by increasing the costs and reducing the benefits of operating in the informal sector and by reducing the costs and increasing the benefits of operating in the formal sector? Or should these entrepreneurs be seen as social actors whose norms, values and beliefs are not aligned with the rules of formal institutions? If they are social actors, is it simply a case of changing these informal entrepreneurs' attitudes towards compliance? Or do the formal institutions also need to change, and if so, how?

To answer these questions, this book advances an understanding of entrepreneurship in the informal sector based on institutional theory. Informal sector entrepreneurship is here explained to result from formal institutional failures and imperfections that lead to an asymmetry between the formal institutions (i.e., the codified laws and regulations) of a society and the informal institutions (i.e., the socially shared norms, values and beliefs of entrepreneurs and citizens). The consequent argument is that if the norms, values and beliefs of entrepreneurs (i.e., entrepreneurial morale) were wholly aligned with the codified laws and regulations (i.e., state morale), there would be no informal sector entrepreneurship. However, because the individual morale of entrepreneurs differs from state morale, for example, due to their lack of trust in government and the rule of law, the result is the prevalence of informal sector entrepreneurship. Entrepreneurship in the informal sector, therefore, is endeavour that is 'illegitimate' in terms of the formal written rules but acceptable in terms of the socially shared norms, values and beliefs of a society's entrepreneurs and its citizens. The result is that the greater the degree of asymmetry between the formal and informal institutions, the higher is the propensity to engage in informal entrepreneurship. This asymmetry arises, moreover, due to formal institutional failures and imperfections. The intention in this book is to identify these formal institutional failures and imperfections that produce this institutional asymmetry and result in the prevalence of informal entrepreneurship.

This theorisation of informal entrepreneurship also has significant and important implications for how such endeavour is tackled. Conventionally, the tendency has been to treat informal entrepreneurs as rational economic actors whose behaviour can be changed by increasing the costs and reducing the benefits of operating in the informal sector and by reducing the costs and increasing the benefits of operating in the formal sector. However, the argument in this book is that entrepreneurs are more social actors whose norms, values and beliefs are not aligned with the rules of formal institutions. The implication is that a shift is required away from purely using hard direct controls that seek to change the costs and benefits confronting entrepreneurs. Instead, it requires more emphasis to be given to developing a high-trust, high-commitment culture by resolving the formal institutional failures that lead to an asymmetry of the formal and informal institutions in societies. On the one hand, this requires the introduction of a raft of policy measures to not only dissuade entrepreneurs from operating in the informal sector but also to incentivise and encourage them to operate in the formal sector by introducing measures that directly increase the costs and reduce the benefits of informality while reducing the costs and increasing the benefits of operating in the formal sector. On the other hand, however, it also requires measures that address the formal institutional failures at the macro-level to reduce the asymmetry between formal and informal institutions. This requires not only alterations in the informal institutions, using measures such as tax education, awareness-raising campaigns and normative appeals but also, and importantly, changes in formal institutions to improve trust in government by developing firstly, greater procedural justice, procedural fairness and redistributive justice and, secondly, changes on a country level in the structural conditions which are associated with greater institutional asymmetry (e.g., public sector corruption, the regulatory burden, low levels of state intervention in the economy and welfare provision).

In this introductory chapter therefore, firstly, a definition of what is here meant by entrepreneurship in the informal sector is provided to understand the scope of the subject matter of this book, secondly, the rationales for studying entrepreneurship in the informal sector are briefly introduced, and third and finally, an outline is provided of the structure and arguments of this book.

Defining Entrepreneurship in the Informal Sector

At the outset of this book, it is necessary to be clear about what is being discussed. After all, some new to the topic of entrepreneurship in the informal sector might think that this book is seeking to understand and tackle drug dealers, pimps and those selling stolen or counterfeit goods on market stalls. To be clear at the outset, even if such endeavour can be interpreted as entrepreneurial (see Friman, 2004; VanderBeken, 2004; Vanduyne, 1993), this type of criminal entrepreneurial activity is not the subject of this book. To understand what is meant by entrepreneurship in the informal sector, firstly, it is necessary to define the informal sector and, secondly, what is here meant by entrepreneurship in the informal sector.

Defining the Informal Sector

How to define the informal sector and distinguish it from the formal sector has been an ongoing debate ever since Hart (1973) first introduced the concept in his study of Ghana nearly half a century ago. Reviewing the vast literature produced over these five decades, nearly all definitions attempt to delineate what is absent from, or insufficient about, the informal sector relative to the formal sector. However, what precisely is denoted as missing or lacking varies according to whether scholars adopt an enterprise-, jobs- or activity-centred definition.

Starting with the enterprise-centred definition, in 1993 at the Fifteenth International Conference of Labour Statisticians (15th ICLS), an attempt was made to solve the ambiguities in meaning that had emerged in the preceding two decades. This defined employment in the informal sector as comprising 'all jobs in informal sector enterprises, or all persons who, during a given reference period, were employed in at least one informal sector enterprise, irrespective of their status of employment and whether it was their main or a secondary job' (Hussmanns, 2005: 3). Informal sector enterprises in this definition were defined as small or unregistered, private, unincorporated enterprises (Hussmanns, 2005). Analysing the component parts of this definition, small refers in this definition to when the numbers employed are below a specific threshold, determined according to national circumstances. An unregistered enterprise in this ICLS definition, furthermore, is one that is not registered under specific forms of national-level legislation (e.g., factories' or commercial acts, tax or social security laws or professional groups' regulatory acts). A private, unincorporated enterprise, meanwhile, is defined by the 15th ICLS as an enterprise owned by an individual or household that is not constituted as a separate legal entity independent of its owner and for which no complete accounts are available that would permit a financial separation of the production activities of the enterprise from the other activities of its owner (Hussmanns, 2005; ILO, 2012, 2013).

One common problem with this enterprise-centred definition was that sometimes all small enterprises were mistakenly classified as informal enterprises. Another major problem was that this enterprise-centred definition omitted to consider informal employment in formal enterprises. In 2003, therefore, the 17th ICLS complemented this enterprise-centred definition with a job-focused definition which enabled the inclusion of informal employment both within and outside of informal enterprises. As the ILO (2012: 12) states, 'informal employment' includes all jobs included in the enterprise-centred definition of 'employment in the informal sector', except those classified as formal jobs in informal sector enterprises, and 'refers to those jobs that generally lack basic social or legal protections or employment benefits and may be found in the formal sector, informal sector or households'.

This job-centred definition therefore recognised the existence of informal jobs in both informal and formal production units and therefore that formal enterprises sometimes employ workers informally, avoiding payment of social security contributions, severance payments and other payments in case of dismissal (Hussmanns, 2005). As such, this jobs-centred definition includes not only employers and own-account workers who are self-employed in their own informal sector enterprises, and contributing family workers and members of informal producers' cooperatives, but also employees whose employment relationship is, in law or in practice, not subject to national labour legislation, income taxation, social protection or entitlement to certain employment benefits, such as severance pay, notice of dismissal and annual paid leave or sick leave (Hussmanns, 2005; ILO, 2012, 2013; Williams and Lansky, 2013).

Although these enterprise- and jobs-centred definitions have tended to dominate how the informal sector has been defined when studying the developing world, they have not dominated scholarship of the informal sector in developed countries and post-socialist transition economies. In the developed and post-socialist worlds, an activity-centred definition of the informal sector has been more commonly used (European Commission, 1998, 2007; OECD, 2012; Williams and Gurtoo, 2013; Williams and Windebank, 1998). The most frequent activity-centred definition adopted is that published in 2002 by the Organisation of Economic Co-operation and Development (OECD), International Monetary Fund (IMF), International Labour Organisation (ILO) and CIS STAT (Interstate Statistical Committee of the Commonwealth of Independent States) as a supplement to the System of National Accounts (SNA) 1993. This defines what it calls 'underground production' (here termed the 'informal sector') as

> all legal production activities that are deliberately concealed from public
> authorities . . . to avoid payment of income, value added or other taxes;
> to avoid payment of social security contributions; to avoid having to

meet certain legal standards such as minimum wages, maximum hours, safety or health standards, etc.

(OECD, 2002: 139)

In this activity-based definition, therefore, what is absent or insufficient about the informal sector is that the activity is not declared to, hidden from or unregistered with the authorities for tax, social security and/or labour law purposes when it should be declared (Williams and Windebank, 1998). If the economic activity possesses additional absences or insufficiencies, it is not defined as part of the informal sector. If the good and/or service which is being traded is illegal (e.g., drug trafficking or selling stolen or counterfeit goods), then this activity is separately defined as part of the wider 'criminal' economy, while if the activity is unpaid, it is excluded and seen as part of the unpaid subsistence economy. There are, nevertheless, some blurred boundaries, such as when activities are reimbursed in kind using reciprocal labour and/or gifts are given instead of money. Usually, however, only paid activities are included (Williams, 2006).

Throughout this book, such an activity-based definition is adopted. The informal sector generally refers to activity that is legal in all respects other than it is not declared to, hidden from or unregistered with the authorities for tax, social security and/or labour law purposes when it should be declared. However, this does not mean that such activity is unregulated. That is a common mistake. As Castells and Portes (1989: 15) erroneously assert, the informal sector is 'a specific form of income generating production . . . unregulated by the institutions of society in a legal and social environment in which similar activities are regulated'. Although they valuably view the informal sector through the lens of the institutions of society, they do not distinguish between the 'legal' (formal) and 'social' (informal) institutions in a society. The result is that they fail to recognise, firstly, that the informal sector, even if unregulated by formal institutions, is regulated by the rules of informal institutions and, secondly, that the endeavour in the informal sector is considered 'legitimate' from the viewpoint of informal institutions even if deemed 'illegal' from the standpoint of the laws and regulations of the formal institutions (Siqueira *et al.*, 2016; Webb *et al.*, 2009).

In consequence, minor additions are required to this activity-based definition to bring clarity to whether the informal sector is regulated or not as well as whether the activity is paid or not. The activity-based definition therefore adopted in this book is that the informal sector is socially legitimate paid activity that is legal in all respects other than that it is not declared to, hidden from or unregistered with the authorities for tax, social security and/or labour law purposes when it should be declared. In consequence, if it is illegal in other respects and/or deemed socially illegitimate, then the activity is not part of the informal sector but rather part of the criminal economy (e.g., forced labour, selling stolen goods or trafficking illegal drugs) which is both illegal from the viewpoint of formal institutions and illegitimate from the viewpoint of informal institutions.

Defining Entrepreneurship

How to define entrepreneurship has for a long time proven a problematical issue (Brockhaus and Horowitz, 1986; Cole, 1969; Hull *et al.*, 1980; Shaver and Scott, 1991), and there is today still no consensus. However, the fact that no consensus has been achieved on how to define entrepreneurship is itself revealing. As Jones and Spicer (2005) argue, the inability of entrepreneurship scholars to achieve a common definition reveals that entrepreneurship as a term is not so much seeking to describe a lived practice but rather is seeking to portray an ideal against which individuals can judge themselves and be judged. This recognition that entrepreneurship is more an object of desire or ideal type, rather than a descriptive subject, is important. Although there is no consensus on how to define entrepreneurship as a lived practice, there is agreement that it is an object of desire or ideal type and should be depicted in a positive and virtuous manner. This is exemplified in portrayals of entrepreneurs as 'economic heroes' (Cannon, 1991) or even 'super heroes' (Burns, 2001). As Burns (2001) asserts, they are 'the stuff of "legends" . . . held in high esteem and held up as role models to be emulated'.

Indeed, this positive ideal type representation of entrepreneurship is apparent across all theoretical approaches towards entrepreneurship (see Cunningham and Lischeron, 1991). It is most explicit in the 'great person' school of entrepreneurship that portrays entrepreneurs as born (rather than made) and asserts that they possess a 'sixth sense' along with energy, vigour, self-esteem, persistence and intuition and contrasts them with mere 'mortals' who 'lack what it takes'. It is also apparent across all of the socially constructed views of entrepreneurship of the classical, leadership, management or intrapreneurship approaches, every one of which depicts the entrepreneur as a positive heroic figurehead who possesses virtuous attributes that 'lesser mortals' do not (Williams and Gurtoo, 2013; Williams and Nadin, 2013a). As Jones and Spicer (2005) therefore conclude, this positive representation across all schools of entrepreneurship thus results in the construction of an unattainable object of desire; this constructed a gap between us as subjects, and this ideal type drives the desire to become an enterprising subject.

The inevitable outcome of this ideal type depiction of entrepreneurship is that those forms of entrepreneurship that do not fully and clearly align with this positive virtuous heroic ideal type are either placed outside the boundaries of entrepreneurship, depicted as temporary or ignored, portrayed as irrelevant or simply consigned to the margins, portraying them as not 'mainstream' entrepreneurship. Indeed it is precisely due to the dominance of this positive ideal type depiction of entrepreneurship as an object of desire, rather than as a lived practice, that entrepreneurship scholars have paid little attention to entrepreneurship in the informal sector. As Williams and

Nadin (2013a) assert, the entrepreneur is popularly portrayed as a heroic figurehead of capitalist society and, as such, somebody who is engaged in for-profit entrepreneurship in the formal market economy. Any form of entrepreneurship that lies beyond this type of entrepreneurship is portrayed as lacking, irrelevant, temporary or not mainstream entrepreneurship. This includes not only all forms of social entrepreneurship (Austin *et al.*, 2006; Defourny and Nyssens, 2010) but also endeavour that is criminal entrepreneurship (McElwee *et al.*, 2011) and informal sector entrepreneurship.

To adopt a definition of entrepreneurship that includes entrepreneurship in the informal sector, there is therefore a need to move beyond such ideal type depictions of entrepreneurship as an object of desire and towards a more lived practice depiction of entrepreneurship. Here, in consequence, the working definition of an entrepreneur adopted is that most commonly used when seeking to delineate the lived practice of entrepreneurship, such as in the Global Entrepreneurship Monitor (GEM). This defines somebody as an entrepreneur if he or she is actively involved in starting a business or the owner/manager of a business less than 36 months old (Harding *et al.*, 2005; Reynolds *et al.*, 2002). This definition, although excluding aspects sometimes included (e.g., intrapreneurship), is fit for the purpose for which it is here intended in this book, namely studying entrepreneurs in the informal sector.

Defining Entrepreneurship in the Informal Sector

Combining these definitions of the informal sector and entrepreneurship, informal sector entrepreneurship is defined as involving somebody actively engaged in starting a business or is the owner/manager of a business that is less than 36 months old who participates in socially legitimate, paid activity that is legal in all respects other than that it is not declared to, hidden from or unregistered with the authorities for tax, social security and/ or labour law purposes when it should be declared. Therefore, the only illegitimate feature of the activity of these entrepreneurs is that some or all of their paid activities are not declared to the authorities when they should be declared. Informal entrepreneurship in consequence does not include activities that cannot be formally registered because they are criminal in nature, such as drug trafficking, gunrunning, human smuggling or protection rackets (Shavell, 2002). Those entrepreneurs are part of the broader criminal economy. It also excludes unpaid activities that are undertaken by individuals, such as agricultural subsistence work. This is part of the unpaid or subsistence economy.

This definition is close to previous definitions of entrepreneurship in the informal sector but differs in some important respects. For example, Cross (2000) adopts a very similar definition, viewing informal entrepreneurship as the production and exchange of legal goods and services that involves the lack of appropriate business permits, violation of zoning codes, failure to report tax liability, non-compliance with labour regulations governing contracts and work conditions and/or the lack of legal guarantees in relations with suppliers and clients. The constant element in this definition is the element of non-compliance with the regulatory provisions governing businesses. This definition, therefore, focuses upon non-compliance with legal, contractual and regulatory provision but ignores its enterprise features as well as its legitimacy in the eyes of informal institutions. The definition adopted in this book and already discussed, in consequence, identifies that this production and exchange of legal goods and services is conducted by an entrepreneur (i.e., somebody actively engaged in starting a business or is the owner/manager of a business that is less than 36 months old), is often considered socially legitimate activity from the viewpoint of informal institutions (even if it is deemed illegal by formal institutions) and adopts more all-encompassing terminology regarding the tax, social security and/ or labour law violations involved.

A further definition of informal entrepreneurship in the previous literature is by Portes *et al.* (1986: 728), who claim that it is

> the sum total of income generating activities outside modern contractual relationships of production (and distribution) which encompasses direct subsistence production, petty commodity production and trade by self-employed individuals for the market and small unregulated enterprises subcontracted by the larger modern ones.

The central elements of this definition are subsistence and petty commodity production, trade by the self-employed and the subcontracting of small, unregulated enterprises. This again pays little attention to defining entrepreneurship, the social legitimacy aspect of such entrepreneurial endeavour and defining precisely the ways in which such entrepreneurial endeavour violates formal institutional regulatory conditions.

Another definition of the informal entrepreneur is that used by Autio and Fu (2015: 67), who assert, 'We define an informal entrepreneur as an individual actively engaged in managing a new venture that sells legitimate goods and services and is not registered with official authorities.' This importantly defines an entrepreneur and also that such entrepreneurs only sell legitimate goods and services to differentiate it from the criminal economy, but nevertheless, they again do not mention the social legitimacy aspect of such endeavour or the precise other ways in which such endeavour violates regulatory conditions beyond the fact that the venture is not registered. In other words, this definition narrowly focuses upon solely unregistered enterprises (i.e., an enterprise-centred definition) when considering what constitutes informal entrepreneurship rather than the full range of informal economic activities which can be conducted by unregistered or registered enterprises (i.e., an activity-centred definition). For example, in this definition, an entrepreneur who operates a registered enterprise but conducts a portion of the trade in the informal sector is not considered to be engaged in entrepreneur-ship in the informal sector.

In sum, and to include various aspects of what constitutes informal entre-preneurship that are missing in other definitions, this book defines informal entrepreneurship as involving somebody actively engaged in starting a busi-ness or is the owner/manager of a business that is less than 36 months old who participates in socially legitimate paid activity that is legal is all respects other than that it is not declared to, hidden from or unregistered with the authorities for tax, social security and/or labour law purposes when it should be declared (see Polese *et al.*, 2017; Sauka *et al.*, 2016; Williams and Nadin, 2013b, 2014). Having outlined how informal entrepreneurship is defined in this book, the next section turns towards understanding why it is important to study.

Rationales for Studying Informal Entrepreneurship

Throughout the twentieth century, the dominant belief was that entrepre-neurship in the informal sector was a minor form of activity which per-sisted only in a few 'backward' enclaves in the global economy and that it was gradually disappearing with the natural and inevitable occurrence of modernisation and economic development. The result was that as a 'left-over' or 'residue' of a pre-modern mode of production, such endeavour was unimportant and considered not worthy of investigation. In consequence, enterprises operating in the formal sector were seen as the 'mainstream' and the appropriate focus of enquiry, and entrepreneurship and enterprise in the informal sector was viewed as some insignificant 'backwater' of little concern.

Over the past few decades, however, it has been recognised that this is a large and persistent sphere. Across the world, it is now recognised that some 60 per cent of the global workforce have their main employment in the informal sector (Jütting and Laiglesia, 2009), 70 per cent of whom are self-employed (ILO, 2013). Extrapolating from this, this means that 42 per cent of the global workforce appears to be engaged in self-employment in the informal sector as their main job. Turning away from jobs to enterprises, although there is a lack of robust comprehensive data on what proportion of all businesses operate in the informal sector, a conservative lower-bound estimate is that some two-thirds of all enterprises are unregistered at start-up (Autio and Fu, 2015), that at least half of all enterprises globally are operating on an unregistered basis (Acs *et al.*, 2013). Such a figure on unreg-istered enterprises as a proportion of all enterprises globally, moreover, does not include all informal entrepreneurship. It does not include the large but so far uncalculated proportion of all registered enterprises globally that con-duct some of their transactions in the informal sector.

Given that the majority of enterprises start up unregistered and that the majority of enterprises globally are either unregistered or registered but conducting a portion of their transactions in the informal sector, this realm of entrepreneurial endeavour is not some marginal enclave. Instead, quite the opposite is the case. On a global level, it is enterprises operating wholly or partially in the informal sector that are the 'mainstream' and omnipresent across the world. It is fully legitimate enterprises that are the minority of enterprises globally. Contrary to common assumption which adopts an ideal type depiction of entrepreneurs and entrepreneurship as playing by the rulebook, therefore, the lived practice of entrepreneurship appears to be somewhat different.

Yet despite the fact that fully formal registered enterprises are a minority of all enterprises globally, little attention has been paid to those enterprises that lie beyond this ideal type depiction and which do not play by the formal rules. This, however, is starting to change. Building upon a small tributary of earlier entrepreneurship scholarship that drew attention to how entrepreneurs do not always play by the rulebook (Bhide and Stevenson, 1990; Kets de Vries, 1977, 1985), this emergent literature on entrepreneurship and enterprise that is not fully legitimate has begun to expand in the past few decades. Studies have begun to reveal how many entrepreneurs participate in criminal activities (Armstrong, 2005; Bruns *et al.*, 2011; De Jong *et al.*, 2012; Fournier, 1998; Gottschalk, 2010; Gottschalk and Smith, 2011; Karjanen, 2011; McElwee, 2009a,b; McElwee *et al.*, 2011; Rehn and Taalas, 2004; Sköld and Rehn, 2007; Smith and McElwee, 2013) and also how many engaged in criminal activities possess entrepreneurial traits and attributes (Bucur *et al.*, 2012; Gottschalk, 2010; Gottschalk and Smith, 2011), including drug dealers (Bouchard and Dion, 2009; Frith and McElwee, 2008), prostitutes and pimps (Smith and Christou, 2009).

Although this literature on the so-called dark side of entrepreneurship (Kets de Vries, 1985) associated with the criminal entrepreneurship has expanded, the majority of the growth in the emergent literature on entrepreneurship and enterprise that is not fully legitimate has focused upon entrepreneurs operating in the informal sector. Table 1.1 charts the rapid expansion of this literature over the past four decades. This examines the number of outputs published on not only the informal economy/sector but also the specific subject of informal sector entrepreneurship. Between 1975 and 1979, for example, just 189 outputs were published with either the 'informal sector' or 'informal economy' in the title, but between 2010 and 2014, there had been more than a tenfold increase in the number of such outputs published, namely 1,981 outputs. In much of the earlier literature on the informal economy/sector, there was an assumption that much of the work in this sphere was dependent waged employment. In the past few decades, however, there has been recognition that a large amount of this work in the informal sector is conducted on an own-account or self-employed basis (ILO, 2013). The result is that such activity has begun to be seen as a form of entrepreneurial endeavour (Williams, 2006).

Table 1.1 Number of Publications With Informal Sector/Economy/Entrepreneurship in Title, 1975–Present

Time period	'Informal sector' (in title of publication)	'Informal economy' (in title of publication)	Both 'informal' and 'entrepreneurship' (in title of publication)
1975–1979	180	9	1
1980–1984	315	39	0
1985–1989	557	117	0
1990–1994	859	212	8
1995–1999	883	242	21
2000–2004	835	506	27
2005–2009	897	620	36
2010–2014	1,158	823	125
2015–Dec. 2016	401	305	64
Total: 1975–Present	6,085	2,873	282

Source: author's calculations based on Google Scholar data

Indeed, in recent years, the number of publications which have both 'informal' and 'entrepreneurship' in the title has started to rapidly expand. The first identified output which had both 'informal' and 'entrepreneurship' in the title was by Paul Kennedy who in 1976 published an article titled 'Cultural Factors Affecting Entrepreneurship and Development in the Informal Economy in Ghana' (Kennedy, 1976). Indeed, and as this book will reveal, his conclusion that '[t]he informal sector is, in many respects, a training ground for a great many entrepreneurs who eventually develop quite large firms' was remarkably prescient (Kennedy, 1976: 21). Yet despite this salient and seminal finding, no further outputs were published with both 'informal' and 'entrepreneurship' in the title until the 1990s, when little more than a handful were published, most of which sought to reread work in the informal sector in developing countries as entrepreneurship. Between 1995 and 2009, there was then a small increase in the number of outputs in each five-year period. However, it is only since 2010 that the study of entrepreneurship in the informal sector has begun to take off, with 189 outputs with 'informal' and 'entrepreneurship' in the title being published.

This compares with 27,200 outputs which have entrepreneurship in the title in the past six years, the vast bulk of which presumably are on entrepreneurship in the formal sector. The result is that for every output published on the vast majority of enterprises globally, 144 are produced on formal sector entrepreneurship. Put another way, just 0.7 per cent of publications with entrepreneurship in the title in the past six years are estimated to be on informal entrepreneurship, despite this form of entrepreneurship being by far the most dominant type of entrepreneurial endeavour globally. To avert the danger that entrepreneurship scholarship continues with its current myopic focus upon formal sector entrepreneurship, therefore, this book contributes to the current small but burgeoning swathe of studies that adopts a more lived practice approach to entrepreneurship and draws attention to the principal form of entrepreneurship in the world today, namely, entrepreneurship in the informal sector.

The intention in this book is therefore to advance understanding and knowledge of what is by all accounts the main type of entrepreneurial endeavour in the world. In doing so, the objective is not only to contribute to establishing within entrepreneurship scholarship a 'sub-discipline' on informal sector entrepreneurship but also to draw to the attention of the wider discipline of business and management studies the ongoing dominance of the informal sector. For too many years, scholarship in not only entrepreneurship but also business and management studies has confined itself to theorising and empirically investigating what is in effect a sphere in which only a minority of employment takes place and businesses operate (i.e., the formal sector). Unless knowledge of the sphere in which the majority of jobs are held and the bulk of businesses operate is advanced, namely, the informal sector, then the subject of business and management studies has little chance of having anything but a partial understanding of the world of work.

Argument of the Book

To advance understanding of informal entrepreneurship, Part I of this book will set out the theoretical framework used and how this book advances this theoretical approach. As Chapter 2 displays, scholarship on entrepreneurship in general, and on entrepreneurship in the informal sector in particular, has increasingly adopted the lens of institutional theory to explain such endeavour (Baumol and Blinder, 2008; Helmke and Levitsky, 2004; North, 1990; Williams and Horodnic, 2016a,b; Williams and Shahid, 2016). From this perspective, all societies have both formal institutions (i.e., codified laws and regulations) that set out the formal legal rules of the game as well as informal institutions which are the 'socially shared rules, usually unwritten, that are created, communicated and enforced outside of officially sanctioned channels' (Helmke and Levitsky, 2004: 727). Informal entrepreneurship has been consequently viewed as endeavour occurring outside of formal institutional prescriptions but within the norms, values and beliefs of informal institutions (Godfrey, 2011; Kistruck *et al.*, 2015; Siqueira *et al.*, 2016; Webb *et al.*, 2009; Welter *et al.*, 2015). In a first wave of institutional theory, informal entrepreneurship was explained as resulting from formal institutional failures, including a range of formal institutional voids, inefficiencies, uncertainty and weaknesses. In a second wave of institutional theory, however, it has been recognised that focusing upon solely formal institutional failures ignores the role played by informal institutions (Godfrey, 2015; Scott, 2008). In consequence, informal entrepreneurship has been increasingly viewed as arising 'because of the incongruence between what is defined as legitimate by formal and informal institutions' (Webb *et al.*, 2009: 495). In this book, however, a third wave of institutional thought will be introduced which synthesises these two previous waves by arguing that formal institutional imperfections and failures produce an asymmetry between formal and informal institutions, and the result is the greater prevalence of entrepreneurship in the informal sector.

In Chapter 3, the determinants of this institutional asymmetry will be identified. Until now, the identification of the formal institutional failures and imperfections that produce institutional asymmetry, and thus the greater prevalence of informal entrepreneurship, has not tended to be based on a theoretically driven approach. In this chapter, however, earlier theoretical perspectives that sought to explain the informal sector and informal entrepreneurship will be used to identify the main formal institutional failures and imperfections that lead to institutional asymmetry and thus the prevalence of informal entrepreneurship. To do this, a review is undertaken of the various formal institutional failures and imperfections identified in three competing theories of informal entrepreneurship, namely: modernisation theory, which views informal entrepreneurship to be a result of economic underdevelopment and a lack of modernisation of governance; neo-liberal theory, which depicts informal entrepreneurship to result from over-regulation of the economy, such as high taxes and burdensome regulations and controls; and political economy theory, which portrays informal entrepreneurship to be a result of inadequate state intervention and a lack of protection of workers. This will then set the scene for an evaluation in Part II of which of these formal institutional failures are significantly associated with the greater prevalence of informal entrepreneurship.

In Part II of this book, therefore, an empirical evaluation is conducted of the prevalence, impacts and determinants of entrepreneurship in the informal sector. Chapter 4 reports the findings regarding the variations in the prevalence of informal entrepreneurship. This will examine not only the cross-national variations in the commonality of informal entrepreneurship but also how informal entrepreneurship varies by sector, the type of business, occupation and various demographic and socio-economic characteristics. Given that conventionally informal entrepreneurship is viewed in a negative manner as deleterious to economic development and growth, Chapter 5 then introduces some potentially positive features of informal entrepreneurship and, in particular, evaluates the relationship between starting up unregistered and future firm performance. This will reveal how enterprises that started up unregistered, and stayed unregistered for longer before registering, display higher levels of future firm performance than those that registered from the outset. Chapter 6 then turns attention towards the reasons for informal entrepreneurship by evaluating not only the institutional asymmetry thesis but also which formal institutional failures and imperfections are significantly associated with the higher prevalence of informal entrepreneurship using a cross-national comparative analysis based on World Bank Enterprise Survey (WBES) data on 142 countries.

Having evaluated the variations in the prevalence of informal entrepreneurship, the positive impacts of such entrepreneurship, including the impacts of starting up unregistered on future firm performance, and identified the formal institutional failures that lead to higher levels of informal entrepreneurship, Part III then turns its attention to the issue of tackling entrepreneurship in the informal sector. To commence, Chapter 7 reviews critically four hypothetical policy goals, namely: taking no action, deregulating formal entrepreneurship, eradicating informal entrepreneurship and formalising informal entrepreneurship. Reviewing the advantages and disadvantages of each of these hypothetical goals of policy, this chapter will reveal that formalising informal entrepreneurship is the most logical and viable goal of policy. The next two chapters then turn towards how formalising informal entrepreneurship can be achieved. The argument is that there are two policy approaches available for achieving this which are not mutually exclusive and can be combined.

In Chapter 8, what are termed 'hard' direct policy measures will be reviewed which not only dissuade entrepreneurs from operating in the informal sector but also incentivise and encourage them to operate in the formal sector. These measures directly increase the costs and reduce the benefits of informality while reducing the costs and increasing the benefits of operating in the formal sector. In doing so, they deal with some of the formal institutional failures, such as the powerlessness of formal institutions, that lead to the greater prevalence of informal entrepreneurship.

However, to tackle the other formal institutional failures that lead to institutional symmetry and the greater prevalence of informal entrepreneurship, namely, the various formal institutional resource misallocations and inefficiencies, voids and weaknesses, Chapter 9 will outline a range of what are here termed 'soft' indirect policy measures. These include not only a range of process innovations that improve the perceived level of procedural and redistributive justice and fairness of government, to reduce institutional symmetry, but also various macro-level economic and social policies that address a range of formal institutional misallocations, inefficiencies and voids, which Part II identified as being significantly associated with greater institutional asymmetry. The concluding Chapter 10 then synthesises the findings and discusses the way forward in terms of both explaining and tackling this realm that covers and includes the vast majority of enterprises and entrepreneurs operating in the world today.

References

Acs, Z., Desai, S., Stenholm, P. and Wuebker, R. (2013). Institutions and the rate of formal and informal entrepreneurship across countries. *Frontiers of Entrepreneurship Research*, 35(15), pp. 1–24.

Armstrong, P. (2005). *Critique of entrepreneurship: People and policy.* Basingstoke: Palgrave Macmillan.

Austin, J., Stevenson, H. and Wei-Skillern, J. (2006). Social and commercial entrepreneurship: Same, different or both? *Entrepreneurship Theory and Practice*, 31(1), pp. 1–22.

Autio, E. and Fu, K. (2015). Economic and political institutions and entry into formal and informal entrepreneurship. *Asia Pacific Journal of Management*, 32(1), pp. 67–94.

Baumol, W.J. and Blinder, A. (2008). *Macroeconomics: Principles and policy.* Cincinnati, OH: South-Western Publishing.

Bhide, A. and Stevenson, H.H. (1990). Why be honest if honesty doesn't pay? *Harvard Business Review*, 68(5), pp. 121–129.

Bouchard, M. and Dion, C.B. (2009). Growers and facilitators: Probing the role of entrepreneurs in the development of the cannabis cultivation industry. *Journal of Small Business and Entrepreneurship*, 22(1), pp. 25–38.

Brockhaus, R.H. and Horowitz, P.S. (1986). The psychology of the entrepreneur. *Entrepreneurship Theory and Practice*, 23(2), pp. 29–45.

Bruns, B., Miggelbrink, J. and Müller, K. (2011). Smuggling and small-scale trade as part of informal economic practices: Empirical findings from the Eastern external EU border. *International Journal of Sociology and Social Policy*, 31(11/12), pp. 664–680.

Bucur, D., Pantea, M. and Dan, L.A. (2012). Profit criminal entrepreneurship. *Journal of Criminal Investigation*, 5(2), pp. 19–39.

Burns, P. (2001). *Entrepreneurship and small business.* Basingstoke: Palgrave.

Cannon, T. (1991). *Enterprise: Creation, development and growth.* Oxford: Butterworth-Heinemann.

Castells, M. and Portes, A. (1989). World underneath: The origins, dynamics and effects of the informal economy. In: A. Portes, M. Castells and L.A. Benton, Eds., *The informal economy: Studies in advanced and less developing countries.* Baltimore: John Hopkins University Press, pp. 1–19.

Cole, A.H. (1969). Definition of entrepreneurship. In: J. Komives, Ed., *Karl A. Bostrum seminar in the study of enterprise.* Milwaukee: Centre for Venture Management, pp. 1–15.

Cross, J.C. (2000). Street vendors, modernity and postmodernity: Conflict and compromise in the global economy. *International Journal of Sociology and Social Policy*, 20(1), pp. 29–51.

Cunningham, J.B. and Lischeron, J. (1991). Defining entrepreneurship. *Journal of Small Business Management*, 29(1), pp. 43–51.

Defourny, J. and Nyssens, M. (2010). Conceptions of social enterprise and social entrepreneurship in Europe and the United States: Convergences and divergences. *Journal of Social Entrepreneurship*, 1(1), pp. 32–53.

De Jong, L., Tu, P.A. and van Ees, H. (2012). Which entrepreneurs bribe and what do they get from it? Exploratory evidence from Vietnam. *Entrepreneurship Theory and Practice*, 36(2), pp. 323–345.

European Commission (1998). *Communication of the commission on undeclared work.* Brussels: European Commission.

European Commission (2007). *Stepping up the fight against undeclared work.* Brussels: European Commission.

Fournier, V. (1998). Stories of development and exploitation: Militant voices in an enterprise culture. *Organization*, 61(1), pp. 107–128.

Friman, H.R. (2004). The great escape? Globalization, immigrant entrepreneurship and the criminal economy. *Review of International Political Economy*, 11(1), pp. 98–131.

Frith, K. and McElwee, G. (2008). An emergent entrepreneur? A story of a drug dealer in a restricted entrepreneurial environment. *Society and Business Review*, 3(2), pp. 270–286.

Godfrey, P.C. (2011). Towards a theory of the informal economy. *Academy of Management Annals*, 5, pp. 231–277.

Godfrey, P.C. (2015). Introduction: Why the informal economy matters to management. In: P.C. Godfrey, Ed., *Management, society, and the informal economy*. London: Routledge, pp. 1–20.

Gottschalk, P. (2010). Entrepreneurship in organised crime. *International Journal of Entrepreneurship and Small Business*, 9(3), pp. 295–307.

Gottschalk, P. and Smith, R. (2011). Criminal entrepreneurship, white-collar criminality and neutralization theory. *Journal of Enterprising Communities*, 5(4), pp. 283–296.

Harding, R., Brooksbank, D., Hart, M., Jones-Evans, D., Levie, J., O'Reilly, J. and Walker, J. (2005). *Global entrepreneurship monitor United Kingdom 2005*. London: London Business School, Global Entrepreneurship Monitor.

Hart, K. (1973). Informal income opportunities and urban employment in Ghana. *Journal of Modern African Studies*, 11(1), pp. 61–89.

Helmke, G. and Levitsky, S. (2004). Informal institutions and comparative politics: A research agenda. *Perspectives on Politics*, 2(4), pp. 725–740.

Hull, D., Bosley, J.J. and Udell, G.G. (1980). Renewing the hunt for the heffalump: Identifying potential entrepreneurs by personality characteristics. *Journal of Small Business*, 18(1), pp. 11–18.

Hussmanns, R. (2005). *Measuring the informal economy: From employment in the informal sector to informal employment*. Geneva: ILO.

ILO (2012). *Statistical update on employment in the informal economy*. Geneva: ILO.

ILO (2013). *Statistical update on employment in the informal economy*. Geneva: ILO.

Jones, C. and Spicer, A. (2005). The sublime object of entrepreneurship. *Organization*, 12(2), pp. 223–246.

Jütting, J. and Laiglesia, J. (2009). Employment, poverty reduction and development: What's new? In: J. Jütting and J. Laiglesia, Eds., *Is informal normal? Towards more and better jobs in developing countries*. Paris: OECD, pp. 129–152.

Karjanen, D. (2011). Tracing informal and illicit flows after socialism: A micro-commodity supply chain analysis in the Slovak Republic. *International Journal of Sociology and Social Policy*, 31(11/12), pp. 648–663.

Kennedy, P. (1976). Cultural factors affecting entrepreneurship and development in the informal economy in Ghana. *The IDS Bulletin*, 8(2), pp. 17–21.

Kets de Vries, M.F.R. (1977). The entrepreneurial personality: A person at the crossroads. *Journal of Management Studies*, 3(1), pp. 34–57.

Kets de Vries, M.F.R. (1985). The dark side of entrepreneurship. *Harvard Business Review*, 63(6), pp. 160–167.

Kistruck, G.M., Webb, J.W., Sutter, C.J. & Bailey, A.V.G. (2015). The double-edged sword of legitimacy in base-of-the-pyramid markets. *Journal of Business Venturing*, 30(3), pp. 436–451.

McElwee, G. (2009a). The ethics of exploring entrepreneurship beyond the boundaries. *Journal of Small Business and Entrepreneurship*, 22(1), pp. iii–x.

McElwee, G. (2009b). Value-adding and value-extracting entrepreneurship at the margins. *Journal of Small Business and Entrepreneurship*, 22(1), pp. 39–54.

McElwee, G., Smith, R. and Somerville, P. (2011). Theorising illegal rural enterprise: Is everyone at it? *International Journal of Rural Criminology*, 1(1), pp. 40–62.

North, D.C. (1990). *Institutions, institutional change and economic performance*. Cambridge: Cambridge University Press.

OECD (2002). *Measuring the non-observed economy*. Paris: OECD.

OECD (2012). *Reducing opportunities for tax non-compliance in the underground economy*. Paris: OECD.

Polese, A., Williams, C.C., Horodnic, I. and Bejakovic, P. (2017). Eds., *The informal economy in global perspective*. Basingstoke: Palgrave Macmillan.

Portes, A., Blitzer, S. and Curtis, J. (1986). The urban informal sector in Uruguay: Its internal structure, characteristics and effects. *World Development*, 14(6), pp. 727–741.

Rehn, A. and Taalas, S. (2004). Znakomstva I Svyazi! [Acquaintances and connections]: Blat, the Soviet Union and mundane entrepreneurship. *Entrepreneurship and Regional Development*, 16(3), pp. 235–250.

Reynolds, P.D., Bygrave, W.D., Autio, E., Cox, L.W. and Hay, M. (2002). *Global entrepreneurship monitor: Executive report*. Kansas City: Kauffman Center for Entrepreneurial Leadership.

Sauka, A., Schneider, F. and Williams, C.C. (2016). Introduction. In: A. Sauka, F. Schneider and C.C. Williams, Eds., *Entrepreneurship and the shadow economy: A European perspective*. Cheltenham: Edward Elgar, pp. 1–7.

Scott, W.R. (2008). *Institutions and organizations: Ideas and interests*. London: Sage.

Shavell, S. (2002). Law versus morality as regulators of conduct. *American Law and Economics Association*, 4, pp. 227–257.

Shaver, K.G. and Scott, L.R. (1991). Person, process, choice: The psychology of new venture creation. *Entrepreneurship Theory and Practice*, 16(2), pp. 23–45.

Siqueira, A.C.O., Webb, J.W. and Bruton, G.D. (2016). Informal entrepreneurship and industry conditions. *Entrepreneurship Theory and Practice*, 40(1), pp. 177–200.

Sköld, D. and Rehn, A. (2007). Makin' it, by keeping it real: Street talk, rap music and the forgotten entrepreneurship from the 'hood'. *Group and Organization Management*, 32(1), pp. 50–78.

Smith, R. and Christou, M.L. (2009). Extracting value from their environment: Some observations on pimping and prostitution as entrepreneurship. *Journal of Small Business and Entrepreneurship*, 22(1), pp. 69–84.

Smith, R. and McElwee, G. (2013). Confronting social constructions of rural criminality: A case story on 'illegal pluriactivity' in the farming community. *Sociologica Ruralis*, 53(1), pp. 112–134.

VanderBeken, T. (2004). Risky business: A risk-based methodology to measure organized crime. *Crime, Law and Social Change*, 41(5), pp. 471–516.

Vanduyne, P.C. (1993). Organized-crime and business-crime enterprises in the Netherlands. *Crime, Law and Social Change*, 19(2), pp. 103–142.

Webb, J.W., Tihanyi, L., Ireland, R.D. and Sirmon, D.G. (2009). You say illegal, I say legitimate: Entrepreneurship in the informal economy. *Academy of Management Review*, 34(3), pp. 492–510.

Welter, F., Smallbone, D. and Pobol, A. (2015). Entrepreneurial activity in the informal economy: A missing piece of the jigsaw puzzle. *Entrepreneurship and Regional Development*, 27(5/6), pp. 292–306.

Williams, C.C. (2006). *The hidden enterprise culture: Entrepreneurship in the underground economy*. Cheltenham: Edward Elgar.

Williams, C.C. and Gurtoo, A. (2013). Beyond entrepreneurs as heroic icons of capitalism: A case study of street entrepreneurs in India. *International Journal of Entrepreneurship and Small Business*, 19(4), pp. 421–437.

Williams, C.C. and Horodnic, I. (2016a). An institutional theory of the informal economy: Some lessons from the United Kingdom. *International Journal of Social Economics*, 43(7), pp. 722–738.

Williams, C.C. and Horodnic, I. (2016b). Cross-country variations in the participation of small businesses in the informal economy: An institutional asymmetry perspective. *Journal of Small Business and Enterprise Development*, 23(1), pp. 3–24.

Williams, C.C. and Lansky, M. (2013). Informal employment in developed and emerging economies: Perspectives and policy responses. *International Labour Review*, 152(3/4), pp. 355–380.

Williams, C.C. and Nadin, S. (2013a). Beyond the entrepreneur as a heroic figurehead of capitalism: Re-representing the lived practices of entrepreneurs. *Entrepreneurship and Regional Development*, 25(7/8), pp. 552–568.

Williams, C.C. and Nadin, S. (2013b). Harnessing the hidden enterprise culture: Supporting the formalization of off-the-books business start-ups. *Journal of Small Business and Enterprise Development*, 20(2), pp. 434–447.

Williams, C.C. and Nadin, S. (2014). Facilitating the formalisation of entrepreneurs in the informal economy: Towards a variegated policy approach. *Journal of Entrepreneurship and Public Policy*, 3(1), pp. 33–48.

Williams, C.C. and Shahid, M. (2016). Informal entrepreneurship and institutional theory: Explaining the varying degrees of (in)formalisation of entrepreneurs in Pakistan. *Entrepreneurship and Regional Development*, 28(1/2), pp. 1–25.

Williams, C.C. and Windebank, J. (1998). *Informal employment in the advanced economies: Implications for work and welfare*. London: Routledge.

Part I

Theorising Entrepreneurship in the Informal Sector

2 An Institutionalist Perspective

Introduction

The aim of Part I of this book is to set out the theoretical framework being used to understand entrepreneurship in the informal sector and how this book is advancing this theoretical lens. To start to do this, this chapter reviews how scholarship on entrepreneurship in general, and on entrepreneurship in the informal sector in particular, has increasingly adopted the lens of institutional theory to explain entrepreneurial endeavour (Baumol and Blinder, 2008; Helmke and Levitsky, 2004; North, 1990). Institutions are the rules of the game that exist in any society, or the 'humanly devised constraints that shape human interaction' (North, 1990: 3), and govern behaviour in society. Structures and mechanisms of social order, institutions or what might be termed governance mechanisms consist of for example governing laws, contracts, property rights and other legal and operational codes, as well as prescribed norms, values and beliefs about what is acceptable. From the perspective of institutionalist theory, moreover, all societies have both formal institutions (i.e., codified laws and regulations) that set out the legal rules of the game as well as informal institutions which are the unwritten, socially shared rules that exist outside of officially sanctioned channels (Helmke and Levitsky, 2004) and are the norms, values and beliefs held by citizens and entrepreneurs reflecting their individual morale about what is right and acceptable (Denzau and North, 1994). In other words, the term 'institution' commonly applies to both informal institutions such as customs, or behaviour patterns important to a society, and to formal institutions created by entities such as the government and public services.

Viewed through this institutionalist lens, formal entrepreneurship is endeavour that occurs within the formal institutional prescriptions set out in the codified laws and regulations. Informal entrepreneurship, in contrast, is endeavour occurring outside of formal institutional prescriptions but within the norms, values and beliefs of informal institutions (Godfrey, 2011; Kistruck et al., 2015; Siqueira et al., 2016; Webb et al., 2009; Welter et al., 2015; Williams and Gurtoo, 2017). Criminal entrepreneurship, meanwhile, occurs not only outside of formal institutional prescriptions but also not within the socially shared rules regarding what is acceptable.

In this chapter, three waves of thought in institutional theory will be outlined regarding how to explain informal entrepreneurship. In a first wave of institutional theory, informal entrepreneurship was explained as resulting from formal institutional failures and imperfections, including formal institutional resource misallocations and inefficiencies, voids, weaknesses and instability. In a second wave of institutional theory, however, it has been recognised that focusing upon solely formal institutional failings and imperfections ignores the role played by informal institutions (Godfrey, 2015; North, 1990; Scott, 2008). In this wave, therefore, greater attention has been paid to these informal institutions, and informal entrepreneurship has been increasingly viewed as arising 'because of the incongruence between what is defined as legitimate by formal and informal institutions' (Webb *et al.*, 2009: 495). In this book, institutional theory on informal entrepreneurship is advanced by offering a third wave of thought that synthesises these two viewpoints. Throughout this book, it will be argued that it is formal institutional failings and imperfections which produce an asymmetry between formal and informal institutions and that this then leads to the greater prevalence of informal entrepreneurship.

To commence, therefore, this chapter reviews the first wave of institutional theory on informal entrepreneurship that viewed formal institutional failures as the direct reason for the prevalence of informal entrepreneurship. Recognising that even if there are formal institutional failings, informal entrepreneurship would not necessarily occur unless the socially shared norms, values and beliefs of entrepreneurs and citizens were not aligned with the formal rules, this chapter then reviews the second wave of thought which asserts that informal entrepreneurship results when there is incongruence between the formal and informal institutions. In the third and final section, meanwhile, a third wave of institutional theory on informal entrepreneurship is advanced by hypothesising that when formal institutional failings and imperfections produce incongruence between formal and informal institutions, the result is a propensity towards informal entrepreneurship.

First Wave Thought: Formal Institutional Failures and Imperfections

In the first wave of institutional thought regarding informal entrepreneurship, it was recognised that entrepreneurship is socially constructed behaviour (Sine and David, 2010; Webb and Ireland, 2015), and institutions defined 'the rules of the game' which prescribe, monitor, enforce and support what is socially acceptable (Baumol and Blinder, 2008; Denzau and North, 1994; Mathias *et al.*, 2014; North, 1990; Webb *et al.*, 2009). All societies, it was recognised, moreover, have codified laws and regulations (i.e., formal institutions) that define the legal rules of the game, and informal institutions that convey the norms, values and beliefs of citizens and entre-preneurs about what is acceptable. Within the first wave of institutional thought, however, the focus was near enough entirely upon the formal insti-tutions when explaining the prevalence of informal entrepreneurship. Little attention was paid to informal institutions, and neither was the issue of whether there is symmetry between formal and informal institutions con-sidered important. Instead the view was that informal entrepreneurship is a direct result of formal institutional failures and imperfections.

In this section, therefore, a brief review is undertaken of the major broad types of formal institutional failure that are seen to result in a greater prev-alence of informal entrepreneurship. These will be returned to in greater depth in the next chapter, which evaluates competing theoretical expla-nations about which specific formal institutional failures determine the prevalence of informal entrepreneurship. Here, therefore, four types of for-mal institutional failure are briefly introduced and reviewed, namely, formal institutional resource misallocations and inefficiencies, formal institutional voids and weaknesses, formal institutional powerlessness and formal insti-tutional instability and uncertainty (for an alternative review, see Webb and Ireland, 2015).

Formal Institutional Resource Misallocations and Inefficiencies

A first set of formal institutional failures relate to resource misallocations, or inefficiencies, by formal institutions (Qian and Strahan, 2007). These resource misallocations and inefficiencies, in large part, are the result of either the lack of modernisation of government organisations and/or due to formal institutions acting in a corrupt manner to protect or maximise economic rents for elites. Here each issue is considered in turn.

Resource misallocations and inefficiencies that result from the lack of modernisation of public services take at least three forms. Firstly, public ser-vices which have not modernised tend to be lacking in terms of redistribu-tive justice. In the context of this book, this refers to whether entrepreneurs feel that they receive the goods and services they deserve given the taxes and social contributions that they pay (Kinsey and Gramsick, 1993; Richardson and Sawyer, 2001; Thurman *et al.*, 1984). Taxes and social contributions are the price citizens and businesses pay for the goods and services that a government provides. When the price paid does not correspond to the per-ceived value of the goods and services received, entrepreneurs will be more likely to operate in the informal sector. Secondly, governments that have not modernised tend to lack procedural justice, which here refers to whether entrepreneurs view the government as dealing with them in a respectful, impartial and responsible manner (Braithwaite and Reinhart, 2000; Murphy, 2005). When entrepreneurs view the state administrative bodies for exam-ple as not treating them in such a manner, then they are more likely to be non-compliant (Hartner *et al.*, 2008; Murphy, 2003; Murphy *et al.*, 2009).

Third, and finally, public services which have not modernised tend to lack procedural fairness, which here refers to whether entrepreneurs feel they are being treated in a fair manner relative to others and that they pay their fair share compared with others (Kinsey and Gramsick, 1993). Entrepreneurs perceiving that they do not receive procedurally fair treatment are more likely to be non-compliant (Bird *et al.*, 2006; McGee *et al.*, 2008; Molero and Pujol, 2012). In consequence, resource misallocations and inefficiencies result from a lack of modernisation of state bodies in terms of the existence of procedural and distributive justice and fairness.

Besides resource misallocations and inefficiencies resulting from the lack of modernisation of state authorities, there are also resource misallocations and inefficiencies that result from the state seeking to protect or maximise economic rents for elites (Acemoglu and Robinson, 2012) and/or the existence of corruption (Aidis and Van Praag, 2007; Khan and Quaddus, 2015; Round *et al.*, 2008; Tonoyan *et al.*, 2010). Corruption in this context is of three varieties, each of which has a different impact on informal entrepreneurship.

The first and most common type of corruption is the 'misuse of public office for private gain' (Bardhan, 1997; Pope, 2000; Shleifer and Vishny, 1993; Svensson, 2005). This is the practice whereby government officials demand or receive gifts, bribes and other payments (e.g., a portion of a given contract) from private sector firms and individual entrepreneurs and provide a service in return. This might include speeding up the granting of an operating license, not producing a negative outcome from a workplace inspection or helping avoid delays in some other regulatory process requiring the approval of public sector officials, such as the granting of a construction permit. Such corruption not only leads to resource misallocations and inefficiencies, and acts as an additional tax that formal entrepreneurs have to pay, but also arguably forces entrepreneurs into the informal sector to escape being subject to such extortion from public officials. A number of studies reveal that countries with a high level of such corruption display relatively lower levels of firm performance (De Rosa *et al.*, 2010; Faruq and Webb, 2013; Gaviria, 2002; Lavallée and Roubaud, 2011; Mauro, 1995; Teal and McArthur, 2002). As Myrdal (1968) explains, corrupt civil servants cause delays that would not otherwise occur simply to provide themselves with the opportunity to receive a corrupt payment to speed up the process. Other studies further develop this argument by revealing that although individual entrepreneurs and enterprises paying bribes to public officials have higher subsequent firm performance levels than those refusing to pay bribes, the net impact of such bribery on the economy as a whole is negative (Williams and Kedir, 2016; Williams and Martinez-Perez, 2016; Williams *et al.*, 2016b).

Besides such low-level public sector corruption usually involves the payment of relatively small amounts by firms to public officials, resource misallocations and inefficiencies also result from a second type of corruption that has been less studied, namely, state capture. This is the process whereby firms or groups of firms influence the formulation of laws and other government policies to their own advantage through illicit or non-transparent means (Fries *et al.*, 2003). The outcome is that they receive preferential treatment, and state resources are diverted towards supporting them. For those who are not part of these elites who capture the resources of the state, the outcome is commonly overly burdensome taxes, and registration and licensing regulations and costs, which act as an entry barrier to formality for new entrepreneurs and relatively fewer public services in return for the taxes and social contributions they pay (De Soto, 1989; Siqueira *et al.*, 2016; Williams *et al.*, 2016a).

A third and final form of corruption which again is seldom studied in the entrepreneurship literature that leads to resource misallocations and inefficiencies is when consumers and entrepreneurs use personal connections to gain preferential access to public goods and services and/or to circumvent formal procedures, including gaining access to contracts in the case of entrepreneurs and educational and health services for consumers. This more agency-oriented form of corruption on the part of entrepreneurs (and citizens) is variously referred to as *guanxi* in China (Chen *et al.*, 2012), *wasta* in the Arab world (Smith *et al.*, 2011), *jeitinho* in Brazil (Ferreira *et al.*, 2012), 'pulling strings' in English-speaking countries (Smith *et al.*, 2012), *blat* in post-Soviet spaces (Ledeneva, 2013; Williams and Onoshchenko, 2014, 2015), *vrski* in FYR Macedonia (Williams and Bezeredi, 2017), *veze* in Serbia, Croatia and Bosnia and Herzegovina and *vruzki* in Bulgaria (Williams and Yang, 2017). It is generally identified as widespread in all countries where it has been studied and also seen as a 'natural' part of doing business. Indeed it is seldom seen in a negative light as resulting in cronyism, corruption and nepotism, despite its negative consequences on those who play by the formal rulebook (see Williams and Yang, 2017).

Formal Institutional Voids and Weaknesses

Beyond resource misallocations and inefficiencies, another formal institutional failing and imperfection that is seen to result in the prevalence of informal entrepreneurship relates to the existence of formal institutional voids and weaknesses. Until now, there has been a considerable debate regarding which institutional voids and weaknesses lead to a greater prevalence of informal entrepreneurship and which do not. Indeed institutional voids seen as a weakness of economies by some commentators are seen as strengths by other commentators.

To explain, a key debate has been whether entrepreneurs are driven into the informal sector by their exclusion from the formal sector as a result of too little state intervention or voluntarily decide to exit the formal sector because of too much state interference. On the one hand, therefore, there is a group of largely neo-liberal scholars who explain informal entrepreneurship to result from entrepreneurs deciding to operate in the informal sector as a matter of choice, such as due to the burdensome regulatory environment and the existence of an excessively intrusive state (Becker, 2004; De Soto, 1989, 2001; London and Hart, 2004; Nwabuzor, 2005; Sauvy, 1984). For these commentators, informal entrepreneurship is a rational economic decision to escape the over-regulated formal sector (De Soto, 1989, 2001; Schneider and Williams, 2013). Informal entrepreneurs voluntarily operate informally to avoid the costs, time and effort of formal registration (De Soto, 1989, 2001; Perry and Maloney, 2007; Small Business Council, 2004). The formal institutional weakness for these commentators, therefore, is that there is an over-intrusive state which stifles the spirit of entrepreneurs through its imposition of high taxes and a vast array of state-imposed institutional constraints (De Soto, 1989, 2001; Perry and Maloney, 2007; Small Business Council, 2004). The consequent policy approach is to pursue tax reductions and reductions in the 'regulatory burden'.

On the other hand, however, and in stark contrast to the neo-liberal perspective, a political economy perspective asserts that entrepreneurs operate in the informal sector as a result of too little state intervention and a lack of worker protection. This leads them to being excluded from the formal sector and turning to informal entrepreneurship out of necessity as a survival tactic and last resort (Castells and Portes, 1989; Davis, 2006; Slavnic, 2010). Informal entrepreneurship, in consequence, is depicted to result from the advent of a deregulated, open world economy and too little state intervention in the economy in deregulatory regimes (Davis, 2006; Gallin, 2001; Portes, 1994; Sassen, 1996; Slavnic, 2010). Informal entrepreneurs are thus viewed as those excluded from the formal sector as a result of too little state intervention and a result of a lack of help given to them to formalise their operations (e.g., Barbour and Llanes, 2013; Copisarow, 2004; Copisarow and Barbour, 2004; ILO, 2002). The solution, therefore, is to increase the amount of state intervention in the economy to prevent the need for citizens to turn to informal entrepreneurship as a survival strategy and to facilitate the formalisation of these informal enterprises through the provision of not only much greater business advice and support but also finance to enable them to start up formally (Community Links and the Refugee Council, 2011; Dellot, 2012; Katungi *et al.*, 2006; Llanes and Barbour, 2007; Small Business Council, 2004; Williams *et al.*, 2012a,b). It is an approach based on greater rather than less state intervention in the economy.

Formal Institutional Powerlessness

Other formal institutional failings and imperfections that are seen to result in the prevalence of informal entrepreneurship relate to the existence of formal institutional powerlessness. This powerlessness is expressed in not only a lack of capacity to enforce policies (Webb *et al.*, 2009) but also a lack of power in terms of the ability to provide incentives to encourage adherence to the formal rules. From this perspective, and taking power to mean the ability to get somebody else to do something that they were not going to do before in the way in which you want them to do it, formal institutions currently lack power. They are unable to encourage businesses and citizens to adhere to the formal rules (i.e., the codified laws and regulations).

It might be assumed that the power of authorities to influence behaviour refers to their ability to detect and punish informal entrepreneurs. However, this is only one aspect. Two basic tools are at the disposal of formal institutions for achieving adherence to the rules. On the one hand, they can indeed use deterrence measures that seek to increase the penalties and risks of detection for engaging in non-compliant behaviour (i.e., 'sticks'). On the other hand, however, they can use incentives and rewards to try to encourage entrepreneurs and enterprises to participate in compliant behaviour ('carrots'). The argument here is that many formal institutions do not possess the capacity and capability to implement effective 'sticks' and 'carrots' so that informal entrepreneurship does not occur.

To see this lack of power of state authorities, one has only to recognise the low costs and high benefits of informal entrepreneurship, coupled with the low benefits and high costs of formalisation, in many developing countries. The result is that many entrepreneurs weigh up the costs and benefits and decide to operate on an informal basis. This is because the benefits of operating in the formal sector in developing countries are insufficient to outweigh the benefits of participating in the informal sector. Possible benefits of registration might include access to credit markets, property rights, training from formal institutions (for which informal institutions cannot act as an efficient substitute), belonging to business associations, contracts with large firms, access to public sector procurement contracts and the ability to become more capital intensive (Fajnzylber *et al.*, 2011; Skousen and Mahoney, 2015). Given that these benefits are underdeveloped in many developing countries, such benefits are often outweighed by the costs of registration and benefits of participating in the informal sector. For example, McKenzie and Sakho (2010) in Bolivia and McCulloch *et al.* (2010), in rural Indonesia, find that registration and thus operating formally only increases firm profitability and sales growth for mid-sized firms, suggesting that delaying registration and formalisation until firms reach a certain size may be optimal. Registration, therefore, can be portrayed as simply another significant cost imposed by the formal institutional environment that comes with little benefit for entrepreneurs in many developing countries.

By avoiding this cost, those delaying registration and operating in the informal sector may also lay a stronger foundation by being able to focus their scarce resources on overcoming other internal and external liabilities of newness beyond registration (Stinchcombe, 1965). Internally, a new venture may lack operational routines, as well as trust, camaraderie and cohesion, resulting in significant competitive (e.g., cost) disadvantages relative to more established competitors. Entrepreneurs must therefore learn unfamiliar roles, which requires significant time and other resources and, in turn, may lead to internal inefficiencies and missed opportunities. Externally, new ventures' lack of a track record makes it difficult for them to convince potential stakeholders (e.g., suppliers, investors and customers) to engage in business with them. Without these external resources (e.g., raw materials, capital and sales), however, a new venture cannot survive. By avoiding the costs of registration, resources can be potentially devoted to overcoming these other internal and external liabilities of newness, thus enabling them to outperform those devoting resources to registration, which may reap few benefits in many developing countries. It can be consequently proposed that delaying registration may give new ventures a head start that enables them to forge ahead of those registered from the outset in terms of firm performance.

This will be particularly beneficial in contexts where 'weak' formal institutions fail to provide sufficient benefits to warrant formalisation (Kistruck *et al.*, 2015; Wunsch-Vincent *et al.*, 2015) and the costs of registration thus outweigh the benefits. Although in the developed world, therefore, the point where the benefits of registration outweigh the costs of continuing unregistered may be very quickly reached, this is less likely and may be much longer in developing countries where the costs of registration may lead to major financial difficulties (Hulme and Shepherd, 2003), while the weak formal institutions result in fewer benefits from registration (De Mel *et al.*, 2012; Thai and Turkina, 2014).

This lack of power of authorities to influence the benefits of formality and costs of informality is therefore an important formal institutional failure and imperfection that results in informal entrepreneurship being more prevalent. The consequent solution is to increase the ability of the authorities to alter the cost/benefit ratio. Firstly, this requires authorities to be able to simplify and reduce the costs of registration and formality, which studies in Kenya (Devas and Kelly, 2001), Uganda (Sander, 2003), Bolivia (Garcia-Bolivar, 2006) and Peru (Jaramillo, 2009) reveal lead to an increase in registration. Secondly, state authorities need to be able to increase the benefits of registration and formality, although De Mel *et al.* (2012) in Sri Lanka find that even a financial offer equivalent to two months' profits led to only 50 per cent of firms registering. This is perhaps because even if the power of authorities to increase the costs of informality and benefits of formality are improved, other formal institutional failings remain, including a perception that these benefits might not last due to a perception of the instability and uncertainty of the formal rules. In other words, the power of authorities to implement formalisation is also limited by the lack of trust of entrepreneurs in authorities in the medium to long term.

Formal Institutional Instability and Uncertainty

The fourth and final formal institutional failing therefore relates to the perceived and/or actual instability and uncertainty of the formal rules. Formal institutional instability and uncertainty is a direct product of continuous changes in laws and regulations (Levitsky and Murillo, 2009; Williams and Shahid, 2016). This is especially the case in many developing and transition economies where entrepreneurs and enterprises have been confronted with continuous changes in the formal rules, so much so that they do not expect rules that apply today to remain in force in the future. In many transition economies, for example, citizens and entrepreneurs see little point in paying compulsory contributory payments for pensions, or social contributions so that they can claim unemployment benefits, because they do not believe that when in the future they may wish to benefit, the same rules will apply. This perceived lack of permanency of the formal rules is therefore a major problem for governments in such transition economies and leads many to seek to evade payments.

Furthermore, in many developing and transition economies, there is often a widespread perception that the formal rules that exist are not indigenous to the country and/or are being imposed from the outside. This was especially the case during the early stages of transition in the post-socialist countries of East Central Europe (see Williams *et al.*, 2013). However, it is also the case in many developing countries, not least when the International Monetary Fund imposes specific structural conditions onto countries, and citizens and enterprises therefore do not see the formal rules as decided by, or belonging to, the national government but as imposed from the outside. In such situations, particularly when the laws and regulations (i.e., 'state morale') are continuously changing, the outcome is that entrepreneurs and enterprises turn elsewhere for a more permanent set of values, norms and understandings.

In these situations, populations and businesses turn to the informal institutions as a source of more permanent shared norms, values and beliefs in relation to what is acceptable and what is not. This is because these informal rules of the game are seen as longer lasting, and the tendency is to revert to these rules when confronted by the continuously changing rules and morale of the formal institutions. Indeed, it can be asserted that developing economies are defined so precisely because they have underdeveloped formal institutions. In these situations, therefore, it is perhaps unsurprising that entrepreneurs and enterprises draw upon existing socially shared norms, values and beliefs to facilitate, govern and structure their economic activities instead of relying on formal codified laws and regulations (London *et al.*, 2014; Mair *et al.*, 2012), which can be very fluid and temporary in nature.

Based on this recognition of the prominent role that can be played by informal institutions, recent years have started to see this first wave thought that focused upon formal institutional failings and imperfections transcended when explaining the prevalence of informal entrepreneurship.

Second Wave Thought: Informal Institutions and Institutional Asymmetry

In a second wave of institutional theory, there has been a move beyond solely studying formal institutional failings when explaining informal entrepreneurship. From the perspective of this second wave of thought, the focus upon solely formal institutional failures and imperfections in first wave thought ignores the role played by cognitive and normative institutions, which can be joined together under the broad category of informal institutions (Godfrey, 2015; North, 1990; Scott, 2008). This second wave of thought thus recognises that even if there are formal institutional failings, informal entrepreneurship does not necessarily result from these failings and imperfections unless the socially shared norms, values and beliefs of enterprises and entrepreneurs are not aligned with the formal rules (Godfrey, 2015; Webb *et al.*, 2009; Williams and Horodnic, 2015a,b).

From this neo-institutional theoretical perspective, therefore, organisations as well as individual entrepreneurs and citizens, and their behaviours, are shaped by the institutional environments in which they are embedded. According to Scott (2008), such institutional environments comprise three components, or pillars, namely, the regulative, normative and cultural cognitive. The regulatory pillar can be understood as the formal rules, laws and associated sanctions that promote certain behaviours and restrict others. In the context of this book, the regulatory pillar thus relates to formal rules about for example the payment of taxation, declaring work, the terms and conditions of employment and so forth. The second normative pillar refers to wider norms and values present in a society about what constitutes appropriate and acceptable behaviour. In this book, these pertain to attitudes towards informal economic activity (i.e., the social acceptability of. e.g., evading tax, engaging in informal work or purchasing goods and services from the informal sector). The final cultural-cognitive pillar relates to how certain behaviours become taken for granted based on shared understandings. This relates to how informal activities are enacted unthinkingly, for instance, routine purchasing from an informal vendor or not expecting or asking for receipts. Indeed to see the existence of this cultural-cognitive pillar, one has only to consider how informal practices are often referred to as 'cultural' or culturally embedded, such as when the populations of countries state that informality is part of for example the Balkan mind-set, Slavic culture, the African mentality and so forth or when corruption is sometimes stated to be part of the national political culture.

This second wave of institutional theory regarding informal entrepreneurship thus posits that organisations, groups and individual entrepreneurs and citizens behave in ways which reflect the regulatory, normative and cognitive rules of their institutional environments, adherence to which ensures legitimacy. In the regulatory pillar, this legitimacy is gained through compliance with legal requirements, in the normative pillar it is based on conformity with a moral basis, and in the cultural-cognitive pillar it comes from adopting a common frame of meaning or approach (Scott, 2008). It is suggested that institutions exert pressure for compliance on organisations, groups and individual entrepreneurs and citizens through mechanisms of isomorphism, with different variants of isomorphism primarily associated with each of the pillars.

Coercive isomorphism is largely associated with the formal regulatory institutional pillar and the enforcement of formal rules and laws and relates to providing either 'sticks', which detect and punish non-compliant behaviour to enforce compliance, or 'carrots' to reward and encourage compliant behaviour and a commitment to compliance. Normative isomorphism meanwhile is associated with the normative pillar and pressures to conform to wider societal expectations. Finally, mimetic isomorphism is related to the cultural-cognitive pillar, whereby organisations and individuals act in ways that reflect shared understandings and common beliefs and which are culturally supported. The latter two from here onwards are conflated under the umbrella of informal institutions, as is the norm in the scholarship explaining the prevalence of informal entrepreneurship from this second wave perspective.

In recent years, that is, a body of work has emerged that has, firstly, examined the asymmetry between informal and formal institutions, and, secondly and more recently, sought to develop a theory of informal adjustments, which refers to individual entrepreneurs and citizens drawing upon the norms, values and beliefs within their society to facilitate, govern and structure their economic activities instead of relying on formal laws, regulations and supporting apparatuses to do so. This is based on the assumption that the informal sector is society's mechanism to provide for itself in socially legitimate ways when formal organisations fail to do so (Webb and Ireland, 2015). Importantly, these norms, values and beliefs can become the basis for collective shared rules, whether implicitly held or formally codified. Indeed, London *et al.* (2014) display that the influence of informal institutions becomes stronger in the presence of formal institutional failures and imperfections.

As such, from the viewpoint of second wave thought, formal institutional failings per se do not necessarily lead to a greater prevalence of informal entrepreneurship. This is because the norms, values and beliefs of a society's informal institutions can be either 'complementary' if they reinforce formal institutions or 'substitutive' if the rules they prescribe are incompatible with the formal institutions (Helmke and Levitsky, 2004; North, 1990). If formal and informal institutions are complementary and thus align, then informal entrepreneurship will not occur when there are formal institutional failings and populations turn to informal institutions for their moral compass. The only reason informal entrepreneurship will occur is because entrepreneurs and enterprises unintentionally do not comply with the formal rules, for example, due to the rules being not simple enough to understand or too complex to fulfil.

Formal institutional failings and imperfections only lead to informal entrepreneurship if there is incongruence between the formal and informal institutions, and thus the rules of informal institutions are substitutive and incompatible with those of the formal institutions (see Godfrey, 2011, 2015; Webb *et al.*, 2009; Williams and Shahid, 2016; Williams *et al.*, 2015; Windebank and Horodnic, 2017). This is sometimes referred to as 'institutional asymmetry' (Williams *et al.*, 2016a). When formal and informal institutions do not align, therefore, non-compliance is more prevalent. Indeed, and based on this recognition, informal entrepreneurship is viewed as arising 'because of the incongruence between what is defined as legitimate by formal and informal institutions' (Webb *et al.*, 2009: 495). If formal and informal institutions do not align, as is common in many developing countries, the result is informal entrepreneurship which, although formally illegal, is deemed socially legitimate (De Castro *et al.*, 2014; Kistruck *et al.*, 2015; Siqueira *et al.*, 2016; Webb *et al.*, 2013, 2014). Indeed the greater the degree of incongruence (i.e., non-alignment) between formal and informal institutions, the higher is the level of informal entrepreneurship (Williams and Shahid, 2016). Informal entrepreneurship is thus here represented as endeavour occurring outside of formal institutional prescriptions but within the norms, values and beliefs of informal institutions (Godfrey, 2011; Kistruck *et al.*, 2015; Siqueira *et al.*, 2016; Webb *et al.*, 2009; Welter *et al.*, 2015). For example, although avoiding registration laws is formally illegal, in many developing economies registration requirements are seen as overly burdensome, due to the formal institutional imperfections, and their circumvention thus deemed socially legitimate (De Soto, 1989; Webb *et al.*, 2013).

As a result, this second wave of institutional thought has used proxy measures to evaluate what is socially legitimate from the viewpoint of informal institutions. Webb *et al.* (2009) for example argue that when the ends are formally illegal (e.g., human trafficking or illegal drug peddling), informal institutions deem them illegitimate, but legitimate when only the means are formally illegal, thus explaining why the informal sector is deemed 'legitimate' but the criminal economy 'illegitimate'. In practice however, this simplistic distinction is not always valid. In societies with a high level of trust in government and small informal economies, not declaring one's income for tax, social security or labour law purposes may well be deemed socially illegitimate, and in societies where opposition to formal institutions is high, criminal activities may well be deemed socially legitimate (see, e.g., Leonard, 1994 on Catholic West Belfast).

In consequence, one way forward is to evaluate and measure whether informal economic practices are deemed socially legitimate by informal institutions. 'Tax morale', defined as the intrinsic motivation to pay taxes owed (Torgler and Schneider, 2007; Enste, 2011), provides such a measure of the acceptability of informal economic practices and thus the degree of asymmetry between formal and informal institutions in relation to such practices. Sometimes referred to as 'civic duty' (Orviska and Hudson, 2003), tax morale thus measures social norms regarding the acceptability of participating in the informal sector.

In the 2013 Eurobarometer survey for example, this is measured by asking participants to rate how acceptable they feel various informal practices are using a 10-point scale where 1 means 'absolutely unacceptable' and 10 means 'absolutely acceptable'. The six behaviours examined are: someone receives welfare payments without entitlement; a firm is hired by another firm and does not report earnings; a firm hires a private person and all or part of their salary is not declared; a firm is hired by a household and doesn't report earnings; someone evades taxes by not or only partially declaring income; and a person hired by a household does not declare earnings when they should be declared. An aggregate 'tax morale' index is then calculated (Williams and Horodnic, 2015a,b,c). Similar approaches are used in other surveys including the International Social Survey (Torgler, 2005b), the World Values Survey (Alm and Torgler, 2006; Torgler, 2006), the European Values Surveys (Hug and Spörri, 2011; Lago-Peñas and Lago-Peñas, 2010), the British Social Attitudes Survey (Orviska and Hudson, 2003), the Latinbarometro (Torgler, 2005a) and the Afrobarometer (Cummings *et al.*, 2009).

The common finding has been that there is a strong correlation between the propensity to engage in the informal sector and the level of tax morale, with Pearson r values between -0.51 and -0.66 (Alm and Torgler, 2006; Alm *et al.*, 2006; Barone and Mocetti, 2009; Frey, 1997; Halla, 2010; Lewis, 1982; Pommerehne and Weck-Hannemann, 1996; Riahi-Belkaoui, 2004; Richardson, 2006; Torgler, 2005a, 2011; Torgler and Schneider, 2009). The higher the level of tax morale, the lower is the prevalence of the informal sector. Alm and Torgler (2006) focus on Europe and the United States. They find a strong negative correlation (Pearson r $= -0.460$) significant at the 0.05 level. Analysing the linear relationship in a simple regression indicates that the variable tax morale can explain more than 20 per cent of the total variance of the size of the informal sector. If tax morale is declining, therefore, the informal sector is likely to increase. In transition economies, meanwhile, Alm *et al.* (2006) again find a strong negative correlation (-0.657). A simple linear regression suggests that a decrease of tax morale by one unit would lead to an increase of the informal sector by 20 percentage points and that the variable tax morale can explain more than 30 per cent of the total variance of the size of informal sector.

Until now, in the tax morale literature, and to explain institutional asymmetry, exploratory analyses have evaluated the influence of a range of variables, including trust in government and the judiciary, the level of perceived corruption, dissatisfaction with public services and national pride (Daude *et al.*, 2013; Lago-Peñas and Lago-Peñas, 2010; Martínez-Vázquez and Torgler, 2009; Torgler, 2004; Torgler and Schneider, 2007). The finding is that tax morale increases with trust in government and the judiciary, lower levels of perceived corruption, satisfaction with public services and national pride. Other country-level variables investigated, albeit by fewer studies, include trust in others to obey the law (Dong *et al.*, 2012;

Giachi, 2014), social security expenditure (Kanniainen and Pääkkönen, 2009) and tax rates (Horodnic and Williams, 2016; Lago-Peñas and Lago-Peñas, 2010; Ostapenko and Williams, 2016). The finding is that lower tax morale is associated with a lower trust in others to obey the law, lower levels of social expenditure and lower tax rates. In this book, however, a more structured approach is adopted. Using the modernisation, neo-liberal and political economy explanations for the wider informal sector in general, and informal entrepreneurship more particularly, which are reviewed in depth in the next chapter, country-level variables are selected that evaluate the various tenets of each of these explanatory theoretical frameworks.

Studies have also started to evaluate not just the prevalence but also the impacts of the asymmetry between formal and informal institutions, and a greater reliance on informal institutions as a guiding framework for populations. The dominant view has been that this has largely negative impacts. Enterprises and entrepreneurs operating under the guiding framework of the informal institutional environment are argued to be less efficient and poorer performing than those operating in formal institutional environments (Benjamin and Mbaye, 2012; La Porta and Shleifer, 2008, 2014). Entrepreneurs and enterprises operating in the formal sector are asserted to have higher levels of revenue and profits, to employ more workers and to be more capital intensive than their informal counterparts (Fajnzylber *et al.*, 2011; McKenzie and Sakho, 2010). It has also been asserted that that registration by informal firms leads to higher firm performance than if they had remained unregistered (Demenet *et al.*, 2016; Fajnzylber *et al.*, 2011; Rand and Torm, 2010). Whether formal firms starting up unregistered also witness lower subsequent levels of firm performance than enterprises starting up registered, however, is open to debate (see Williams *et al.*, 2017) and will be returned to in Chapter 5.

In sum, in second wave thought, informal entrepreneurship is viewed as more extensive in some economies due to the existence of incongruence between formal and informal institutions, resulting in the use of informal institutions as an alternative guiding framework (Mair *et al.*, 2012; Godfrey, 2015). When symmetry exists between these formal and informal institutions, little or no informal entrepreneurship will occur since the socially shared norms, values and beliefs of entrepreneurs will be aligned with the formal rules. However, when there is asymmetry between the formal and informal institutions, such as when there is a lack of trust in government and the rule of law, practices will emerge grounded in the socially shared norms that are illegitimate in terms of the formal rules. Informal sector entrepreneurship is one such practice. This second wave of institutional thought, therefore, has explained informal entrepreneurship as resulting from the incongruence between formal and informal institutions.

Third Wave Thought: Institutional Asymmetry as an Outcome of Formal Institutional Failures

In this book, the intention is to further advance institutional theory on informal entrepreneurship by offering a third wave perspective that synthesises the previous two viewpoints. In this first wave of thought, the view was that formal institutional failings and imperfections result in the prevalence of informal entrepreneurship. In the second wave of thought, however, it has been recognised that even if there are formal institutional failings, informal entrepreneurship would not necessarily result unless the socially shared norms, values and beliefs of entrepreneurs and citizens are not aligned with the formal rules, that is, unless they are substitutive. As such, informal entrepreneurship has been explained as resulting from the incongruence between formal and informal institutions.

In third wave thought, however, the argument will be that informal entrepreneurship is not solely produced by institutional asymmetry per se. Such institutional asymmetry is itself a result of formal institutional failings and imperfections. Here, therefore, and in what is here termed third wave thought, it will be argued that it is formal institutional failings and imperfections that produce an asymmetry between formal and informal institutions and that this then leads to the greater prevalence of informal entrepreneurship. The ways in which, and whether, formal institutional failings and imperfections produce institutional asymmetry is a complex and multifaceted process that will vary in different institutional environments. In some institutional contexts, such as when formal and informal institutions are complementary, and thus aligned, formal institutional failings may not lead to the greater prevalence of informal entrepreneurship. This, however, although hypothetically a possibility, is here considered not to be generally the case in most institutional environments and entrepreneurial ecosystems. It might be hypothetically the case, for example, in some long-standing and slow-to-change developed economies where the formal institutions over many decades have managed to both shape, and be shaped by, the informal institutions so that they become complementary through a process of iterative shaping of each other. However, it is not generally the case.

Much more commonly it is here believed that formal and informal institutions are substitutive, meaning that formal institutional failings and imperfections produce institutional asymmetry which in turn results in the acceptability and prevalence of informal entrepreneurship. The key issues that need to be analysed to put some flesh on this third wave thought, therefore, are, firstly, the precise formal institutional imperfections that lead to institutional asymmetry and thus the prevalence of informal entrepreneurship and, secondly, how these formal institutional failings and imperfections can be tackled. Indeed, these are the two key objectives addressed in this book.

In the next chapter, therefore, and to start to address these two objectives, attention turns to the theoretical explanations that have sought to determine the structural or country-level determinants of informal entrepreneurship to set the scene for a theoretically informed evaluation of the formal institutional failings that result in informal entrepreneurship. This, it should be noted, is a departure on many past studies which, when evaluating the determinants of institutional asymmetry, have tended to randomly select a range of variables to evaluate rather than to select them in a structured, theoretically informed manner. Part II of this book will then evaluate the validity of these determinants before turning attention in Part III to how to tackle these formal institutional failings that result in institutional asymmetry and thus the greater prevalence of informal entrepreneurship. The first step in consequence is to identify in a theoretically informed manner the range of formal institutional failings and imperfections that can lead to institutional asymmetry and thus the prevalence of entrepreneurship in the informal sector. This is the subject matter of the next chapter.

References

Acemoglu, D. and Robinson, J.A. (2012). *Why nations fail: The origins of power, prosperity and poverty*. London: Profile Books.

Aidis, R. and Van Praag, M.V. (2007). Illegal entrepreneurship experience: Does it make a difference for business performance and motivation? *Journal of Business Venturing*, 22(2), pp. 283–310.

Alm, J., Martinez-Vazque, E. and Torgler, B. (2006). Russian attitudes toward paying taxes: Before, during and after the transition. *International Journal of Social Economics*, 33(12), pp. 832–857.

Alm, J. and Torgler, B. (2006). Culture differences and tax morale in the United States and in Europe. *Journal of Economic Psychology*, 27(2), pp. 224–246.

Barbour, A. and Llanes, M. (2013). *Supporting people to legitimise their informal businesses*. York: Joseph Rowntree Foundation.

Bardhan, P. (1997). Corruption and development: A review of issues. *Journal of Economic Literature*, 35, pp. 1320–1346.

Barone, G. and Mocetti, S. (2009). *Tax morale and public spending in efficiency*. Rome: Economic Working Paper no. 732, Bank of Italy.

Baumol, W.J. and Blinder, A. (2008). *Macroeconomics: Principles and policy*. Cincinnati, OH: South-Western Publishing.

Becker, K.F. (2004). *The informal economy*. Stockholm: Swedish International Development Agency.

Benjamin, N.C. and Mbaye, A. (2012). The informal sector, productivity, and enforcement in West Africa: A firm-level analysis. *Review of Development Economics*, 16(4), pp. 472–492.

Bird, R., Martinez-Vazquez, J. and Torgler, B. (2006). Societal institutions and tax effort in developing countries. In: J. Alm, J. Martinez-Vazquez and M. Rider, Eds., *The challenges of tax reform in the global economy*. New York: Springer, pp. 283–338.

Braithwaite, V. and Reinhart, M. (2000). *The taxpayers' charter: Does the Australian tax office comply and who benefits*. Canberra: Centre for Tax System Integrity Working Paper no. 1, Australian National University.

Castells, M. and Portes, A. (1989). World underneath: The origins, dynamics and effects of the informal economy. In: A. Portes, M. Castells and L. Benton, Eds.,

The informal economy: Studies in advanced and less developing countries. Baltimore: John Hopkins University Press, pp. 19–41.

Chen, C.C., Chen, X.-P. and Huang, S. (2012). Chinese guanxi: An integrative review and new directions for future research. *Management and Organization Review*, 9(1), pp. 167–207.

Community Links and the Refugee Council. (2011). *Understanding the informal economic activity of refugees in London.* London: Community Links and the Refugee Council.

Copisarow, R. (2004). *Street UK: A micro-finance organisation: Lessons learned from its first three years' operations.* Birmingham: Street UK.

Copisarow, R. and Barbour, A. (2004). *Self-employed people in the informal economy: Cheats or contributors?* London: Community Links.

Cummings, R.G., Martinez-Vazquez, J., McKee, M. and Torgler, B. (2009). Tax morale affects tax compliance: Evidence from surveys and an artefactual field experiment. *Journal of Economic Behaviour and Organization*, 70(3), pp. 447–457.

Daude, C., Gutiérrez, H. and Melguizo, A. (2013). What drives tax morale? A focus on emerging economies. *Review of Public Economics*, 207(4), pp. 9–40.

Davis, M. (2006). *Planet of slums.* London: Verso.

De Castro, J.O., Khavul, S. and Bruton, G.D. (2014). Shades of grey: How do informal firms navigate between macro and meso institutional environments? *Strategic Entrepreneurship Journal*, 8, pp. 75–94.

Dellot, B. (2012). *Untapped enterprise: Learning to live with the informal economy.* London: Royal Society of the Arts.

De Mel, S., McKenzie, D. and Woodruff, C. (2012). The demand for, and consequences of, formalization among informal firms in Sri Lanka. *American Economic Journal: Applied Economics*, 5(2), pp. 122–150.

Demenet, A., Razafindrakoto, M. and Roubaud, F. (2016). Do informal businesses gain from registration and how? Panel data evidence from Vietnam. *World Development*, 84, pp. 326–341.

Denzau, A.T. and North, D. (1994). Shared mental models: Ideologies and institutions. *Kyklos*, 47, pp. 3–30.

De Rosa, D., Gooroochurn, N. and Gorg, H. (2010). *Corruption and productivity: Firm-level evidence from the Beeps survey.* Washington, DC: World Bank Policy Research Working Paper no. 5348, World Bank.

De Soto, H. (1989). *The other path: The invisible revolution in the third world.* New York: Harper and Row.

De Soto, H. (2001). *The mystery of capital: Why capitalism triumphs in the West and fails everywhere else.* London: Black Swan.

Devas, N. and Kelly, R. (2001). Regulation or revenue? An analysis of local business licenses, with a case study of the single business permit reform in Kenya. *Public Administration and Development*, 21, pp. 381–391.

Dong, B., Dulleck, U. and Torgler, B. (2012). Conditional corruption. *Journal of Economic Psychology*, 33, pp. 609–627.

Enste, D.H. (2011). Who is working illicitly and why? Insights from representative survey data in Germany. In: F. Schneider, Ed., *Handbook of the shadow economy.* Cheltenham: Edward Elgar, pp. 324–344.

Fajnzylber, P., Maloney, W.F. and Montes-Rojas, G.V. (2011). Does formality improve micro-firm performance? Evidence from the Brazilian SIMPLES program. *Journal of Development Economics*, 94(2), pp. 262–276.

Faruq, H. and Webb, M. (2013). Corruption, bureaucracy and firm productivity in Africa. *Review of Development Economics*, 17, pp. 117–129.

Ferreira, M.C., Fischer, R., Barreiros Porto, J., Pilati, R. and Milfont, T.L. (2012). Unravelling the history of Brazilian Jeitinho: A cultural exploration of social norms. *Personality and Social Psychology Bulletin*, 38(3), pp. 331–344.

Frey, B. (1997). *Not just for money: An economic theory of personal motivation*. Cheltenham: Edward Elgar.

Fries, S., Lysenko, T. and Polanec, S. (2003). *The 2002 business environment and enterprise performance survey: Results from a survey of 6,100 firms*. EBRD Working Paper no. 84. Available at: www.ebrd.com/pubs/find/index.html (last accessed 6 June 2017).

Gallin, D. (2001). Propositions on trade unions and informal employment in time of globalisation. *Antipode*, 19(4), pp. 531–549.

Garcia-Bolivar, O. (2006). *Informal economy: Is it a problem, a solution or both? The perspective of the informal business*. Berkeley, CA: Bepress Legal Series Paper no. 1065.

Gaviria, A. (2002). Assessing the effects of corruption and crime on firm performance: Evidence from Latin America. *Emerging Markets Review*, 3, pp. 245–268.

Giachi, S. (2014). Social dimensions of tax evasion: Trust and tax morale in contemporary Spain. *Revista Española de Investigaciones Sociológicas*, 145, pp. 73–98.

Godfrey, P.C. (2011). Toward a theory of the informal economy. *Academy of Management Annals*, 5(1), pp. 231–277.

Godfrey, P.C. (2015). Introduction: Why the informal economy matters to management. In: P.C. Godfrey, Ed., *Management, society, and the informal economy*. London: Routledge, pp. 1–20.

Halla, M. (2010). *Tax morale and compliance behaviour: First evidence on a causal link*. Bonn: IZA Discussion Paper no. 4918, IZA.

Hartner, M., Rechberger, S., Kirchler, E. and Schabmann, A. (2008). Procedural justice and tax compliance. *Economic Analysis and Policy*, 38(1), pp. 137–152.

Helmke, G. and Levitsky, S. (2004). Informal institutions and comparative politics: A research agenda. *Perspectives on Politics*, 2(6), pp. 725–740.

Horodnic, I. and Williams, C.C. (2016). An evaluation of the shadow economy in Baltic states: A tax morale perspective. *International Journal of Entrepreneurship and Small Business*, 28(2/3), pp. 339–358.

Hug, S. and Spörri, F. (2011). Referendums, trust and tax evasion. *European Journal of Political Economy*, 27(1), pp. 120–131.

Hulme, D. and Shepherd, A. (2003). Conceptualizing chronic poverty. *World Development*, 31(3), pp. 403–423.

ILO (2002). *Decent work and the informal economy*. Report VI for the 90th International Labour Conference. Geneva: ILO.

Jaramillo, M. (2009). *Is there demand for formality among informal firms? Evidence from microfirms in downtown Lima*. Bonn: German Development Institute Discussion Paper no. 12/2009, German Development Institute.

Kanniainen, V. and Pääkkönen, J. (2009). Do the catholic and protestant countries differ by their tax morale? *Empirica*, 37, pp. 271–290.

Katungi, D., Neale, E. and Barbour, A. (2006). *People in low-paid informal work*. York: Joseph Rowntree Foundation.

Khan, E.A. and Quaddus, M. (2015). Examining the influence of business environment on socio-economic performance of informal microenterprises: Content analysis and partial least square approach. *International Journal of Sociology and Social Policy*, 35(3/4), pp. 273–288.

Kinsey, K. and Gramsick, H. (1993). Did the tax reform act of 1986 improve compliance? Three studies of pre- and post-TRA compliance attitudes. *Law and Policy*, 15, pp. 239–325.

Kistruck, G.M., Webb, J.W., Sutter, C.J. and Bailey, A.V.G. (2015). The double-edged sword of legitimacy in base-of-the-pyramid markets. *Journal of Business Venturing*, 30(3), pp. 436–451.

Lago-Peñas, I. and Lago-Peñas, S. (2010). The determinants of tax morale in comparative perspective: Evidence from European countries. *European Journal of Political Economy*, 26, pp. 441–453.

La Porta, R. and Shleifer, A. (2008). The unofficial economy and economic development. *Brookings Papers on Economic Activity*, 47(1), pp. 123–135.

La Porta, R. and Shleifer, A. (2014). Informality and development. *Journal of Economic Perspectives*, 28(3), pp. 109–126.

Lavallée, E. and Roubaud, F. (2011). *Corruption and informal enterprise performance: West African evidence*. Amsterdam: International Institute of Social Studies.

Ledeneva, A.V. (2013). *Can Russia modernise? Sistema, power networks and informal governance*. Cambridge: Cambridge University Press.

Leonard, M. (1994). *Informal economic activity in Belfast*. Aldershot: Avebury.

Levitsky, S. and Murillo, M.V. (2009). Variation in institutional strength. *Annual Review of Political Science*, 12(1), pp. 115–133.

Lewis, A. (1982). *The psychology of taxation*. Oxford: Martin Robertson.

Llanes, M. and Barbour, A. (2007). *Self-employed and micro-entrepreneurs: Informal trading and the journey towards formalization*. London: Community Links.

London, T., Esper, H., Grogan-Kaylor, E. and Kistruck, G.M. (2014). Connecting poverty to purchase in informal markets. *Strategic Entrepreneurship Journal*, 8, pp. 37–55.

London, T. and Hart, S.L. (2004). Reinventing strategies for emerging markets: Beyond the transnational model. *Journal of International Business Studies*, 35(5), pp. 350–370.

Mair, J., Marti, I. and Ventresca, M. (2012). Building inclusive markets in rural Bangladesh: How intermediaries work institutional voids. *Academy of Management Journal*, 55, pp. 819–850.

Martínez-Vázquez, J. and Torgler, B. (2009). The evolution of tax morale in modern Spain. *Journal of Economic Issues*, 43(1), pp. 1–28.

Mathias, B.D., Lux, S., Crook, T.R., Autry, C. and Zaretzki, R. (2014). Competing against the unknown: The impact of enabling and constraining institutions on the informal economy. *Journal of Business Ethics*, 127(2), pp. 251–264.

Mauro, P. (1995). Corruption and growth. *Quarterly Journal of Economics*, 110(3), pp. 681–712.

McCulloch, N., Schulze, G. and Voss, J. (2010). *What determines firms' decisions to formalize?* Frieburg: Discusiion Paper Series no. 13, University of Frieburg Department of International Economic Policy.

McGee, R.W., Alver, J. and Alver, L. (2008). The ethics of tax evasion: A survey of Estonian opinion. In: R.W. McGee, Ed., *Taxation and public finance in transition and developing countries*. Berlin: Springer, pp. 119–136.

McKenzie, D. and Sakho, Y.S. (2010). Does it pay firms to register for taxes? The impact of formality on firm profitability. *Journal of Development Economics*, 91(1), pp. 15–24.

Molero, J.C. and Pujol, F. (2012). Walking inside the potential tax evader's mind: Tax morale does matter. *Journal of Business Ethics*, 105, pp. 151–162.

Murphy, K. (2003). Procedural fairness and tax compliance. *Australian Journal of Social Issues*, 38(3), pp. 379–408.

Murphy, K. (2005). Regulating more effectively: The relationship between procedural justice, legitimacy and tax non-compliance. *Journal of Law and Society*, 32(4), pp. 562–589.

Murphy, K., Tyler, T. and Curtis, A. (2009). Nurturing regulatory compliance: Is procedural fairness effective when people question the legitimacy of the law? *Regulation and Governance*, 3, pp. 1–26.

Myrdal, G. (1968). *Asian drama: An inquiry into the poverty of nations*. New York: Pantheon.

North, D.C. (1990). *Institution, institutional change and economic performance.* Cambridge: Cambridge University Press.

Nwabuzor, A. (2005). Corruption and development: New initiatives in economic openness and strengthened rule of law. *Journal of Business Ethics*, 59(1/2), pp. 121–138.

Orviska, M. and Hudson, J. (2003). Tax evasion, civic duty and the law abiding citizen. *European Journal of Political Economy*, 19, pp. 83–102.

Ostapenko, N. and Williams, C.C. (2016). Determinants of entrepreneurs' views on the acceptability of tax evasion and the informal economy in Slovakia and Ukraine: An institutional asymmetry approach. *International Journal of Entrepreneurship and Small Business*, 28(2/3), pp. 121–145.

Perry, G.E. and Maloney, W.F. (2007). Overview: Informality: Exit and exclusion. In: G.E. Perry, W.F. Maloney, O.S. Arias, P. Fajnzylber, A.D. Mason and J. Saavedra-Chanduvi, Eds., *Informality: Exit and exclusion.* Washington, DC: World Bank, pp. 1–20.

Pommerehne, W.W. and Weck-Hannemann, H. (1996). Tax rates, tax administration, and income tax evasion in Switzerland. *Public Choice*, 88, pp. 161–170.

Pope, J. (2000). *Confronting corruption: The elements of a national integrity system.* Berlin, Germany: Transparency International Source Book.

Portes, A. (1994). The informal economy and its paradoxes. In: N.J. Smelser and R. Swedberg, Eds., *The handbook of economic sociology.* Princeton: Princeton University Press, pp. 142–165.

Qian, J.U.N. and Strahan, P.E. (2007). How laws and institutions shape financial contracts: The case of bank loans. *Journal of Finance*, 62, pp. 2803–2834.

Rand, J. and Torm, N. (2010). *The benefits of formalization: Evidence from Vietnamese SMEs.* Copenhagen: Development Economics Research Group (DERG), Department of Economics, University of Copenhagen.

Riahi-Belkaoui, A. (2004). Relationship between tax compliance internationally and selected determinants of tax morale. *Journal of International Accounting, Auditing and Taxation*, 13(2), pp. 135–143.

Richardson, G. (2006). Determinants of tax evasion: A cross-country investigation. *Journal of International Accounting, Auditing and Taxation*, 15(2), pp. 150–169.

Richardson, M. and Sawyer, A. (2001). A taxonomy of the tax compliance literature: Further findings, problems and prospects. *Australian Tax Forum*, 16(2), pp. 137–320.

Round, J., Williams, C.C. and Rodgers, P. (2008). Corruption in the post-Soviet workplace: The experiences of recent graduates in contemporary Ukraine. *Work, Employment and Society*, 22(1), pp. 149–166.

Sander, C. (2003). *Less is more: Better compliance and increased revenues by streamlining business registration in Uganda.* London: Department for International Development.

Sassen, S. (1996). Service employment regimes and the new inequality. In: E. Mingione, Ed., *Urban poverty and the underclass.* Oxford: Basil Blackwell, pp. 142–159.

Sauvy, A. (1984). *Le travail noir et l'economie de demain.* Paris: Calmann-Levy.

Schneider, F. and Williams, C.C. (2013). *The shadow economy.* London: Institute of Economic Affairs.

Scott, W.R. (2008). *Institutions and organizations: Ideas and interests.* London: Sage.

Shleifer, A. and Vishny, R.W. (1993). Corruption. *Quarterly Journal of Economics*, 108, pp. 599–617.

Sine, W.D. and David, R.J. (2010). Institutions and entrepreneurship. In: W.D. Sine and R.J. David, Eds., *Institutions and entrepreneurship: Research in the sociology of work.* Bingley: Emerald, pp. 1–26.

Siqueira, A.C.O., Webb, J.W. and Bruton, G.D. (2016). Informal entrepreneurship and industry conditions. *Entrepreneurship Theory and Practice*, 40(1), pp. 177–200.

Skousen, B.R. and Mahoney, J.T. (2015). Factors influencing the registration decision in the informal economy. In: P.C. Godfrey, Ed., *Management, society, and the informal economy*. London: Routledge, pp. 95–112.

Slavnic, Z. (2010). Political economy of informalization. *European Societies*, 12(1), pp. 3–23.

Small Business Council (2004). *Small business in the informal economy: Making the transition to the formal economy*. London: Small Business Council.

Smith, P., Huang, H.J., Harb, C. and Torres, C. (2012). How distinctive are indigenous ways of achieving influence? A comparative study of guanxi, wasta, jeitinho, svyazi and pulling strings. *Journal of Cross-Cultural Psychology*, 43(1), pp. 135–150.

Smith, P., Torres, C., Leong, C.H., Budhwar, P., Achoui, M. and Lebedeva, N. (2011). Are indigenous approaches to achieving influence in business organizations distinctive? A comparative study of guanxi, wasta, jeitinho, svyazi and pulling strings. *International Journal of Human Resource Management*, 23(2), pp. 333–348.

Stinchcombe, A.L. (1965). Social structure and organizations. In: J.G. March, Ed., *Handbook of organizations*. Chicago, IL: Rand McNally, pp. 142–193.

Svensson, J. (2005). Eight questions about corruption. *Journal of Economic Perspectives*, 19, pp. 19–42.

Teal, F. and McArthur, J. (2002). *Corruption and firm performance in Africa*. Oxford: University of Oxford Department of Economics Working Paper no. 2002–10.

Thai, M.T.T. and Turkina, E. (2014). Macro-level determinants of formal entrepreneurship versus informal entrepreneurship. *Journal of Business Venturing*, 29(4), pp. 490–510.

Thurman, Q.C., St. John, C. and Riggs, L. (1984). Neutralisation and tax evasion: How effective would a moral appeal be in improving compliance to tax laws? *Law and Policy*, 6(3), pp. 309–327.

Tonoyan, V., Strohmeyer, R., Habib, M. and Perlitz, M. (2010). Corruption and entrepreneurship: How formal and informal institutions shape small firm behaviour in transition and mature market economies. *Entrepreneurship Theory and Practice*, 34(5), pp. 803–831.

Torgler, B. (2004). Tax morale in Asian countries. *Journal of Asian Economics*, 15(2), pp. 237–266.

Torgler, B. (2005a). Tax morale and direct democracy. *European Journal of Political Economy*, 21, pp. 525–531.

Torgler, B. (2005b). Tax morale in Latin America. *Public Choice*, 122(1), pp. 133–157.

Torgler, B. (2006). The importance of faith: Tax morale and religiosity. *Journal of Economic Behavior and Organization*, 61, pp. 81–109.

Torgler, B. (2011). *Tax morale and compliance: Review of evidence and case studies for Europe*. Washington, DC: World Bank Policy Research Working Paper no. 5922, World Bank.

Torgler, B. and Schneider, F. (2007). What shapes attitudes toward paying taxes? Evidence from multicultural European countries. *Social Science Quarterly*, 88(2), pp. 443–470.

Torgler, B. and Schneider, F. (2009). The impact of tax morale and institutional quality on the shadow economy. *Journal of Economic Psychology*, 30, pp. 228–245.

Webb, J.W., Bruton, G.D., Tihanyi, L. and Ireland, R.D. (2013). Research on entrepreneurship in the informal economy: Framing a research agenda. *Journal of Business Venturing*, 28(5), pp. 598–614.

Webb, J.W. and Ireland, R.D. (2015). Laying the foundation for a theory of informal adjustments. In: P.C. Godfrey, Ed., *Management, society, and the informal economy*. London: Routledge, pp. 21–41.

Webb, J.W., Ireland, R.D. and Ketchen, D.J. (2014). Toward a greater understanding of entrepreneurship and strategy in the informal economy. *Strategic Entrepreneurship Journal*, 8, pp. 1–15.

Webb, J.W., Tihanyi, L., Ireland, R.D. and Sirmon, D.G. (2009). You say illegal, I say legitimate: Entrepreneurship in the informal economy. *Academy of Management Review*, 34(3), pp. 492–510.

Welter, F., Smallbone, D. and Pobol, A. (2015). Entrepreneurial activity in the informal economy: A missing piece of the jigsaw puzzle. *Entrepreneurship and Regional Development*, 27(5/6), pp. 292–306.

Williams, C.C. and Bezeredi, S. (2017). Evaluating the use of personal connections to bypass formal procedures: A study of *vrski* in FYR Macedonia. *UTMS Journal of Economics*, 8(2), pp. 1–19.

Williams, C.C. and Gurtoo, A. (2017). The institutional environment of entrepreneurship in developing countries: An introductory overview. In: C.C. Williams and A. Gurtoo, Eds., *Routledge handbook of entrepreneurship in developing economies*. London: Routledge, pp. 13–16.

Williams, C.C. and Horodnic, I. (2015a). Evaluating the prevalence of the undeclared economy in Central and Eastern Europe: An institutional asymmetry perspective. *European Journal of Industrial Relations*, 21(4), pp. 389–406.

Williams, C.C. and Horodnic, I. (2015b). Explaining and tackling the shadow economy in Estonia, Latvia and Lithuania: A tax morale approach. *Journal of Baltic Economics*, 15(2), pp. 81–98.

Williams, C.C. and Horodnic, I. (2015c). Explaining the prevalence of the informal economy in the Baltics: An institutional asymmetry perspective. *European Spatial Research and Policy*, 22(2), pp. 127–144.

Williams, C.C., Horodnic, I. and Windebank, J. (2015). Explaining participation in the informal economy: An institutional incongruence perspective. *International Sociology*, 30(3), pp. 294–313.

Williams, C.C. and Kedir, A. (2016). The impacts of corruption on firm performance: Some lessons from 40 African countries. *Journal of Developmental Entrepreneurship*, 21(4), pp. 1–18.

Williams, C.C. and Martinez-Perez, A. (2016). Evaluating the impacts of corruption on firm performance in developing economies: An institutional perspective. *International Journal of Business and Globalisation*, 16(4), pp. 401–422.

Williams, C.C., Martinez-Perez, A. and Kedir, A.M. (2016b). Does bribery have a negative impact on firm performance? A firm-level analysis across 132 developing countries. *International Journal of Entrepreneurial Behaviour and Research*, 22(3), pp. 398–415.

Williams, C.C., Martinez-Perez, A. and Kedir, A.M. (2017). Informal entrepreneurship in developing economies: The impacts of starting-up unregistered on firm performance. *Entrepreneurship Theory and Practice*, doi: 10.1111/etap.12238

Williams, C.C., Nadin, S. and Rodgers, P. (2012a). Evaluating competing theories of informal entrepreneurship: Some lessons from Ukraine. *International Journal of Entrepreneurial Behaviour and Research*, 18(5), pp. 528–543.

Williams, C.C., Nadin, S., Barbour, A. and Llanes, M. (2012b). *Enabling enterprise: Tackling the barriers to formalisation*. London: Community Links.

Williams, C.C. and Onoshchenko, O. (2014). Evaluating the role of *blat* in finding graduate employment in post-Soviet Ukraine: The 'dark side' of job recruitment? *Employee Relations*, 36(3), pp. 254–265.

Williams, C.C. and Onoshchenko, O. (2015). An evaluation of the persistence of blat in post-Soviet societies: A case study of Ukraine's health services sector. *Studies in Transition States and Societies*, 7(2), pp. 46–63.

Williams, C.C., Round, J. and Rodgers, P. (2013). *The role of informal economies in the post-Soviet world: The end of transition?* London: Routledge.

Williams, C.C. and Shahid, M. (2016). Informal entrepreneurship and institutional theory: Explaining the varying degrees of (in)formalisation of entrepreneurs in Pakistan. *Entrepreneurship and Regional Development*, 28(1/2), pp. 1–25.

Williams, C.C., Shahid, M. and Martinez, A. (2016a). Determinants of the level of informality of informal micro-enterprises: Some evidence from the city of Lahore, Pakistan. *World Development*, 84, pp. 312–325.

Williams, C.C. and Yang, J. (2017). Evaluating the use of personal networks to circumvent formal processes: A case study of *vruzki* in Bulgaria. *The South East European Journal of Economics and Business*, 12(1), pp. 57–67.

Windebank, J. and Horodnic, I.A. (2017). Explaining participation in undeclared work in France: Lessons for policy evaluation. *International Journal of Sociology and Social Policy*, 37(3/4), pp. 203–217.

Wunsch-Vincent, S., de Beer, J. and Fu, K. (2015). What we know and do not know about innovation in the informal economy. In: E. Kraemer-Mbula and S. Wunsch-Vincent, Eds., *The informal economy in developing nations: Hidden engine of innovation? New economic insights and policies*. Cambridge: Cambridge University Press, pp. 142–160.

3 Determinants of Institutional Asymmetry

Introduction

In the last chapter, a theoretical explanation for informal entrepreneurship was set out based on institutionalist theory. This argued that formal institutional failures and imperfections lead to the development of asymmetry between formal and informal institutions, which results in a greater prevalence of informal entrepreneurship. In this chapter, the formal institutional failings and imperfections that are determinants of this institutional asymmetry will be discussed. Until now, analyses of the formal institutional failures and imperfections that lead to the development of institutional asymmetry, and thus the greater prevalence of informal entrepreneurship, have tended to adopt a random, or what might be termed scattergun, approach to the selection of variables to evaluate. In this chapter, however, the intention is to draw upon earlier theories that sought to explain the prevalence of informal entrepreneurship to identify the main formal institutional failures and imperfections to evaluate.

To do this, a review is conducted of the various formal institutional failures and imperfections identified in the three major competing theories of informal entrepreneurship, namely, modernisation theory which pinpoints economic underdevelopment and unmodern systems of governance, manifested in high levels of corruption, as key determinants of informal entrepreneurship; neo-liberal theory which focuses upon too much government intervention in the form of high taxes and burdensome regulations and controls as key determinants; and political economy theory which conversely identifies inadequate state intervention and the lack of protection of workers as the key determinants of informal entrepreneurship. This will then set the scene for a critical evaluation in Part II of this book regarding which of these formal institutional failures and imperfections are significantly associated with the development of institutional asymmetry and thus the greater prevalence of entrepreneurship in the informal sector.

To commence, therefore, the first section of this chapter will review modernisation theory and set out each of key factors which it views as determining the prevalence of informal entrepreneurship. The second section then turns its attention to political economy theory and its view that inadequate state intervention and protection of workers determine the level of informal entrepreneurship. Thirdly and finally, neo-liberal theory is addressed and how it views too much government intervention in the form of high taxes and burdensome regulations as the key drivers of entrepreneurship in the informal sector.

Modernisation Theory

Modernisation theory was the dominant perspective towards the informal sector in general and informal entrepreneurship, more particularly, throughout the twentieth century. In this theoretical approach, work in the informal sector is portrayed as a remnant or leftover from a pre-modern mode of production and as fading as the modern formal sector takes hold (Geertz, 1963; Gilbert, 1998; Lewis, 1959; Packard, 2007). As Bromley (2007: xv) asserts, from this modernisation perspective, the informal sector is viewed as 'unimportant and destined to disappear'. This sector is therefore portrayed as a by-product of underdevelopment and will disappear with economic advancement and the modernisation of governance. Sometimes referred to as 'residue' or 'dual economy' theory, the informal sector is nothing more than a leftover or residue from an earlier mode of production and consumption and, as such, will fade from view as a result of economic advancement and modernisation.

Conceptually, therefore, the view is that the informal sector is separate from the formal sector and informal entrepreneurship discrete from formal entrepreneurship. Viewed from a broader philosophical perspective, this view corresponds with the theory of binary oppositions discussed by Derrida (1967). For him, Western thought is based on conceptualising binaries or dualisms whereby activity is viewed in either/or terms as discrete and separate binary opposites. Often, moreover, as Derrida (1967) suggests in his thesis of hierarchical binary thought, these either/or opposites are ordered in a hierarchical normative relationship and temporal sequencing with each other. One binary opposite is considered superordinate, while the other is subordinate. In modernisation theory, it is informality and informal entrepreneurship that is viewed as subordinate and viewed negatively in both normative and temporal terms and seen as associated with underdevelopment. The formal sector and formal entrepreneurship, meanwhile, is viewed as superordinate, positive and connected with progress and as growing and emerging (Williams and Round, 2008; Williams, 2014a).

For Chen (2006, 2012, 2014), however, this view of the informal sector and informal entrepreneurship in binary hierarchical thought has to be rethought, not least due to the fact the informal sector is extensive and has grown in many places and various new forms have even emerged. Table 3.1 provides a summary of the main differences between this 'old' hierarchical binary view of the informal sector (i.e., modernisation theory) and 'new' ways of viewing this phenomenon.

Table 3.1 Old and New Views of the Informal Sector

The old view	The new view
The informal sector is the traditional economy that will disappear with modernisation and economic growth.	The informal sector is 'here to stay' and expanding in contemporary capitalist society.
It is only marginally productive.	It is a major provider of employment, goods and services, especially for lower-income groups, and is a significant share of GDP.
It exists separately from the formal sector.	It is linked to the formal sector – it produces for, trades with, distributes for and provides services to the formal sector.
It represents a reserve pool of surplus labour.	Much of the recent rise in informal employment is due to the decline in formal employment or the informalisation of previously formal employment relationships.
It is comprised mostly of street traders and very small-scale producers.	It is made up of a wide range of informal occupations – both 'resilient old forms' such as casual day labour in construction and agriculture as well as 'emerging new ones' such as temporary and part-time jobs plus homework for high-tech industries.
Most of those in the sector are entrepreneurs who run illegal and unregistered enterprises to avoid regulation and taxation.	It is made up of non-standard wage workers as well as entrepreneurs and self-employed persons producing legal goods and services, albeit through irregular or unregulated means. Most entrepreneurs and the self-employed are amenable to, and would welcome, efforts to reduce barriers to registration and related transaction costs and to increase benefits from regulation; most informal wage workers would welcome more stable jobs and workers' rights.
Work in the informal sector is comprised mostly of survival activities and thus is not a subject for economic policy.	Informal enterprises include not only survival activities but also stable enterprises and dynamic growing businesses, and informal employment includes not only self-employment but also wage employment. All forms of informal employment are affected by most (if not all) economic policies.

Source: adaptation and revision of Chen *et al.* (2004: 20)

In temporal terms, therefore, the superordinate formal sector, and formal entrepreneurship, is viewed as growing and replacing the subordinate informal sector and informal entrepreneurship, which is seen as disappearing. In the middle of the last century, for example, there was a widespread belief that industrialisation, economic development and modernisation would pull workers in developing countries out of the supposedly unproductive informal sector and into the modern industrial formal sector. This theory stemmed from the experience of rebuilding Europe and Japan following World War II and the expansion of industrialisation in the United States and Britain.

The assumption was therefore that there is a mono-dimensional linear pattern of economic development in which less developed countries would, naturally and inevitably, follow the path of capitalist economic development 'enjoyed' by the advanced economies. This took no account of the differential histories and that the global economic and political situation facing Africa, Asia and Latin America were markedly different from those experienced by Europe and North America. Neither was account taken of the fact that global power relations remain heavily skewed in favour of those already 'modern' advanced economies. Indeed one of the main reasons for the refutation of modernisation theory is 'a widespread recognition that the informal sector is not some weak and disappearing realm but strong, persistent and even growing in the contemporary global economy' (Williams and Round, 2007: 32).

In normative terms, it is similarly the case that the superordinate formal sector, as well as formal entrepreneurship, is depicted as a virtuous, positive and beneficial phenomenon. Meanwhile, the informal sector, and informal entrepreneurship, is depicted in harmful, negative and deleterious terms. Nowhere is this more prominently displayed in the entrepreneurship literature than in the work of Baumol (1990), who discusses formal entrepreneurship as 'productive' entrepreneurship and informal entrepreneurship as 'unproductive' entrepreneurship.

However, it is not just the temporal and normative hierarchical sequencing of formal and informal entrepreneurship in modernisation theory that is important. Potts (2008) sees the main problem of the dualistic conceptualisation of the formal and informal sector, and formal and informal entrepreneurship, to be the fallacious view of 'disconnection' between the two sectors and argues that this modernisation perspective 'has descriptive value but is dangerously misleading if translated into policy that is founded on an idea that the sectors are functionally separate' (Potts, 2008: 152–153).

This notion of representing the economy in discrete dualistic terms is associated with scholars such as Boeke (1942), in relation to their studies on South-East Asia, and the economist Lewis (1954). The discrete dualistic depiction of the formal and informal economies differed in some ways to the then dominant neo-classical economic models, although Lewis was in that tradition. At the core of the dualist view was that less developed countries had two different sectors. One was capitalist in its mode of production, modernising, progressive, dynamic and often depicted as capital intensive. The other, the 'subsistence' or 'peasant' sector (or in later terminology the 'marginal' sector), was portrayed as a pre-capitalist mode of production reliant on family labour, unsophisticated in its production and operations, using low technology and possessing poor productivity. These were viewed as separate. For Lewis (1954), economic development involved the fading away of the latter sector as it was absorbed by and transformed into the former. Boeke (1942), developing the notion of 'social dualism', portrayed a culture clash between the imported social systems (e.g., capitalism) and the indigenous social systems, thus transcending the notion of merely two purely economic systems by depicting them as also two separate social systems incorporating different social values. He did not believe that the two separate societies could coexist successfully and argued that governments needed to adopt separate policies for each. The approach was to 'transform' the traditional pre-capitalist sector into a 'modern' one.

From the perspective of modernisation theory, therefore, the size of the informal sector and informal entrepreneurship in a country indicates its position on a one-dimensional linear trajectory towards formalisation. Classifying countries in this way thus enables the relative level of economic advancement and modernisation to be measured and for countries to be placed according to their place in the development queue with nations at the fore with small informal economies being 'advanced', 'modern' and 'progressive' and nations at the back of the queue with large informal economies being deemed 'backward', 'traditional' and 'underdeveloped' (Geertz, 1963; Gilbert, 1998; Lewis, 1959; Packard, 2007). According to this perspective, therefore, informal entrepreneurs are the antithesis of everything modern and signal underdevelopment and backwardness (Potts, 2008; Williams and Gurtoo, 2012; Williams and Round, 2007).

To evaluate the validity of the view in modernisation theory that informal entrepreneurship is more prevalent in less economically developed economies, therefore, there is a need to evaluate the relationship between cross-national variations in the prevalence of informal entrepreneurship and cross-national variations in gross domestic product (GDP) per capita (ILO, 2013). If the modernisation theory is correct, then the finding will be that there is a significant positive association between increasing levels of GDP per capita and decreasing levels of informal entrepreneurship. Using a simple bivariate analysis, many studies have revealed a strong association between higher levels of GDP per capita and lower levels of work in the informal sector and informal entrepreneurship (Bologna, 2014; ILO, 2013; Williams, 2015a,b,c). Bologna (2014), for example, evaluates Brazilian municipalities and finds that an increase in the size of the informal sector is associated with a decrease in GDP per capita.

To evaluate the validity of the view in modernisation theory that informal entrepreneurship is more prevalent in societies where there is poor quality governance and corruption, meanwhile, there is a need to evaluate the relationship between cross-national variations in the prevalence of informal entrepreneurship and cross-national variations in the quality of governance and corruption. Previous studies have revealed that the higher the quality of governance, the greater is the level of institutional symmetry (Daude *et al.*, 2013; Torgler, 2012). More particularly, the higher is the trust in the justice system and government, the greater is the institutional symmetry (Daude *et al.*, 2013; Giachi, 2014; Lago Peñas and Lago Peñas, 2010; Martínez-Vázquez and Torgler, 2009; Torgler, 2005a, 2012; Torgler and Schneider, 2007) and the greater is the satisfaction with public services, the higher is the institutional symmetry (Daude *et al.*, 2013; Russo, 2013; Torgler, 2005b). As Kuehn (2014) reveals in relation to OECD countries, tax rates alone explain only 23 per cent of the cross-national variations in the size of the informal sector. Taking into account both governance quality and tax rates, agreement between the model's results and the data increases to 72 per cent. A policy experiment raising governance quality in Greece, Italy, Spain and Portugal to Finnish standards, it is argued, would reduce the size of the informal sector by 13 percentage points. Thus, the quality of governance appears to be an important determinant of the level of informality.

Many other studies reinforce this relationship among low institutional quality, corruption and the size of the informal sector. Friedman *et al.* (2000), Chong and Gradstein (2007) and Johnson *et al.* (1998) all find a positive relationship among low institutional quality, a large regulatory burden, corruption, and the size of the informal sector. Davis and Henrekson (2005) also find that the relationship between institutional quality and informality holds across a sample of 21 high-income countries, showing the negative relationship between the size of the informal sector and the commonly used World Bank governance indicators on government effectiveness, regulatory quality, rule of law and control of corruption. While slightly weakened, the negative relationship between institutional quality and informality is also robust to the exclusion of the three poorest countries in the sample: Greece, Portugal and Spain.

Hence the relationship between corruption and the informal sector, as well as informal entrepreneurship, from the viewpoint of this modernisation theory, is that greater levels of corruption are associated with higher levels of informality and informal entrepreneurship. From this perspective, corruption by public officials, which can be seen as an additional form of taxation and an additional burdensome form of regulation that needs to be overcome, is driving entrepreneurs out of the formal sector and into the informal sector, where they can be free of such costs of formality. Although there may still be extortion from public officials of those working in the informal sector, the perception is that these will be lower than for entrepreneurs attempting to operate on a formal basis and having to pay bribes for permits and licenses, for instance. From this modernisation perspective, therefore, corruption and informality are complements; increased corruption, which acts like an additional tax increasing the regulatory burden, leads more entrepreneurs to operate informally (Buehn and Schneider, 2012; Dreher and Schneider, 2010; Friedman *et al.*, 2000; Goel and Saunoris, 2014; Hibbs and Piculescu, 2005; Hindriks *et al.*, 1999; Johnson *et al.*, 1997, 1998; Wallace and Latcheva, 2006).

However, others argue that corruption and informality are substitutes; as more entrepreneurs enter the informal sector, this reduces the ability of officials to secure bribes (Choi and Thum, 2005; Dreher *et al.*, 2009; Katsios, 2006; Rose-Ackerman, 1997). Choi and Thum (2005) present a model in which the entrepreneur's option to enter the informal sector constrains the corrupt bureaucrat's ability to ask for bribes. The informal sector thus mitigates imperfections in the formal sector and disables bureaucrats from achieving personal gains. Consequently, the existence of the informal sector reduces corruption. For example, Rose-Ackerman (1997: 21) notes that 'going underground is a substitute for bribery, although sometimes firms bribe officials in order to avoid official taxes'. Yet others have adopted a more nuanced approach, arguing either that they are complements in low-income countries, but that no relationship exists between corruption and informality in high-income countries (Dreher and Schneider, 2010), or that corruption and informality are only significantly associated in the tropics, where they are substitutes, but are not significantly associated elsewhere (Virta, 2010).

In much of the literature, this modernisation theory, which posits that informality is associated with the level of economic development and the quality of governance and level of corruption, is portrayed as an old theoretical perspective that has been superseded. This is because of its binary hierarchical depiction of the two spheres as separate and its view that the subordinate informal sector is declining and fading from view as economies develop and modernise their governance. However, it is far from the case that modernisation theory is some old-fashioned perspective that is no longer adhered to and has been superseded.

Indeed, in recent years, there have been concerted attempts to update conventional modernisation theory. The principal scholars to have done so are La Porta and Shleifer (2008, 2014). They recognise the persistence of informality and its extensiveness but nonetheless maintain the other basic tenets of modernisation theory. That is to say, they continue to maintain a portrayal of the informal and formal economies as disconnected sectors and to adopt a depiction of the informal sector and informal entrepreneurship as a negative phenomenon, portraying informal entrepreneurs as typically uneducated people operating small, unproductive enterprises in separate 'bottom of the pyramid' (BOP) markets producing low-quality products for low-income consumers using little capital and adding little value (La Porta and Shleifer, 2014). The basic tenets of modernisation theory are therefore maintained that the formal and informal economies are discrete and a hierarchical binary, with the formal sector endowed with positive features and the informal sector with negative features. So too is the view that the informal sector and informal entrepreneurship are consequently associated with the level of economic development and quality of governance and corruption.

Political Economy Theory

A second alternative explanation for the prevalence of informal entrepreneurship derives from a loose grouping of scholars who have adopted a political economy perspective and recognise that the formal and informal spheres are not entirely disconnected. This political economy school of thought was propagated by Caroline Moser in the late 1970s (Moser, 1977) and by Portes and colleagues in the late 1980s (see Castells and Portes, 1989; Portes, 1994). Unlike the modernisation perspective, this school moves away from the notion that the informal sector is a residue of traditional economic systems (i.e., economic dualism). Instead it views those in the informal sector as working in subordinate economic units and adopts a view of the structural dependency of the informal sector and the exploitation of the informal workforce by the formal sector (Castells and Portes, 1989). In this perspective, informal entrepreneurship is therefore viewed as a sector that is dependent on the formal sector and performs subordinated functions that reduce the costs of formal manufacturing and distribution, thereby increasing their market competitiveness (see Castells and Portes, 1989). The proponents of this school of thought, therefore, reject the separation of informal entrepreneurship from the formal sector. Instead, they uphold the view that the two economies are functionally related sectors and part of the same economic system, namely, late capitalism (Portes, 1994).

From this perspective, the growth of informal entrepreneurship is viewed as a direct by-product of the emergence of an ever more deregulated and open world economy (Aliyev, 2015; Bhattacharya, 2014; Castells and Portes, 1989; Dibben and Williams, 2012; Dibben *et al.*, 2015; Gallin, 2001; Harriss-White, 2014; Hudson, 2005; Portes, 1994; Sassen, 1996; Slavnic, 2010; Taiwo, 2013). The increasing functional integration of a single global economic system results in subcontracting and outsourcing becoming a primary means of integrating employment in the informal sector and informal entrepreneurship into contemporary capitalism, causing a further downward pressure on wages and the erosion of incomes, social services and benefits and the growth of yet more jobs in the informal sector and informal entrepreneurship. For example, one contemporary manifestation of this is that workers who were former employees are now seen to engage in 'false self-employment' for one supplier only in the so-called gig or platform economy (Williams, 2017). As Fernandez-Kelly (2006: 18) states, 'the informal sector is far from a vestige of earlier stages in economic development. Instead, informality is part and parcel of the processes of modernization'. Indeed for Davis (2006: 186), such 'primitive forms of exploitation ... have been given new life by postmodern globalization'. Informal enterprises are integrated into contemporary capitalism to reduce production costs (Castells and Portes, 1989; Davis, 2006; Meagher, 2010; Slack *et al.*, 2017; Slavnic, 2010; Taiwo, 2013).

The growth of the informal sector and informal entrepreneurship, therefore, is seen as part of what Piore and Sabel (1984) describe as the reorganisation of production into small-scale, decentralised and more flexible economic units as part of the shift away from Fordist mass production and towards 'flexible specialisation'. The outcome, they argue, has been the informalisation of employment relations. Standard wage jobs (i.e., regular full-time jobs) were being turned into non-standard wage jobs (including part-time, temporary and contract jobs) with hourly wages but few benefits or into piece-rate jobs with no benefits; self-employment persisted or expanded; and production of goods and services was being subcontracted to small-scale informal units and industrial outworkers. As such, the informal sector and informal entrepreneurship have become a permanent, but subordinate and dependent, feature of capitalist development. Meanwhile, structural adjustment in Africa and economic transition in the former Soviet Union and in Central and Eastern Europe were also associated with an expansion of the informal sector. This is because, in response to global competition, formal firms hire all but a few core workers under informal arrangements or outsource the production of goods and services to other firms and countries. Informality, therefore, is not simply an outcome of excess labour supply or over-regulation (Yusuff, 2011: 628). Instead, the informal sector and informal entrepreneurship 'exists to serve the needs of the larger firms by supplying cheaper goods and services' (Dellot, 2012: 16). As a result, the 'rich formal sector extracts value from the poor informal sector' to lock in a persistent inequitable world system (Godfrey, 2011: 246).

Moreover, the resultant diminishing state involvement in social protection and economic intervention accompanying deregulation are seen to have led to those excluded from the formal labour market and social protection being pushed into informal entrepreneurship as a survival strategy (Chen, 2012; ILO, 2014; Meagher, 2010; Mešić, 2016; Sasaki *et al.*, 2016; Taiwo, 2013). Consequently, although recognising informal entrepreneurship as intertwined with the formal realm, it remains depicted as having negative impacts. Firstly, this is because economies are viewed as losing 'natural' competitiveness because productive formal enterprises suffer unfair competition from unproductive informal enterprises (Leal Ordóñez, 2014; Levy, 2008; Lewis, 2004). Secondly, governments are viewed as losing both regulatory control over work conditions (ILO, 2014) and tax revenue (Bajada and Schneider, 2005) and, thirdly, customers as lacking legal recourse and certainty that health and safety regulations have been followed (Williams and Martinez-Perez, 2014). Informal entrepreneurs, meanwhile, are viewed as 'necessity driven' (Castells and Portes, 1989; Gallin, 2001), lacking access to capital, credit and financial services (ILO, 2014), which when combined with the need to keep their business small to stay 'under the radar' of the authorities (Williams *et al.*, 2012), lack of advice and support (Barbour and Llanes, 2013) and an inability to secure formal intellectual property rights to process and product innovations (De Beer *et al.*, 2013) mean that they become locked in a 'poverty trap' (McKenzie and Woodruff, 2006).

Entrepreneurs who operate in the informal sector are thus assumed in this political economy perspective to be low-paid, marginalised populations who engage in this endeavour out of necessity, pushed into this enterprise as a survival strategy in the absence of alternative options (e.g., Barsoum, 2015; Castells and Portes, 1989; Gallin, 2001; Lagos, 1995; Maldonado, 1995). As Travers (2002: 2) puts it, '[i]t is usually said that people do the work to earn extra money and left at that'. From street sellers in the Dominican Republic (e.g. Itzigsohn, 2000) and Somalia (Little, 2003), through informal garment businesses in India (e.g., Das, 2003; Unai and Rani, 2003) and the Philippines (Doane *et al.*, 2003), to home-based microenterprises in Mexico (e.g., Staudt, 1998) and Martinique (Browne, 2004) and waste pickers in the Global South (Coletto and Bisschop, 2017), the assumption is that this is a sphere which people enter out of necessity as a survival strategy (e.g., Itzigsohn, 2000; Otero, 1994; Rakowski, 1994). As Bhowmik (2005: 96) puts it, for the marginalised populations who engage in this endeavour, informal sector entrepreneurship 'is the only means for survival'. The characteristics of those active in the informal sector, as opposed to those in the formal, are quite specific and can be considered under the general heading of downgraded labour (Sassen, 1996).

This negative portrayal of the informal sector and informal entrepreneurship is thus mirrored in descriptions of the labour involved and their working conditions. That those employed in the informal sector are asserted to receive little legal or social protection and are unable to enforce contracts or have security of property rights (ILO, 2014). Venkatesh (2006: 385) epitomises this in his depiction of the informal sector as enabling poor communities to survive and as populated by those excluded from the social mainstream and composed of discriminatory practices, lack of regulations and exploitative practices. In this view, informal entrepreneurs are forced to work in the informal sector because they are unable to compete with low-wage workers in foreign countries or to find formal employment given their limited education levels (see also Castells and Portes, 1989; Valenzuela, 2003). Informal entrepreneurs are 'survivalists' pursuing informal economic activities out of necessity and as a last resort.

From this political economy perspective, therefore, the argument is that the informal sector in general and informal entrepreneurship, more particularly, are a result of low state intervention in the economy and welfare, and there is a lack of protection of workers. As such, informal entrepreneurship is asserted to be higher when taxes are lower, public expenditure as a proportion of GDP is lower, and there are lower levels of social protection. High taxes are thus not a cause of informal entrepreneurship. Rather, countries with high tax rates are viewed as having lower levels of informal entrepreneurship, mostly because they have higher levels of tax morale and can raise higher levels of public expenditure via taxes to fund social protection programmes, such as welfare safety nets and active labour market policies that reduce the necessity of engaging in informal entrepreneurship as a survival practice (Williams and Horodnic, 2015a,b,c).

Neo-Liberal Theory

For a group of neo-liberal commentators, informal entrepreneurship is not so much a necessity-driven endeavour undertaken as a last resort and survival practice but more a matter of choice and a response to the over-regulation of the formal sector. It is seen as a populist reaction to high taxes and too much interference in the free market. For such neo-liberals, informal entrepreneurs are seen as casting off the shackles of high taxes and an excessively intrusive and burdensome state (e.g., De Soto, 1989; Sauvy, 1984) by participating in informal entrepreneurship as a rational economic decision that enables them to escape the over-regulated formal sector (Becker, 2004; De Soto, 1989, 2001; London and Hart, 2004; Nwabuzor, 2005; Sauvy, 1984; Schneider and Williams, 2013). Informal entrepreneurs are thus seen to voluntarily operate in the informal sector to avoid the financial costs of formal registration along with the associated time and effort required (De Soto, 1989, 2001; Perry and Maloney, 2007; Small Business Council, 2004). As Nwabuzor (2005: 126) asserts, '[i]nformality is a response to burdensome controls, and an attempt to circumvent them', or as Becker (2004: 10) puts it, 'informal work arrangements are a rational response by micro-entrepreneurs to over-regulation by government bureaucracies'. For De Soto (1989: 255) in consequence, 'the real problem is not so much informality as formality'.

A prominent advocate of this view of informal entrepreneurship has been Peruvian economist Hernando De Soto, whose central hypothesis is that the costs of formalisation and over-regulation impede entrepreneurs and that deregulation and simplification of the registration procedure can result in economic freedom and enable entrepreneurship to flourish in developing countries (De Soto, 1989). For such neo-liberal scholars, those currently operating as informal entrepreneurs could positively contribute to economic growth and development but are currently constrained from doing so by cumbersome government regulations supporting mercantilist interests (De Soto, 1989: xix). Informal entrepreneurship, in this sense, is a revolutionary movement of free market enterprise against over-regulation. Such entrepreneurs want to work legally but cannot do so due to the heavy costs of formalisation and bureaucracy, which makes it almost impossible for them to operate as legitimate entrepreneurs. Informal entrepreneurs therefore find themselves in a situation where violating regulations is more economically beneficial to them than compliance.

Informal entrepreneurship is thus the people's 'spontaneous and creative response to the state's incapacity to satisfy the basic needs of the impoverished masses' (De Soto, 1989: xiv–xv). It is a rational economic strategy pursued by entrepreneurs whose spirit is stifled by high taxes and state-imposed institutional constraints (De Soto, 1989, 2001; Perry and Maloney, 2007; Small Business Council, 2004).

Indeed to contextualise this neo-liberal perspective on informal entrepreneurship in the context of the evolution of different waves of neo-liberal thought, Bhattacharya (2014) identifies seven waves of neo-liberal anti-labour discourse. Sequentially, these have: (1) attacked labour 'rigidities' rather than focused on labour's hard-won rights; (2) treated low-cost labour as a comparative advantage; (3) viewed labour rights as obstacles and luxuries; (4) adopted the doctrine and practice of flexibilisation in advanced countries; (5) pursued the paradigm of informality and the gulfs between formal and informal labour in developing countries; (6) called to formalise informal workers and disguised the informalisation of formal workers and (7) celebrated enterprise culture and informal entrepreneurialism.

The recent neo-liberal wave of writing on informal entrepreneurship, in consequence, is more celebratory of these workers than either modernisation theory or political economy theory. It views these entrepreneurs as the vanguard of the movement against excessive state control and overburdensome regulations. They are depicted as voluntarily deciding to engage in such endeavour (Adom and Williams, 2012a,b, 2014; Cross, 2000; Gerxhani, 2004; Gurtoo and Williams, 2009; Maloney, 2004; Snyder, 2004). For example, Cross (2000) argues that although street vendors have been conventionally depicted as necessity-driven entrepreneurs, most that he studied did so out of choice to avoid the costs, time and effort of formal registration (see also Cross and Morales, 2007). In other words, informal entrepreneurship offers them potential benefits that they cannot find in the formal sector, including flexible hours, job training, opportunity for economic independence, better wages and the avoidance of taxes and inefficient government regulation (Maloney, 2004).

The policy approach advocated, therefore, is to pursue tax reductions and reduce the 'regulatory burden' and state over-interference. De Soto (1989) famously proposed that government, and Peru's specifically, pushes firms into the informal sector by raising the barriers and costs of formalisation. By excluding firms from the formal sector, these barriers stifle entrepreneurship and reduce the dynamism of the private sector. Others such as Levy (2008) have claimed that the high levels of informality display the level of escape from this overburdensome system by small firms. This 'exit' view leads to a vicious cycle: firms escape because the state does not make a formal status appealing. For example, financial markets and courts may be dysfunctional, and public procurement processes may be corrupt. By being in the informal sector, firms avoid paying taxes that would provide resources the state might use to improve the provision of public goods or to facilitate firms to become formal. The result is that even more entrepreneurs escape, creating a spiral of ever more entrepreneurs into informality.

For neo-liberal commentators (Loayza, 2007; Schneider and Enste, 2000; Schneider and Klinglmair, 2004; Schneider *et al.*,2010), therefore, the main drivers of the informal are tax and social security contribution burdens (Cebula, 1997; Feld and Schneider, 2010; Friedman *et al.*, 2000; Giles, 1999; Giles and Tedds, 2002; Hill and Kabir, 1996; Johnson *et al.*, 1998; Schneider, 2005; Tanzi, 1999) and the intensity of regulations since it implies an increase in costs that discourages entrepreneurs from operating in the formal sector (Johnson *et al.*, 1997). According to Schneider and Klinglmair (2004), the most important factors influencing the growth in the informality are taxation and social security burdens: 'The bigger the difference between the total cost of labour in the formal sector and the after-tax earnings (from work), the greater is the incentive to avoid this difference'. Given that this difference is broadly based on the social security burden and the tax burden, these are viewed as key determinants of the size of the informal sector and level of informal entrepreneurship.

In connection with the tax burden (i.e., the amount of income, property or sales tax levied on individuals or businesses, measured by the effective tax rate, which is the ratio of tax revenue to GDP), Cebula (1997) for example, argues that stemming this will stop the growth of the informal sector. However, Johnson *et al.* (1998) and Schneider (2002) are more cautious, arguing that it is not higher tax rates that increase the size of the informal sector but the ineffective and discretionary application of the tax system and regulations by governments.

Evaluations of the Competing Theoretical Perspectives

Most previous studies of the informal sector and informal entrepreneurship have tended to adopt the singular logic of one or the other of these three competing theoretical perspectives. For example, La Porta and Shleifer (2008, 2014) adopt the singular logic of modernisation theory, De Soto (1989) the singular logic of neo-liberal theory and Castells and Portes (1989), Davis (2006) and Slavnic (2010) the singular logic of political economy theory. All such theoretical perspectives contain an internal consistency in their logic and appear to their adherents to be sufficient as explanations.

However, in recent years, it has been recognised that these competing theoretical perspectives are not mutually exclusive. When studying the prevalence of the informal sector, for example, numerous studies have evaluated the validity of these three contrasting theoretical perspectives. To do this, evaluations have been conducted of the association between cross-national variations in the prevalence of the informal sector and cross-national variations of the key casual factors in each of these three theoretical perspectives. First of all, there have been numerous studies analysing simple bivariate correlations between the size of the informal sector and the various determinants highlighted in each of the theoretical perspectives, analysing cross-national variations at the level of the European Union (Williams, 2008b,

2013, 2014a,b; Williams and Windebank, 2015), Central and Eastern Europe (Williams, 2015a,c,e), Latin America (Williams and Youssef, 2014a,b) and the wider developing world (Williams, 2015b,d). These studies examining solely the bivariate correlations all confirm the validity of the modernisation and political economy perspectives and refute the tenets of the neo-liberal theory.

There have also been multivariate analyses of the relationship between cross-national variations in the size of the informal sector and the key determinants in each of these theoretical perspectives, including at the level of Central and Eastern Europe (Williams and Horodnic, 2015a), the Baltics (Williams and Horodnic, 2015b,c) and South-East Europe (Williams and Horodnic, 2015d). These more sophisticated multivariate analyses again confirm the validity of the modernisation and political economy perspectives but do not confirm the tenets of the neo-liberal theory. All these studies, however, evaluate the relevance of these theories in relation to the size of the informal sector rather than the prevalence of informal entrepreneurship.

However, there have been studies that similarly evaluate these theories as explanations for the prevalence of informal entrepreneurship. In doing so, these have begun to display that these theoretical perspectives are not always mutually exclusive. Put another way, there has been a growing recognition that if informal entrepreneurship is to be more fully understood, it is necessary to be more open to explanations that lie beyond the single logics of individual theoretical perspectives. Over the past decade, for example, a series of studies, mostly in the Global North and based on small-scale studies, have begun to seek to conjoin the neo-liberal and political economy perspectives by evaluating the ratios of necessity-to-opportunity informal entrepreneurship in different contexts. These studies conducted in England (Williams, 2006a,b,c, 2007a,b,c, 2008a, 2009b), Ukraine (Round and Williams, 2008; Williams, 2009a,c; Williams and Round, 2007; Williams *et al.*, 2009) and Russia (Round *et al.*, 2008; Williams and Round, 2008, 2009; Williams, 2009b) reveal the socio-spatial contingency of informal entrepreneurs' motives in terms of the ratio of necessity-to-opportunity entrepreneurship with greater proportions of necessity-driven informal entrepreneurship in deprived populations and opportunity entrepreneurship in more affluent populations. In the Global South, meanwhile, the studies so far conducted, mostly in Latin America (see Perry *et al.*, 2007) but also India (Williams and Gurtoo, 2011, 2012) and Brazil (Williams and Youssef, 2015), again reveal the prevalence of opportunity drivers in informal entrepreneurs' rationales.

The outcome is to show that the political economy and neo-liberal perspectives should not be seen as mutually exclusive. Rather, they depict the motives of different groups of informal entrepreneurs and the ratio of necessity-to-opportunity entrepreneurs in any context will differ, reflecting how the relative importance of each explanation varies in different contexts. As Perry and Maloney (2007: 2) succinctly point out, '[t]hese two lenses, focusing, respectively, on informality driven by exclusion from state benefits and on voluntary exit decisions resulting from private cost-benefit calculations, are complementary rather than competing analytical frameworks'.

There have also been studies which evaluate the association between cross-national variations in the prevalence of informal entrepreneurship and cross-national variations in the key determinants in each of the three theoretical perspectives. Again, some of these studies are simple bivariate correlations between the prevalence of informal entrepreneurship and the various causal factors highlighted in each of the theoretical perspectives, analysing cross-national variations across the developing world (Williams, 2014c,d). These again confirm the tenets of the modernisation and political economy theses but do not confirm the tenets of the neo-liberal thesis. There are also some multivariate regression analyses conducted at the level of the European Union. However, these are limited to examining the tendency of small businesses to falsely declare the salaries of their employees by paying them two salaries, namely, a declared salary and an undeclared (envelope) wage (Williams and Horodnic, 2016) and a study of the self-employed working in the informal sector (Williams and Martinez-Perez, 2014). All these studies again confirm the validity of the modernisation and political economy perspectives but do not confirm the tenets of the neo-liberal theory. Until now, however, few if any studies have evaluated the validity of these competing theoretical perspectives as determinants of the prevalence of informal entrepreneurship using multivariate analysis. In Part II of this book, therefore, this significant gap in the literature will start to be filled by evaluating the validity of these three theoretical explanations for the prevalence of informal entrepreneurship and thus which formal institutional failings and imperfections result in the growth of informal entrepreneurship.

Conclusions

This chapter has reviewed the competing perspectives regarding which specific formal institutional failures and imperfections result in the growth of the informal sector in general and informal entrepreneurship more particularly. This has revealed that modernisation theory pinpoints economic underdevelopment and unmodern systems of governance, manifested in high levels of corruption as the key determinants of informal entrepreneurship. Meanwhile, neo-liberal theory asserts that the major determinant is too much government intervention in the form of high taxes and burdensome regulations and controls, while political economy theory conversely identifies inadequate state intervention and a lack of protection of workers as the key determinants of informal entrepreneurship.

Part I of this book has therefore argued that formal institutional failures and imperfections lead to the development of an asymmetry between formal and informal institutions in societies and that the greater is the institutional asymmetry, the greater is the prevalence of informal entrepreneurship (see

Chapter 2). In this chapter, and to put greater flesh on the characteristics of these formal institutional failures and imperfections, the competing theories have been reviewed regarding which specific formal institutional failures and imperfections are seen to result in the growth of the informal sector in general and informal entrepreneurship more particularly.

Having reviewed these theoretical explanations for the prevalence of informal entrepreneurship, Part II will now turn towards evaluating the relationship between theory and lived practice, including which of these formal institutional failures and imperfections are significantly associated with variations in the level of informal entrepreneurship across countries. Until now, these have been seen largely as mutually exclusive theories. In Part I of this book, however, not only has institutional theory been used to provide an umbrella theoretical framework within which these existing theories can be contextualised, but in so doing, it has been revealed that these theoretical perspectives need not necessarily be treated as mutually exclusive. With this in mind, attention now turns towards an evaluation of the lived practices of informal entrepreneurship in the contemporary world.

References

Adom, K. and Williams, C.C. (2012a). Evaluating the explanations for the informal economy in third world cities: Some evidence from Koforidua in the eastern region of Ghana. *International Entrepreneurship and Management Journal*, 8(3), pp. 309–324.

Adom, K. and Williams, C.C. (2012b). Evaluating the motives of informal entrepreneurs in Koforidua, Ghana. *Journal of Developmental Entrepreneurship*, 17(1), pp. 1–21.

Adom, K. and Williams, C.C. (2014). Evaluating the explanations for the informal economy in third world cities: Some evidence from Koforidua in the eastern region of Ghana. *International Entrepreneurship and Management Journal*, 10(2), pp. 427–445.

Aliyev, H. (2015). Post-Soviet informality: Towards theory-building. *International Journal of Sociology and Social Policy*, 35(3/4), pp. 182–198.

Bajada, C. and Schneider, F. (2005). Introduction. In: C. Bajada and F. Schneider, Eds., *Size, causes and consequences of the underground economy: An international perspective*. Aldershot: Ashgate, pp. 1–14.

Barbour, A. and Llanes, M. (2013). *Supporting people to legitimise their informal businesses*. York: Joseph Rowntree Foundation.

Barsoum, G. (2015). Striving for job security: The lived experience of employment informality among educated youth in Egypt. *International Journal of Sociology and Social Policy*, 35(5/6), pp. 340–358.

Baumol, W.J. (1990). Entrepreneurship: Productive, unproductive, destructive. *Journal of Political Economy*, 98(5), pp. 893–921.

Becker, K.F. (2004). *The informal economy*. Stockholm: Swedish International Development Agency.

Bhattacharya, S. (2014). Is labour still a relevant category for praxis? Critical reflections on some contemporary discourses on work and labour in capitalism. *Development and Change*, 45(5), pp. 941–962.

Bhowmik, S. (2005). Street vendors in Asia: A review. *Economic and Political Weekly*, May 28–June 4, pp. 2256–2264.

Boeke, J.H. (1942). *Economies and economic policy in dual societies.* Harlem: Tjeenk Willnik.

Bologna, J. (2014). *The effect of informal employment and corruption on income levels in Brazil.* Available at: http://papers.ssrn.com/sol3/papers.cfm?abstract_id=2489057 (last accessed 6 June 2017).

Bromley, G. (2007). Foreword. In: J. Cross and A. Morales, Eds., *Street entrepreneurs: People, place and politics in local and global perspective.* London: Routledge, pp. 1–12.

Browne, K.E. (2004). *Creole economics: Caribbean cunning under the French flag.* Austin: University of Texas.

Buehn, A. and Schneider, F. (2012). Corruption and the shadow economy: Like oil and vinegar, like water and fire? *International Tax and Public Finance,* 19, pp. 172–194.

Castells, M. and Portes, A. (1989). World underneath: The origins, dynamics, and effects of the informal economy. In: A. Portes, M. Castells and L.A. Benton, Eds., *The informal economy: Studies in advanced and less developed countries.* Baltimore: The Johns Hopkins University Press, pp. 11–37.

Cebula, R. (1997). An empirical analysis of the impact of government tax and auditing policies on the size of the underground economy: The case of the United States, 1993–94. *American Journal of Economics and Sociology,* 56(2), pp. 173–185.

Chen, M. (2006). Rethinking the informal economy: Linkages with the formal economy and the formal regulatory environment. In: B. Guha-Khasnobis, R. Kanbur and E. Ostrom, Eds., *Linking the formal and informal economy: Concepts and policies.* Oxford: Oxford University Press, pp. 75–92.

Chen, M. (2012). *The informal economy: Definitions, theories and policies.* Manchester: Women in Informal Employment Global and Organising.

Chen, M. (2014). Informal employment and development: Patterns of inclusion and exclusion. *European Journal of Development Research,* 26(4), pp. 397–418.

Chen, M., Vanek, J. and Carr, M. (2004). *Mainstreaming informal employment and gender in poverty reduction: A handbook for policy-makers and other stakeholders.* London: The Commonwealth Secretariat.

Choi, J.P. and Thum, M. (2005). Corruption and the shadow economy. *International Economic Review,* 46(3), pp. 817–836.

Chong, A. and Gradstein, M. (2007). Inequality and informality. *Journal of Public Economics,* 91(1/2), pp. 159–179.

Coletto, D. and Bisschop, L. (2017). Waste pickers in the informal economy of the global South: Included or excluded? *International Journal of Sociology and Social Policy,* 37(5/6), pp. 280–294.

Cross, J.C. (2000). Street vendors, modernity and postmodernity: Conflict and compromise in the global economy. *International Journal of Sociology and Social Policy,* 20(1), pp. 29–51.

Cross, J.C. and Morales, A. (2007). Introduction: Locating street markets in the modern/postmodern world. In: J. Cross and A. Morales, Eds., *Street entrepreneurs: People, place and politics in local and global perspective.* London: Routledge, pp. 1–20.

Das, K. (2003). Income and employment in informal manufacturing: A case study. In: R. Jhabvala, R.M. Sudarshan and J. Unni, Eds., *Informal economy centrestage: New structures of employment.* London: Sage, pp. 42–69.

Daude, C., Gutiérrez, H. and Melguizo, A. (2013). What drives tax morale? A focus on emerging economies. *Review of Public Economics,* 207(4), pp. 9–40.

Davis, M. (2006). *Planet of slums.* London: Verso.

Davis, S.J. and Henrekson, M. (2005). Tax effects on work activity, industry mix and shadow economy size: Evidence from rich-country comparisons. In:

R. Gomez-Salvador, A. Lamo, B. Petrongolo, M. Ward and E. Wasmer, Eds., *Labour supply and incentives to work in Europe*. Northampton, MA: Edward Elgar, pp. 44–104.

De Beer, J., Fu, K. and Wunsch-Vincent, S. (2013). *The informal economy, innovation and intellectual property: Concepts, metrics and policy considerations*. Geneva: Economic Research Working Paper no. 10, World Intellectual Property Organization.

Dellot, B. (2012). *Untapped enterprise: Learning to live with the informal economy*. London: Royal Society of the Arts.

Derrida, J. (1967). *Of grammatology*. Baltimore: John Hopkins University Press.

De Soto, H. (1989). *The other path: The invisible revolution in the third world*. New York: Harper and Row.

De Soto, H. (2001). *The mystery of capital: Why capitalism triumphs in the West and fails everywhere else*. London: Black Swan.

Dibben, P. and Williams, C.C. (2012). Varieties of capitalism and employment relations: Informally dominated market economies. *Industrial Relations: A Review of Economy & Society*, 51(S1), pp. 563–582.

Dibben, P., Wood, G. and Williams, C.C. (2015). Towards and against formalization: Regulation and change in informal work in Mozambique. *International Labour Review*, 154(3), pp. 373–392.

Doane, D., Srikajon, D. and Ofrenco, R. (2003). Social protection for informal workers in the garment industry. In: F. Lund and J. Nicholson, Eds., *Chains of production, ladders of protection: Social protection for workers in the informal economy*. Durban: School of Development Studies, University of Natal, pp. 101–142.

Dreher, A., Kotsogiannis, C. and McCorriston, S. (2009). How do institutions affect corruption and the shadow economy? *International Tax and Public Finance*, 16, pp. 773–796.

Dreher, A. and Schneider, F. (2010). Corruption and the shadow economy: An empirical analysis. *Public Choice*, 144, pp. 215–238.

Feld, L.P. and Schneider, F. (2010). Survey on the shadow economy and undeclared earnings in OECD countries. *German Economic Review*, 11(2), pp. 109–149.

Fernandez-Kelly, P. (2006). Introduction. In: P. Fernandez-Kelly and J. Shefner, Eds., *Out of the shadows: Political action and the informal economy in Latin America*. Pennsylvania: Pennsylvania State University Press, pp. 1–19.

Friedman, E., Johnson, S., Kaufmann, D. and Zoido-Lobaton, P. (2000). Dodging the grabbing hand: The determinants of unofficial activity in 69 countries. *Journal of Public Economics*, 76(3), pp. 459–493.

Gallin, D. (2001). Propositions on trade unions and informal employment in time of globalisation. *Antipode*, 19(4), pp. 531–549.

Geertz, C. (1963). *Old societies and new states: The quest for modernity in Asia and Africa*. Glencoe, IL: Free Press.

Gerxhani, K. (2004). The informal sector in developed and less developed countries: A literature survey. *Public Choice*, 120(3/4), pp. 267–300.

Giachi, S. (2014). Social dimensions of tax evasion: Trust and tax morale in contemporary Spain. *Revista Española de Investigaciones Sociológicas*, 145, pp. 73–98.

Gilbert, A. (1998). *The Latin American city*. London: Latin American Bureau.

Giles, D. (1999). Measuring the hidden economy: Implications for econometric modeling. *Economic Journal*, 109(456), pp. 370–380.

Giles, D. and Tedds, L. (2002). *Taxes and the Canadian underground economy*. Toronto: Canadian Tax Foundation.

Godfrey, P.C. (2011). Toward a theory of the informal economy. *Academy of Management Annals*, 5(1), pp. 231–277.

Goel, R.K. and Saunoris, J.W. (2014). Global corruption and the shadow economy: Spatial aspect. *Public Choice*, 161(1/2), pp. 119–139.

Gurtoo, A. and Williams, C.C. (2009). Entrepreneurship and the informal sector: Some lessons from India. *International Journal of Entrepreneurship and Innovation*, 10(1), pp. 55–62.

Harriss-White, B. (2014). Labour and petty production. *Development and Change*, 45(5), pp. 981–1000.

Hibbs, D.A. and Piculescu, V. (2005). *Institutions, corruption and tax evasion in the unofficial economy*. Göteborg: Department of Economics.

Hill, R. and Kabir, M. (1996). Tax rates, the tax mix, and the growth of the underground economy in Canada: What can we infer? *Canadian Tax Journal/Revue Fiscale Canadienne*, 64(6), pp. 1552–1583.

Hindriks, J., Muthoo, A. and Keen, M. (1999). Corruption, extortion and evasion. *Journal of Public Economics*, 74, pp. 395–430.

Hudson, R. (2005). *Economic geographies: Circuits, flows and spaces*. London: Sage.

ILO (2013). *Women and men in the informal economy: Statistical picture*. Geneva: ILO.

ILO (2014). *Transitioning from the informal to the formal economy*. Geneva: ILO.

Itzigsohn, J. (2000). *Developing poverty: The state, labor market deregulation and the informal economy in Costa Rica and the Dominican Republic*. Pennsylvania: Pennsylvania State University Press.

Johnson, S., Kaufmann, D. and Shleifer, A. (1997). The unofficial economy in transition. *Brookings Papers on Economic Activity*, 2, pp. 159–239.

Johnson, S., Kaufmann, D. and Zoido-Lobatón, P. (1998). Regulatory discretion and the unofficial economy. *The American Economic Review*, 88(2), pp. 387–392.

Katsios, S. (2006). The shadow economy and corruption in Greece. *South-Eastern Europe Journal of Economics*, 1, pp. 61–80.

Kuehn, Z. (2014). Tax rates, governance and the informal economy in high-income countries. *Economic Inquiry*, 52(1), pp. 405–430.

Lago Peñas, I. and Lago Peñas, S. (2010). The determinants of tax morale in comparative perspective: Evidence from European countries. *European Journal of Political Economy*, 26(4), pp. 441–453.

Lagos, R.A. (1995). Formalising the informal sector: Barriers and costs. *Development and Change*, 26(1), pp. 110–131.

La Porta, R. and Shleifer, A. (2008). The unofficial economy and economic development. *Brookings Papers on Economic Activity*, 47(1), pp. 123–135.

La Porta, R. and Shleifer, A. (2014). Informality and development. *Journal of Economic Perspectives*, 28(3), pp. 109–126.

Leal Ordóñez, J.C. (2014). Tax collection, the informal sector and productivity. *Review of Economic Dynamics*, 17, pp. 262–286.

Levy, S. (2008). *Good intentions, bad outcomes: Social policy, informality and economic growth in Mexico*. Washington, DC: Brookings Institution.

Lewis, A.W. (1954). Economic development with unlimited supplies of labor. *Manchester School of Economics and Social Studies*, 22(1), pp. 139–191.

Lewis, A.W. (1959). *The theory of economic growth*. London: Allen and Unwin.

Lewis, W.W. (2004). *The power of productivity: Wealth, poverty, and the threat to global stability*. Chicago: University of Chicago Press.

Little, P.D. (2003). *Somalia: Economy without state*. Bloomington: Indiana University Press.

Loayza, N. (2007). *The causes and consequences of informality in Peru*. Lima: Working Papers no. 18, Banco Central de Reserva del Perú.

London, T. and Hart, S.L. (2004). Reinventing strategies for emerging markets: Beyond the transnational model. *Journal of International Business Studies*, 35(5), pp. 350–370.

Maldonado, C. (1995). The informal sector: Legalization or laissez-faire? *International Labour Review*, 134(6), pp. 705–728.

Maloney, W.F. (2004). Informality revisited. *World Development*, 32(7), pp. 1159–1178.

Martínez-Vázquez, J. and Torgler, B. (2009). The evolution of tax morale in modern Spain. *Journal of Economic Issues*, 43(1), pp. 1–28.

McKenzie, D. and Woodruff, C. (2006). Do entry costs provide an empirical basis for poverty traps? Evidence from microenterprises. *Economic Development and Cultural Change*, 55(1), pp. 3–42.

Meagher, K. (2010). *Identity economics: Social networks and the informal economy in Nigeria*. New York: James Currey.

Mešić, N. (2016). Paradoxes of European free movement in times of austerity: The role of social movement actors in framing the plight of Roma berry pickers in Sweden. *International Journal of Sociology and Social Policy*, 36(5/6), pp. 289–303.

Moser, C. (1977). The dual economy and marginality debate and the contribution of micro analysis: Market sellers in Bogotá. *Development and Change*, 8(4), pp. 465–489.

Nwabuzor, A. (2005). Corruption and development: New initiatives in economic openness and strengthened rule of law. *Journal of Business Ethics*, 59(1/2), pp. 121–138.

Otero, M. (1994). The role of governments and private institutions in addressing the informal sector in Latin America. In: C.A. Rakowski, Ed., *Contrapunto: The informal sector debate in Latin America*. New York: State University of New York Press, pp. 129–142.

Packard, T. (2007). *Do workers in Chile choose informal employment? A dynamic analysis of sector choice*. Washington, DC: World Bank Latin American and the Caribbean Region Social Projection Unit.

Perry, G.E. and Maloney, W.F. (2007). Overview: Informality: Exit and exclusion. In: G.E. Perry, W.F. Maloney, O.S. Arias, P. Fajnzylber, A.D. Mason and J. Saavedra-Chanduvi, Eds., *Informality: Exit and exclusion*. Washington, DC: World Bank, pp. 1–19.

Perry, G.E., Malone, W.F., Arias, O.S., Fajnzylber, R., Mason, A.D. and Saavedra-Chanduvi, J. (2007). Eds., *Informality: Exit and exclusion*. Washington, DC: World Bank.

Piore, M.J. and Sabel, C.F. (1984). *The second industrial divide*. New York: Basic books.

Portes, A. (1994). The informal economy and its paradoxes. In: N.J. Smelser and R. Swedberg, Eds., *The handbook of economic sociology*. Princeton: Princeton University Press, pp. 142–165.

Potts, D. (2008). The urban informal sector in sub-Saharan Africa: From bad to good (and back again? *Development Southern Africa*, 25(2), pp. 151–167.

Rakowski, C. (1994). The informal sector debate, part II: 1984–1993. In: C.A. Rakowski, Ed., *Contrapunto: The informal sector debate in Latin America*. New York: State University of New York Press, pp. 121–152.

Rose-Ackerman, S. (1997). *Corruption and development*. Washington, DC: World Bank.

Round, J. and Williams, C.C. (2008). Everyday tactics and spaces of power: The role of informal economies in post-Soviet Ukraine. *Social and Cultural Geography*, 9(2), pp. 171–185.

Round, J., Williams, C.C. and Rodgers, P. (2008). Corruption in the post-Soviet workplace: The experiences of recent graduates in contemporary Ukraine. *Work, Employment and Society*, 22(1), pp. 149–166.

Russo, F.F. (2013). Tax morale and tax evasion reports. *Economics Letters*, 121, pp. 110–114.

Sasaki, S., Kyoko Kusakabe, K. and Doneys, P. (2016). Exploring human (in-)security from a gender perspective: A case study of subcontracted workers in Thailand. *International Journal of Sociology and Social Policy*, 36(5/6), pp. 304–318.

Sassen, S. (1996). Service employment regimes and the new inequality. In: E. Mingione, Ed., *Urban poverty and the underclass*. Oxford: Basil Blackwell, pp. 142–159.

Sauvy, A. (1984). *Le Travail Noir et l'Economie de Demain*. Paris: Calmann-Levy.

Schneider, F. (2002). *Size and measurement of the informal economy in 110 countries around the world*. Paper presented at a Workshop of Australian National Tax Centre, ANU, Canberra, Australia, July.

Schneider, F. (2005). Shadow economies around the world: What do we really know. *European Journal of Political Economy*, 21(3), pp. 598–642.

Schneider, F., Buehn, A. and Montenegro, C.E. (2010). New estimates for the shadow economies all over the world. *International Economic Journal*, 24(4), pp. 443–461.

Schneider, F. and Enste, D.H. (2000). Shadow economies: Size, causes, and consequences. *Journal of Economic Literature*, 38(1), pp. 77–114.

Schneider, F. and Klinglmair, R. (2004). *Shadow economies around the world: What do we know?* Bonn: IZA Discussion Papers no. 1043, Institute for the Study of Labor (IZA).

Schneider, F. and Williams, C.C. (2013). *The shadow economy*. London: Institute of Economic Affairs.

Slack, T., Cope, M.R., Jensen, L. and Tickamyer, A.R. (2017). Social embeddedness, formal labor supply, and participation in informal work. *International Journal of Sociology and Social Policy*, 37(3/4), pp. 248–264.

Slavnic, Z. (2010). Political economy of informalisation. *European Societies*, 12(1), pp. 3–23.

Small Business Council (2004). *Small business in the informal economy: Making the transition to the formal economy*. London: Small Business Council.

Snyder, K.A. (2004). Routes to the informal economy in New York's East village: Crisis, economics and identity. *Sociological Perspectives*, 47(2), pp. 215–240.

Staudt, K. (1998). *Free trade? Informal economies at the US-Mexico border*. Philadelphia: Temple, University Press.

Taiwo, O. (2013). Employment choice and mobility in multi-sector labour markets: Theoretical model and evidence from Ghana. *International Labour Review*, 152(3/4), pp. 469–492.

Tanzi, V. (1999). Uses and abuses of estimates of the underground economy. *Economic Journal*, 109(456), pp. 338–347.

Torgler, B. (2005a). Tax morale in Latin America. *Public Choice*, 122, pp. 133–157.

Torgler, B. (2005b). Tax morale and direct democracy. *European Journal of Political Economy*, 21, pp. 525–531.

Torgler, B. (2012). Tax morale, Eastern Europe and European enlargement. *Communist and Post-Communist Studies*, 45, pp. 11–25.

Torgler, B. and Schneider, F. (2007). *Shadow economy, tax morale, governance and institutional quality: A panel analysis*. Bonn: IZA Discussion Paper no. 2563, IZA.

Travers, A. (2002). *Prospects for enterprise: An investigation into the motivations of workers in the informal economy*. London: Community Links.

Unai, J. and Rani, U. (2003). Employment and income in the informal economy: A micro-perspective. In: R. Jhabvala, R.M. Sudarshan and J. Unni, Eds.,

Informal economy centrestage: New structures of employment. London: Sage, pp. 142–169.

Valenzuela, A. (2003). Day labor work. *Annual Review of Sociology*, 29, pp. 307–333.

Venkatesh, S.A. (2006). *Off the books: The underground economy of the urban poor.* Cambridge, MA: Harvard University Press.

Virta, H. (2010). The linkage between corruption and shadow economy size: Does geography matter? *International Journal of Development Issues*, 9(1), pp. 4–24.

Wallace, C. and Latcheva, R. (2006). Economic transformation outside the law: Corruption, trust in public institutions and the informal economy in transition countries of Central and Eastern Europe. *Europe-Asia Studies*, 58(1), pp. 81–102.

Williams, C.C. (2006a). *The hidden enterprise culture: Entrepreneurship in the underground economy.* Cheltenham: Edward Elgar.

Williams, C.C. (2006b). Harnessing the hidden enterprise culture: The Street (UK) community development finance initiative. *Local Economy*, 21(1), pp. 13–24.

Williams, C.C. (2006c). Beyond the sweatshop: Off-the-books work in contemporary England. *Journal of Small Business and Enterprise Development*, 13(1), pp. 89–99.

Williams, C.C. (2007a). Do entrepreneurs always play by the rulebook? *Management Online Review*, April, pp. 1–18.

Williams, C.C. (2007b). Entrepreneurs operating in the informal economy: Necessity or opportunity driven? *Journal of Small Business and Entrepreneurship*, 20(3), pp. 309–320.

Williams, C.C. (2007c). Small businesses and the informal economy: Evidence from the UK. *International Journal of Entrepreneurial Behaviour and Research*, 13(6), pp. 349–366.

Williams, C.C. (2008a). Beyond ideal-type depictions of entrepreneurship: Some lessons from the service sector in England. *The Service Industries Journal*, 28(7/8), pp. 1041–1053.

Williams, C.C. (2008b). Cross-national variations in undeclared work: Results from a survey of 27 European countries. *International Journal of Economic Perspectives*, 2(2), pp. 46–63.

Williams, C.C. (2009a). Beyond legitimate entrepreneurship: The prevalence of off-the-books entrepreneurs in Ukraine. *Journal of Small Business and Entrepreneurship*, 22(1), pp. 55–68.

Williams, C.C. (2009b). Entrepreneurship and the off-the-books economy: Some lessons from England. *International Journal of Management and Enterprise Development*, 7(4), pp. 429–444.

Williams, C.C. (2009c). Explaining participation in off-the-books entrepreneurship in Ukraine: A gendered evaluation. *International Entrepreneurship and Management Journal*, 5(4), pp. 497–513.

Williams, C.C. (2013). Tackling Europe's informal economy: A critical evaluation of the neo-liberal de-regulatory perspective. *Journal of Contemporary European Research*, 9(3), pp. 261–279.

Williams, C.C. (2014a). *Confronting the shadow economy: Evaluating tax compliance and behaviour policies.* Cheltenham: Edward Elgar.

Williams, C.C. (2014b). Out of the shadows: A classification of economies by the size and character of their informal sector. *Work, Employment and Society*, 28(5), pp. 735–753.

Williams, C.C. (2014c). Explaining cross-national variations in the commonality of informal sector entrepreneurship: An exploratory analysis of 38 emerging economies. *Journal of Small Business and Entrepreneurship*, 27(2), pp. 191–212.

Williams, C.C. (2014d). Tackling enterprises operating in the informal sector in developing and transition economies: A critical evaluation of the neo-liberal policy approach. *Journal of Global Entrepreneurship Research*, 4(1), pp. 1–17.

Williams, C.C. (2015a). Explaining cross-national variations in the informalisation of employment: Some lessons from Central and Eastern Europe. *European Societies*, 17(4), pp. 492–512.

Williams, C.C. (2015b). Explaining cross-national variations in the scale of informal employment: An exploratory analysis of 41 less developed economies. *International Journal of Manpower*, 36(2), pp. 118–135.

Williams, C.C. (2015c). Explaining the informal economy: An exploratory evaluation of competing perspectives. *Relations Industrielles/Industrial Relations*, 70(4), pp. 741–765.

Williams, C.C. (2015d). Out of the margins: Classifying economies by the prevalence and character of employment in the informal economy. *International Labour Review*, 154(3), pp. 331–352.

Williams, C.C. (2015e). Tackling informal employment in developing and transition economies: A critical evaluation of the neo-liberal approach. *International Journal of Business and Globalisation*, 14(3), pp. 251–270.

Williams, C.C. (2017). *Dependent self-employment: Trends, challenges and policy responses in the EU*. Geneva: ILO.

Williams, C.C. and Gurtoo, A. (2011). Evaluating competing explanations for street entrepreneurship: Some evidence from India. *Journal of Global Entrepreneurship Research*, 1(2), pp. 3–19.

Williams, C.C. and Gurtoo, A. (2012). Evaluating competing theories of street entrepreneurship: Some lessons from Bangalore, India. *International Entrepreneurship and Management Journal*, 8(4), pp. 391–409.

Williams, C.C. and Horodnic, I. (2015a). Evaluating the prevalence of the undeclared economy in Central and Eastern Europe: An institutional asymmetry perspective. *European Journal of Industrial Relations*, 21(4), pp. 389–406.

Williams, C.C. and Horodnic, I. (2015b). Explaining and tackling the shadow economy in Estonia, Latvia and Lithuania: A tax morale approach. *Journal of Baltic Economics*, 15(2), pp. 81–98.

Williams, C.C. and Horodnic, I. (2015c). Explaining the prevalence of the informal economy in the Baltics: An institutional asymmetry perspective. *European Spatial Research and Policy*, 22(2), pp. 127–144.

Williams, C.C. and Horodnic, I. (2015d). Tackling the informal economy in South East Europe: An institutional approach. *Journal of South East European and Black Sea Studies*, 15(4), pp. 519–539.

Williams, C.C. and Horodnic, I. (2016). Cross-country variations in the participation of small businesses in the informal economy: An institutional asymmetry perspective. *Journal of Small Business and Enterprise Development*, 23(1), pp. 3–24.

Williams, C.C. and Martinez-Perez, A. (2014). Entrepreneurship in the informal economy: A product of too much or too little state intervention? *International Journal of Entrepreneurship and Innovation*, 15(4), pp. 227–237.

Williams, C.C., Nadin, S. and Rodgers, P. (2012). Evaluating competing theories of informal entrepreneurship: Some lessons from Ukraine. *International Journal of Entrepreneurial Behaviour and Research*, 18(5), pp. 528–543.

Williams, C.C. and Round, J. (2007). Entrepreneurship and the informal economy: A study of Ukraine's hidden enterprise culture. *Journal of Developmental Entrepreneurship*, 12(1), pp. 119–136.

Williams, C.C. and Round, J. (2008). The hidden enterprise culture of Moscow: Entrepreneurship and off-the-books working practices. *Journal of Developmental Entrepreneurship*, 13(4), pp. 445–462.

Williams, C.C. and Round, J. (2009). Evaluating informal entrepreneurs' motives: Some lessons from Moscow. *International Journal of Entrepreneurial Behaviour and Research*, 15(1), pp. 94–107.

Williams, C.C., Round, J. and Rodgers, J. (2009). Evaluating the motives of informal entrepreneurs: Some lessons from Ukraine. *Journal of Developmental Entrepreneurship*, 14(1), pp. 59–71.

Williams, C.C. and Windebank, J. (2015). Evaluating competing theories of informal employment: Some lessons from a 2013 European survey. *International Journal of Business and Globalisation*, 15(1), pp. 45–62.

Williams, C.C. and Youssef, Y.A. (2014a). Tackling informal entrepreneurship in Latin America: A critical evaluation of the neo-liberal policy approach. *Journal of Entrepreneurship and Organization Management*, 3(1), pp. 1–9.

Williams, C.C. and Youssef, Y.A. (2014b). Classifying Latin American economies: A degrees of informalisation approach. *International Journal of Business Administration*, 5(3), pp. 73–85.

Williams, C.C. and Youssef, Y.A. (2014c). Is informal sector entrepreneurship necessity- or opportunity-driven? Some lessons from urban Brazil. *Business and Management Research*, 3(1), pp. 41–53.

Williams, C.C. and Youssef, Y.A. (2015). Theorizing entrepreneurship in the informal sector in urban Brazil: A product of exclusion or exit? *Journal of Entrepreneurship*, 24(2), pp. 148–168.

Yusuff, O.S. (2011). A theoretical analysis of the concept of informal economy and informality in developing countries. *European Journal of Social Sciences*, 20(4), pp. 624–636.

Part II

Informal Sector Entrepreneurship in Global Perspective

4 Prevalence of Informal Entrepreneurship

Introduction

In Part II of this book, the intention is to advance understanding of the prevalence, impacts and determinants of informal entrepreneurship. To do so, each of these issues is considered in turn. This chapter examines the prevalence of informal entrepreneurship, followed in Chapter 5 by an evaluation of its impacts, and Chapter 6 explores the reasons for informal entrepreneurship.

The aim of this chapter is to provide an introductory overview of the prevalence of entrepreneurship in the informal sector across the world. In the first section of this chapter, therefore, one of the first known overviews is provided of the prevalence of informal entrepreneurship not only at the global scale but also across global regions and how its prevalence varies cross-nationally. To do this, two main sources of data are used. On the one hand, an analysis of the ILO survey on the informal sector conducted in 2013 in 38 developing countries will be reported. On the other hand, data from the WBES will be analysed. This collects data on the informal sector and informal entrepreneurship in a large number of countries across the globe. Here in this chapter, the results from 127 countries are reported.

The second section then turns its attention to non-spatial aspects of the distribution of informal entrepreneurship across the world. This commences by analysing the variations in the prevalence of informal entrepreneurship across different sectors of the global economy, followed by an analysis of how the prevalence of informal entrepreneurship varies according to firm age, by the size of firm, export orientation, ownership characteristics, the structure of the workforce and so forth. The outcome will be an introductory statistical portrait of the prevalence of entrepreneurship in the informal sector across the world. This will set the scene for the next two chapters, which examine the impacts of entrepreneurship in the informal sector and the reasons for informal entrepreneurship, respectively.

Magnitude of Informal Entrepreneurship: A Global Perspective

Numerous small-scale and national-level studies have been conducted that estimate the prevalence of informal entrepreneurship in individual countries (e.g., Chepurenko, 2016; Dana, 1995; Denisova-Schmidt and Prytula, 2016; Godfrey and Dyer, 2015; London *et al.*, 2014; Williams, 2010; Williams and Martinez-Perez, 2014a,b; Yu and Bruton, 2015). There are also some small-scale cross-national comparisons (Williams, 2008; Williams *et al.*, 2016). A study comparing Russia, Ukraine and England, for example, finds that 96 per cent, 51 per cent and 23 per cent of entrepreneurs operate in the informal sector, respectively. The problem, however, is that these findings are based on interviews with just 130 entrepreneurs in England, 331 in Ukraine and 81 in Moscow (Williams, 2008).

Until now, few studies have evaluated the overall prevalence of informal entrepreneurship on a global level and whether and how its magnitude varies across global regions and cross-nationally. This section, therefore, provides a review of the various data sets and estimates available to provide one of the first overviews of the magnitude of informal entrepreneurship on a worldwide scale and how its prevalence varies across global regions and cross-nationally.

To evaluate the prevalence of informal entrepreneurship at the worldwide, global regional and cross-national scale, three major data sets currently exist that can be used. Firstly, there is the GEM. This has a very broad coverage of countries and Autio and Fu (2015) for instance have used this to derive estimates of the prevalence of informal entrepreneurship at the global regional and cross-national scales. Secondly, the WBES data have questions within that provide three indicators of the scale of the informal sector and informal entrepreneurship, including one that enables estimates to be produced of the proportion of currently formal businesses that started up unregistered and two which examine the impacts of the informal sector. And thirdly and finally, the ILO has collated data on the magnitude of the informal sector and informal employment in 47 countries (ILO, 2011, 2012), although data on the scale of informal entrepreneurship can only be derived for 38 of these countries.

What follows is a focus upon reporting in depth two of these data sets, namely the ILO and WBES, on the prevalence of informal entrepreneurship. The results from the remaining data set, namely the GEM, have already been reported in some depth elsewhere (Autio and Fu, 2015; Dau and Cuervo-Cazurra, 2014). Here, therefore, it will suffice to summarise these results.

Several studies have derived estimates of the prevalence of informal entrepreneurship using data from the GEM, even though this survey does not directly ask any questions on whether entrepreneurs are operating in the formal or informal sector. Examining two such studies to have estimated the prevalence of informal entrepreneurship using GEM data, the finding is that a sizeable proportion of all businesses start up without registration. Dau and Cuervo-Cazurra (2014) examining 51 countries find that 3.37 informal enterprises are created annually for every 100 people, while Autio and Fu (2015) using a similar measure find that some two-thirds of businesses start up without registration in the informal sector not only in emerging and transition economies (where 0.62 informal businesses compared with 0.37 formal businesses are created annually for every 100 people) but also in OECD countries (where 0.62 informal businesses compared with 0.43 formal businesses are annually created for every 100 people).

To derive these estimates, both studies combine the GEM with other data sets to estimate the level of informal entrepreneurship. This is achieved by subtracting World Bank estimates of the number of registered businesses from the GEM estimates of the total number of new enterprises in each country. This, however, can be only a very tentative estimate. For this reason, and to transcend this potentially very problematic way of estimating informal entrepreneurship, more straightforward measures of the prevalence of informal entrepreneurship will be here reported. These are firstly, an ILO survey of informal entrepreneurship and, secondly, the responses to a question in the WBES on whether the formal businesses surveyed had registered before they commenced operations or whether they were unregistered at start-up.

ILO Survey of 38 Developing Economies

To understand how the ILO data can be used to evaluate the prevalence of informal entrepreneurship, it is first necessary to understand the definitions of the informal sector and informal employment developed by the 15th and 17th International Conferences of Labour Statisticians (ICLSs) (Hussmanns, 2005; ILO, 2011, 2012), as discussed in Chapter 1. As Table 4.1 displays, the informal sector can be defined using either enterprises or jobs as the unit of analysis. If enterprises are used as the unit of analysis, then the informal sphere is defined in terms of 'employment in the informal sector' (A+B), while if employment is the unit of analysis, then the informal sphere is defined in terms of 'informal employment' (A+C).

To define informal sector entrepreneurship, therefore, the first step is to use enterprises as the unit of analysis to define the 'informal sector' and,

Table 4.1 A Typology of the Informal Sphere

	Informal jobs	*Formal jobs*
Informal economic units	A	B
Formal economic units	C	D

Source: ILO (2012)

secondly, to use employment as the unit of analysis to identify entrepreneurs who operate in the informal sector. Starting with the enterprise-based definition that uses enterprises as the unit of analysis to define the 'informal sector', the 15th ICLS in 1993 defines the 'informal sector' as comprising private unincorporated enterprises that are unregistered or small in terms of the number of employed persons (Hussmanns, 2005). Unpacking the various components of this definition, an 'unincorporated' enterprise is defined as a production unit not constituted as a separate legal entity independent of the individual (or group of individuals) who owns it and for which no complete set of accounts is kept. Meanwhile, an enterprise that is 'unregistered' is defined as one not registered under specific forms of national legislation (e.g., factories' or commercial acts, tax or social security laws or professional groups' regulatory acts). The issuing of a trade license or business permit under local regulations does not qualify as registration. The final component of this definition is what is meant by small. This is determined as being when an enterprise falls below a specific threshold size in terms of employment (e.g., five employees), and this level is determined by national circumstances (Hussmanns, 2005; ILO, 2011, 2012). The informal sector, in sum, is comprised of these private unincorporated enterprises (i.e., not constituted as a separate legal entity independent of the person/s owning and for which no complete set of accounts is kept) and which are either unregistered or small in terms of the number employed in them.

Importantly, not everybody operating in the informal sector as defined here is an entrepreneur. Many operating in these informal sector enterprises will be employees (i.e., 'A' in Table 4.1), and others operating in the informal sector enterprises may be in formal employment (i.e., 'B' in Table 4.1). For this reason, a jobs-based definition of 'informal employment' was adopted by the 17th ICLS in 2003. This enabled, as will be seen, the identification and enumeration of those working in the informal sector who can be considered to be entrepreneurs. Informal employment in this 17th ICLS definition encompasses five categories of worker: (1) own-account workers and employers employed in their own informal enterprises; (2) members of informal producers' cooperatives (not established as legal entities); (3) own-account workers producing goods exclusively for their own final use by their household (if considered employed given that the production comprises an important contribution to the total household consumption and is included in the national definition of employment); (4) contributing family workers in formal or informal enterprises and (5) employees who are treated as informal employees if they are not covered by social security or are not entitled to other employment benefits. Here, only those in Category 1, namely own-account workers and employers employed in their own informal enterprises, are deemed to be 'entrepreneurs'. Informal sector 'entrepreneurs', therefore, here include two groups: (1) own-account workers employed in their own informal sector enterprises or (2) employers employed in their own informal sector enterprises (ILO, 2011, 2012).

Using these widely accepted and used ILO enterprise- and jobs-based definitions, therefore, informal sector entrepreneurs are defined for the purposes of analysing the ILO data as own-account workers or employers operating an unregistered and/or small unincorporated private enterprise engaged in the production of goods or services for sale or barter. The major advantage of using this ILO data set to evaluate the magnitude of informal entrepreneurship is that this definition of entrepreneurship in the informal sector is used across all the countries included. Moreover, there is also a similar methodology used to evaluate its magnitude. For each country, the Bureau of Statistics of the ILO sends a common questionnaire to all statistical offices of each country requesting that each national office completes detailed statistical tables regarding the level of employment in the informal sector and informal employment. For each country to provide this data, either the ILO Department of Statistics questionnaire sent to each country is used or information from their national labour force or informal sector surveys (for further details, see ILO, 2012). The only difference among countries is that when defining the informal sector and informal employment (and thus informal sector entrepreneurship), there is some minor variation across nations vis-à-vis what is defined as 'small' (e.g., employing less than five employees) and 'unregistered' due to different national-level laws applying. On the whole, therefore, the data evaluated is comparable across countries.

Here the findings on the prevalence of informal sector entrepreneurship are reported. Before doing so, however, an important clarification is required. These ILO surveys only measure non-agricultural employment. Employment in agriculture, hunting, forestry and fishing is excluded from the analysis. The consequence is that these estimates of the level of informal entrepreneurship may well be lower-bound estimates. The prevalence of informal entrepreneurship in each country may be higher if agriculture were to be included since this sector is composed of a high level of own-account work in developing countries. It is also important to recognise that persons with more than one job are classified on the basis of their self-reported main job. Again, this may result in these estimates being lower-bound estimates since many may have second jobs that are defined as informal sector entrepreneurship.

Table 4.2 reports the findings for the 38 developing countries for which data on the level of informal sector entrepreneurship are available. This reveals that the simple unweighted average is that one-quarter (25.3 per cent) of the non-agricultural workforce engage in informal sector entrepreneurship as their main job. However, given the variable workforce size across countries, a weighted figure is used; one in six (16.6 per cent) of the non-agricultural workforce participate in informal sector entrepreneurship as their main job on average across these 38 countries. Informal sector entrepreneurship, therefore, is not some minor economic activity but is the main job of one in six of the non-agricultural workforce in these countries.

Table 4.2 Percentage of Non-Agricultural Workforce Engaged in Informal Entrepreneurship as Their Main Employment (Unweighted and Weighted) By Global Region

Global region	% of non-agricultural workforce in informal entrepreneurship as main job		% of non-agricultural workforce in informal sector enterprises		No. of countries
	Unweighted	Weighted	Unweighted	Weighted	
All countries	25.3	16.6	40.6	31.5	38
East Asia & Pacific	24.1	18.6	49.5	33.7	4
Europe & Central Asia	7.7	8.5	15.6	20.6	5
Latin America & Caribbean	27.6	22.7	40.6	33.3	16
Middle East & North Africa	11.1	11.1	23.2	23.2	1
South Asia	28.4	10.0	63.7	28.6	3
Sub-Saharan Africa	32.0	26.1	48.0	38.8	9

Source: author's own calculations from ILO (2012) data set

Indeed it has to be remembered that this is a lower-bound estimate. If the agricultural workforce were to be included, as well as those who engage in informal entrepreneurship as a second job, then the proportion of the total workforce involved in informal sector entrepreneurship would be doubtless considerably higher than this figure of one in six of the workforce.

When the workers employed by these informal entrepreneurs are included, the finding is that just under one-third (31.5 per cent) of the workforce across these 38 countries is either informal sector entrepreneurs or has a main job in informal sector enterprises. Entrepreneurship in the informal sector, therefore, does not reside in the margins of the global economy. One in six of the non-agricultural workforce is an informal entrepreneur as a main job, and nearly one in three workers is either an informal entrepreneur or works in informal sector enterprises. This is a large proportion of the total non-agricultural workforce in these 38 countries.

The proportion of the workforce operating as informal entrepreneurs for their main job, however, is not the same across all global regions. Some global regions have much higher proportions of their workforce engaged in informal entrepreneurship than others. Using the World Bank classification of global regions, the 38 countries for which data is available on informal entrepreneurship can be broken down into six regions as displayed in Table 4.2. The weighted share of the workforce who are informal entrepreneurs for their main job varies from just over one-quarter (26.1 per cent) in sub-Saharan Africa, through nearly one in four (22.7 per cent) in Latin America and the Caribbean, to one in eleven (8.5 per cent) in Europe and Central Asia. The proportion of the workforce engaged as informal entrepreneurs in their main job, therefore, is not evenly distributed globally.

When the employees employed by informal entrepreneurs are included, the finding is that the share of the workforce engaged as either informal sector entrepreneurs or with their main job in informal sector enterprises varies from 38.8 per cent in sub-Saharan Africa to 20.6 per cent in Europe and Central Asia. Even in the global region with the smallest proportions, therefore, more than one in five in the workforce is engaged as an informal entrepreneur for a main job or have a main job in informal sector enterprises. This figure, moreover, excludes the significant agricultural workforce working on an own-account basis and the large number of employees who have a second job in which they operate as an informal entrepreneur.

Besides these variations among global regions, Table 4.3 reveals that there are also considerable cross-national variations in the share of the non-agricultural workforce engaged in informal sector entrepreneurship, ranging from 58.5 per cent in Mali to just 2.3 per cent in Serbia. Although sub-Saharan countries are in general clustered among the countries with the highest proportions of the workforce engaged in informal sector entrepreneurship as their main job, and European and Central Asian countries are in general clustered among the countries with the lowest proportions, with Latin American and Caribbean countries, South Asian as well as East Asian and Pacific countries somewhere in between, there are many exceptions.

In many countries, furthermore, the majority of the workforce has their main employment in informal sector enterprises. As Table 4.3 reveals, in 16 (42 per cent) of the 38 countries surveyed, informal enterprises employ the majority of the non-agricultural workforce. Informal entrepreneurship and the employment created by such informal entrepreneurs, in consequence, is not a minor aspect of the labour market and of limited importance. It is the dominant sector in the economy. Indeed it is the formal sector, and formal entrepreneurs and formal enterprises more particularly, that in some countries, is in the minority. However, there are again marked cross-national variations in the share of the non-agricultural workforce with a main job in informal enterprises either as an informal entrepreneur or waged employee. This ranges from 73 per cent in Pakistan and 71.4 per cent in Mali through to 7.0 per cent in Moldova and 3.5 per cent in Serbia.

In sum, this ILO data set highlights the importance of informal entrepreneurship both in terms of the number directly employed as informal entrepreneurs and in terms of the numbers employed in their main job in informal enterprises. These figures, moreover, are lower-bound estimates since they exclude agriculture, where a large proportion of the workforce is composed

Table 4.3 Cross-National Variations in the Share of the Non-Agricultural Work-force Engaged in Informal Entrepreneurship as Their Main Employment

Country	% of non-agricultural workforce in informal entrepreneurship as main job	% of non-agricultural workforce in informal sector enterprises	Year	Global region
Mali	58.5	71.4	2004	Sub-Saharan Africa
Liberia	42.5	49.5	2010	Sub-Saharan Africa
Tanzania	41.5	51.7	2005/6	Sub-Saharan Africa
Colombia	37.9	52.2	2010	Latin America & Caribbean
Uganda	36.9	59.8	2010	Sub-Saharan Africa
Honduras	36.6	58.3	2009	Latin America & Caribbean
Peru	34.8	49.0	2009	Latin America & Caribbean
Zambia	34.6	64.4	2008	Sub-Saharan Africa
Ethiopia	33.9	41.4	2004	Sub-Saharan Africa
El Salvador	33.5	53.4	2009	Latin America & Caribbean
Nicaragua	33.2	54.4	2009	Latin America & Caribbean
Pakistan	32.9	73.0	2009/10	South Asia
Bolivia	32.4	52.1	2006	Latin America & Caribbean
India	31.7	67.5	2009/10	South Asia
Venezuela	30.6	36.3	2009	Latin America & Caribbean
Indonesia	28.4	60.2	2009	East Asia & Pacific
Philippines	26.8	72.5	2008	East Asia and Pacific
Madagascar	26.8	51.8	2005	Sub-Saharan Africa
Vietnam	26.4	43.5	2009	East Asia & Pacific
Dominican Rep	26.2	29.4	2009	Latin America & Caribbean
Panama	25.1	27.7	2009	Latin America & Caribbean
Uruguay	23.9	33.9	2009	Latin America & Caribbean
Paraguay	23.8	37.9	2009	Latin America & Caribbean
Costa Rica	23.3	37.0	2009	Latin America & Caribbean

Country	% of non-agricultural workforce in informal entrepreneurship as main job	% of non-agricultural workforce in informal sector enterprises	Year	Global region
Ecuador	22.7	37.3	2009	Latin America & Caribbean
Argentina	21.9	32.1	2009	Latin America & Caribbean
Kyrgyzstan	20.8	59.2	2009	Europe & Central Asia
Sri Lanka	20.6	50.5	2009	South Asia
Mexico	19.1	34.1	2009	Latin America & Caribbean
Brazil	17.3	24.3	1009	Latin America & Caribbean
China	14.9	21.9	2010	East Asia & Pacific
West Bank & Gaza	11.1	23.2	2010	Middle East & North Africa
South Africa	10.9	17.8	2010	Sub-Saharan Africa
Moldova Rep	6.6	7.3	2009	Europe & Central Asia
Armenia	4.9	10.2	2009	Europe & Central Asia
Macedonia	3.9	7.6	2010	Europe & Central Asia
Lesotho	2.7	49.1	2008	Sub-Saharan Africa
Serbia	2.3	3.5	2010	Europe & Central Asia

Source: author's own calculations from ILO (2012) data set

of own-account workers and also the considerable number of citizens who have second jobs in which they operate as informal entrepreneurs.

World Bank Enterprise Survey (WBES)

The WBES asks three questions that provide estimates of the prevalence of informal entrepreneurship. Firstly, the formal businesses employing five or more employees surveyed in the WBES are asked whether they started operations while still unregistered (and if so, the length of time that they remained unregistered after starting-up operations). This, therefore, provides an estimate of the proportion of formal businesses with more than five employees that started up on an unregistered basis. Secondly, these formal businesses are asked whether they are competing against unregistered firms in the informal sector and, thirdly and finally, these formal businesses are asked whether the informal sector is a major obstacle to their operations.

In this section, WBES data are analysed from 142 countries across the globe. This includes 15 developed countries (including Germany, Spain, Ireland and South Korea) and 127 developing countries, including 41 in Africa, 13 in East Asia and the Pacific region, 29 in Europe and Central Asia, 31 in Latin America and Caribbean, 7 in the Middle East and North Africa, and 6 in South Asia. Of the countries surveyed, 25 are low-income countries, 42 lower middle-income countries, 36 middle-income countries, 4 upper middle-income countries, and 20 high-income countries. All world regions and levels of economic development are thus covered by this survey.

In every country, the WBES collects data using a stratified random sample of non-agricultural, formal, private sector businesses with five or more employees which is stratified by firm size, business sector and geographic region. The firm size strata in the WBES are 5–19 (small), 20–99 (medium), and 100+ employees (large-sized firms), while sector is broken down into manufacturing, services, transportation and construction. Public utilities, government services, health care and financial services sectors are not included, and in larger economies, manufacturing sub-sectors are selected as additional strata on the basis of employment, value added and total number of establishments. Geographical regions within a country are selected based on which cities or regions collectively contain the majority of economic activity. The sampling frame is derived from the universe of eligible firms, normally obtained from the country's statistical office or another government agency such as the tax or business licensing authorities. Since 2006, all national surveys explain the source of the sample frame.

To collect data, a harmonised questionnaire is used across all countries, answered by some 1,200–1,800 business owners and top managers in larger economies, 360 in medium-sized economies and 150 in smaller economies. Although the WBES has collected data since 2002, the sample here is restricted to the 142 countries that since 2006, have used the harmonised questionnaire and common sampling methodology, which assures that data is comparable across countries and over time.

As Table 4.4 reveals, of all formal businesses employing five or more employees surveyed in the WBES, some one in five (19.9 per cent) started up unregistered and operated in the informal sector. This is important because it reveals, contrary to the tenets of the modernisation theory discussed in the last chapter, that the formal and informal economies are not separate. One-fifth of enterprises currently operating in the formal sector started in the informal sector. There is therefore migration from the informal to the formal sector. This in consequence displays the value of pursuing a policy of formalising entrepreneurship in the informal sector. Some one-fifth of currently existing formal enterprises have their origins in the informal sector and would not have existed if a policy of eradicating informal entrepreneurship had been successfully implemented.

Table 4.4 Prevalence of Entrepreneurship in the Informal Sector, By Global Region, 2006–2014

Region	% of formal enterprises that started up unregistered	% of formal enterprises competing against unregistered or informal firms	% of formal enterprises identifying competitors in informal sector as a major constraint
Sub-Saharan Africa	43.2	52.1	32.8
East Asia & Pacific	17.1	45.9	11.9
Europe & Central Asia	5.5	36.7	21.7
Latin American & Caribbean	10.2	42.1	36.6
Middle East & North Africa	21.2	42.1	27.2
South Asia	46.9	26.5	14.6
OECD	7.9	20.5	2.9
All	19.9	41.9	26.9

Source: author's own calculations from the WBES data set

This survey also produces additional measures of the prevalence of informal enterprises. Some 41.9 per cent of formal businesses surveyed across the world identify themselves as competing against unregistered or formal firms on a global scale, and over one-quarter (26.9 per cent) of all formal enterprises surveyed across the world identify that competitors in the informal sector are a major obstacle. A large proportion of the formal business community, therefore, competes against and is constrained to a major degree by the existence of informal enterprises.

The prevalence of entrepreneurship in the informal sector, however, is not evenly spread across all global regions. Instead, and as Table 4.4 reveals, the proportion of formal businesses that started up on an unregistered basis is much higher in Sub-Saharan Africa (43.2 per cent) and South Asia (46.9 per cent) and relatively low in Europe and Central Asia (i.e., just 1 in 20 started up unregistered) and OECD nations (7.9 per cent). This mirrors the findings of the ILO data set regarding the uneven distribution of informal entrepreneurship across global regions. Similar regional variations are identified when the other WBES indicators of the prevalence of informal enterprises are analysed. The share of formal businesses which identify themselves as competing against unregistered or formal firms displays a similar spatial pattern so far as the differences across global regions are concerned, ranging from a high of 52.1 per cent in sub-Saharan Africa to a low of 20.5 per cent in OECD nations. The share of all formal enterprises identifying competitors in the informal sector as a major obstacle again displays a similar spatial pattern, ranging from 36.6 in Latin America and the Caribbean, and 32.8 per cent in sub-Saharan Africa, to 2.9 per cent in OECD nations.

There are also some significant cross-national variations in the prevalence of informal entrepreneurship. Analysing the variations in the proportion of currently formal enterprises with five or more employees that started up unregistered, Table 4.5 reveals that this ranges from countries where

Table 4.5 Cross-National Variations in the Prevalence of Informal Entrepreneurship

Country	% of formal enterprises that started up unregistered	% of formal enterprises competing against unregistered or informal firms	% of formal enterprises identifying competitors in informal sector as a major constraint
Afghanistan	16	43	31
Albania	5	44	33
Angola	74	26	32
Antigua & Barbuda	12	77	33
Argentina	8	41	40
Armenia	2	28	25
Azerbaijan	17	26	17
Bahamas	10	50	14
Bangladesh	60	20	10
Barbados	15	51	18
Belarus	6	38	17
Belize	17	64	33
Benin	17	75	67
Bhutan	2	20	9
Bosnia & Herzegovina	2	49	22
Bolivia	14	41	57
Botswana	59	33	25
Brazil	6	65	44
Bulgaria	4	43	31
Burkina Faso	21	63	53
Burundi	100	20	38
Cameroon	17	84	71
Cape Verde	17	46	42
Central African Republic (CAR)	7	66	45

Country	% of formal enterprises that started up unregistered	% of formal enterprises competing against unregistered or informal firms	% of formal enterprises identifying competitors in informal sector as a major constraint
Chad	20	81	72
Chile	5	30	26
China	5	52	5
Colombia	13	43	47
Congo	21	60	44
Costa Rica	24	72	35
Cote d'Ivoire	45	63	30
Croatia	2	34	16
Czech Republic	5	37	24
Djibouti	3	21	20
Dominica	3	11	11
Dominica Republic	17	72	40
Dem. Rep of Congo (DRC)	53	61	44
Ecuador	11	34	33
El Salvador	23	31	37
Eritrea	3	23	0
Estonia	3	23	6
Ethiopia	4	34	14
Fiji	10	37	14
FYR Macedonia	3	63	42
Gabon	35	69	35
The Gambia	100	17	22
Georgia	7	50	21
Ghana	27	66	24
Grenada	30	67	25
Guatemala	11	43	36
Guinea	100	17	22
Guinea Bissau	100	18	32
Guyana	19	57	29
Honduras	13	35	28
Hungary	3	30	16
India	9	N/A	43
Indonesia	55	54	14
Iraq	40	60	46

(*Continued*)

Table 4.5 (Continued)

Country	% of formal enterprises that started up unregistered	% of formal enterprises competing against unregistered or informal firms	% of formal enterprises identifying competitors in informal sector as a major constraint
Israel	8	21	3
Jamaica	19	53	29
Jordan	3	20	10
Kazakhstan	3	29	21
Kenya	50	30	36
Kosovo	5	49	38
Kyrgyzstan	12	55	35
Laos	11	26	12
Latvia	3	31	21
Lebanon	18	56	36
Lesotho	13	50	20
Liberia	25	60	19
Lithuania	4	43	26
Madagascar	10	64	26
Malawi	15	69	26
Mali	17	69	44
Mauritania	49	39	35
Mexico	10	36	35
Federal States of Micronesia	7	40	12
Moldova	3	30	22
Mongolia	17	42	18
Montenegro	6	39	16
Mozambique	12	77	52
Myanmar	18	28	4
Namibia	100	11	13
Nepal	8	48	21
Nicaragua	21	32	30
Niger	9	77	57
Nigeria	100	59	18
Pakistan	100	32	0
Panama	3	32	14
Paraguay	5	37	50
Peru	6	49	47
Philippines	6	35	21
Poland	3	29	18

Country	% of formal enterprises that started up unregistered	% of formal enterprises competing against unregistered or informal firms	% of formal enterprises identifying competitors in informal sector as a major constraint
Romania	2	27	25
Russia	4	28	15
Rwanda	53	32	25
Samoa	1 /	61	16
Senegal	20	69	42
Serbia	5	49	23
Sierra Leone	13	65	18
Slovakia	1	35	11
Slovenia	1	25	11
South Africa	7	41	10
Sri Lanka	24	43	27
St Kitts & Nevis	16	59	32
St Lucia	3	23	14
St Vincent & the Grenadines	25	51	17
Suriname	2	85	42
Swaziland	100	16	43
Tajikistan	18	33	26
Tanzania	52	44	38
Timor-Leste	19	65	19
Togo	23	72	48
Tonga	12	82	29
Trinidad & Tobago	23	61	24
Turkey	8	53	25
Uganda	63	54	35
Ukraine	7	40	27
Uruguay	5	44	50
Uzbekistan	27	28	17
Vanuatu	14	38	10
Venezuela	3	14	19
Vietnam	15	50	14
West Bank & Gaza	20	45	22
Yemen	25	37	22
Zambia	12	72	37
Zimbabwe	5	70	46

Source: author's own calculations from the WBES data set

all surveyed enterprises asserted that they started up unregistered (i.e., Burundi, The Gambia, Guinea, Guinea Bissau, Namibia, Nigeria, Pakistan and Swaziland) to other countries where just 1 per cent started up unregistered (i.e., Slovenia and Slovakia) and others where just 2 per cent did so (i.e., Armenia, Bhutan, Bosnia and Herzegovina, Croatia and Suriname). It is similarly the case that when examining the proportion of businesses that compete against unregistered or informal firms, this again varies widely, ranging from 85 per cent in Suriname, 84 per cent in Cameron and 82 per cent in Tonga to only 11 per cent in Namibia, 14 per cent in Venezuela and 17 per cent in The Gambia. It is also the case that there are wide cross-national variations in the share of firms identifying competitors in the informal sector as a major constraint, ranging from 72 per cent in Chad, 71 per cent in Cameroon and 67 per cent in Benin through to only 4 per cent in Myanmar, 3 per cent in Israel and no firms in Nigeria and Eritrea.

As such, considerable cross-national variations exist in not only the degree to which enterprises start up unregistered, but also the proportion of formal enterprises that compete with unregistered and informal enterprises, and face major constraints from such competitors. As Chapter 3 displayed, there are three major competing theories regarding the country-level conditions that lead some countries to have larger informal sectors. Here, the intention has been solely to highlight the cross-national variations in the scale and impacts of the informal entrepreneurs and enterprises. In Chapter 6, this topic will be returned to when an evaluation is undertaken of the country-level conditions that influence the scale of informal entrepreneurship across countries. For the moment, however, this is left aside. Here attention turns to how the distribution of entrepreneurship in the informal sector varies not only across global regions and cross-nationally but also across different sectors and how different types of firms appear to be more affected by entrepreneurship in the informal sector than others.

Distribution of Informal Entrepreneurship

The scale of informal entrepreneurship does not only vary across global regions and cross-nationally, but also there are variations in its prevalence and impacts, firstly, by sector and, secondly, by firm characteristics such as firm size, firm age and whether it is a domestic or exporting firm. Each is here considered in turn.

Sectoral Distribution of Informal Entrepreneurship

So far as the economic sectors in which informal entrepreneurship is to be found are concerned, there are often many popular prejudices about the sectors in which it is concentrated. For example, it is often asserted that such entrepreneurship is more likely to be found in the construction sector and textiles industry, not least due to the subcontracting and outsourcing arrangements which characterise these sectors (Mehrotra and Biggeri, 2007) but also in the food, hospitality and tourism industry (Williams and Horodnic, 2017; Williams and Thomas, 1996), manifested in the presence of so many street vendors and hawkers in developing countries operating microenterprises and small kiosks and stalls (Bandyopadhyay, 2015; Bhowmik, 2007; Cross and Morales, 2007; Crossa, 2015; Dunn, 2015; Etzold, 2015; Graaff and Ha, 2015; Kettles, 2007; Khan, 2017; Lyon, 2007; Staudt, 2007).

Table 4.6 evaluates whether such assumptions are indeed valid when adopting a global sectoral perspective. The finding from these descriptive statistics is that there appears to be relatively little variation across sectors in terms of the proportion of formal enterprises with five or more employees

Table 4.6 Prevalence of Informal Entrepreneurship By Sector, 2006–2014

Sector of activity	% of formal enterprises that started up unregistered	% of formal enterprises competing against unregistered or informal firms	% of formal enterprises identifying competitors in informal sector as a major constraint
Textiles	19.6	40.1	29.3
Leather	19.7	33.2	24.0
Garments	19.5	42.7	35.2
Food	19.5	41.9	29.9
Metals & machinery	20.2	40.1	22.4
Electronics	20.0	31.3	17.6
Chemicals & pharmaceuticals	20.1	32.7	27.3
Wood & furniture	19.7	51.7	28.6
Non-metallic & plastic products	20.0	40.5	22.8
Auto & auto components	19.9	42.5	19.7
Other manufacturing	19.1	34.2	29.2
Wholesale & retail trade	21.1	49.3	26.4
Hotel & restaurants	19.9	46.5	21.5
Other services	20.1	42.6	26.9
All manufacturing	17.0	38.8	27.9
All services	21.7	47.3	25.9

Source: author's own calculations from the WBES data set

that started operations unregistered in the informal sector, ranging from 21.1 per cent for the wholesale and retail trade to 19.1 per cent for other manufacturing industries. This, of course, is perhaps unsurprising since this only reveals that similar proportions of enterprises formalise across sectors.

However, there is greater variation when examining the share of formal enterprises competing against unregistered or informal enterprises, which is perhaps a better reflection of the prevalence of informality across sectors. The proportion of formal enterprise with five or more employees competing against unregistered or informal enterprises ranges from 51.7 per cent in the wood and furniture sector and 49.3 per cent in the wholesale and retail trade (perhaps reflecting the prevalence of informal street vendors) to 32.7 per cent in the chemicals and pharmaceutical industry and 31.3 per cent in the electronics sector. Therefore there are some marked variations across sectors in the proportion of formal enterprises competing with unregistered or informal competitors.

This is similarly the case when the share of firms identifying competitors in the informal sector as a major obstacle is analysed. This ranges from 35.6 per cent of formal firms in the garment industry and 29.9 per cent in the food industry (again perhaps reflecting the presence of informal street food hawkers) to 17.6 per cent in the electronics industry, where there are perhaps higher barriers to entry for informal competitors, but nonetheless one in six formal businesses still assert that informal competitors are a major obstacle.

It is not just across sectors, however, that there are variations in the prevalence and impacts of informal entrepreneurship. There are also variations in the prevalence and impacts of informal entrepreneurship according to firm-level variables such as firm size, firm age, export orientation and ownership characteristics. It is to these variations, therefore, that attention now turns.

Distribution of Informal Entrepreneurship: By Firm Size, Age, Export Orientation and Ownership

There is often an assumption that if a firm starts up unregistered, then it is unlikely to grow to the same size as firms that start up legitimately. Viewed through the lens of the liabilities of newness (Stinchcombe, 1965), such new ventures are seen to lack legitimacy and reliability (Choi and Shepherd, 2005; Delmar and Shane, 2004) and are less likely to be perceived as competent, effective and worthy (Zimmerman and Zeitz, 2002). Registering is thus viewed as a means by which new ventures enhance legitimacy and reduce their liabilities of newness (Kistruck et al., 2015; Webb et al., 2009). Non-registration, meanwhile, is seen as leading to a lack of legitimacy and reduces firm performance (Fajnzylber et al., 2009; Farrell, 2004; ILO, 2007; La Porta and Shleifer, 2008; Palmer, 2007). Enterprises starting up unregistered should therefore have worse subsequent performance levels than those registered from the outset, all other things being equal. If this is correct, then firms that started up unregistered should be smaller firms, displaying that they have been unable to grow at the same rate as enterprises that started up registered.

As Table 4.7 reveals, however, this is not the case. Some one in five (21.2 per cent) of formal enterprises with 100+ employees had started up unregistered and 22 per cent of enterprises with 20–99 employees. Conversely, only 15.1 per cent of formal enterprises with 5–19 employees had started up unregistered. This suggests that enterprises starting up unregistered have subsequently outperformed enterprises starting up registered in

Table 4.7 Prevalence of Informal Entrepreneurship By Firm Size, Age, Export Orientation and Ownership, 2006–2014

Firm characteristics	% of formal enterprises that started up unregistered	% of formal enterprises competing against unregistered or informal firms	% of formal enterprises identifying competitors in informal sector as a major obstacle
Firm size:			
Small firm (5–19 employees)	15.1	44.9	28.9
Medium-sized firm (20–99)	22.0	41.3	27.1
Large firm (100+)	21.2	35.6	21.2
Firm age:			
< 5 years old	23.8	40.3	25.0
5–9 years old	20.4	41.4	24.9
10–19 years old	16.8	42.1	25.9
>19 years old	21.9	42.9	29.8
Export orientation:			
Exporting firm	13.5	32.8	21.0
Non-exporting firm	20.8	43.3	27.0
Ownership:			
Foreign owned	15.3	36.0	23.9
Domestic owned	20.5	42.9	27.0
Gender of ownership:			
Female share in ownership	17.1	42.9	27.5
No female involvement	21.6	40.8	25.8

Source: author's own calculations from the WBES data set

terms of employment growth, with a greater proportion growing to become middle-sized or larger-sized enterprises and a small proportion remaining smaller-sized firms than those which started up registered.

Younger formal firms, moreover, are more likely to state that they started up unregistered than older firms. On the one hand, this might very tentatively suggest that enterprises starting up unregistered do not survive into older age. On the other hand, and more likely, it reflects that there has been an increase in the number of formal firms that start up unregistered in recent decades with the advent of a form of global capitalism that has relied ever more on subcontracting and outsourcing to informal and unregistered enterprises (Castells and Portes, 1989; Gallin, 2001).

Starting up unregistered, however, is more common among non-exporting firms than among exporting firms and also among those that are domestic owned compared with those that are foreign owned. This is perhaps because exporting and foreign-owned firms are more visible to registering and regulatory authorities, and a much lower number and proportion of them thus start up unregistered. Finally, and from a gender perspective, the interesting finding is that formal enterprises with five or more employees in which there is the involvement of women in the ownership of the business are less likely to have started up unregistered than enterprises operated purely by men.

Turning to the whether some types of formal enterprises are more likely to be competing against unregistered or informal firms, and also whether some types of formal firms are more likely to identify competitors in the informal sector as a major obstacle, Table 4.7 reveals that this is the case. Commencing with firm size, the finding is that a greater proportion of small firms (44.9 per cent) report that they are competing against unregistered or informal firms than medium- and large-sized firms (41.3 and 35.6 per cent, respectively) and that also a greater proportion of small firms (28.9 per cent) identify competitors in the informal sector as a major obstacle compared with medium- and large-sized firms (27.1 and 22.1 per cent, respectively). This reinforces previous studies (Dana and Ratten, 2017; Kuzilwa and Nyamsogoro, 2017; Wijebandara and Coonay, 2017). Small formal firms are more likely to witness competition from informal competitors and to view them as a major obstacle. Whether this remains the case when controlling for other variables such as sector will be returned to in the next chapter.

Interestingly it is not the case that younger enterprises are more likely to witness competition from informal and unregistered providers, and neither is it the case that they are more likely to state that competing against unregistered or informal firms is a major obstacle. Instead the older the firm, the more likely they are in both cases to state that this is the case. Competition from the informal sector, and informal competitors as an obstacle, are not new venture problems. Instead it prevails more among older enterprises. Why this is the case will be returned to in what follows and also in the next chapter.

It is the case however, that both exporting firms and foreign-owned firms are less likely to witness competition from informal and unregistered providers and to view competing against unregistered or informal firms as a major obstacle. This can tentatively be asserted to be doubtless due to the markets that they serve. Finally, and from a gender perspective, the interesting finding is that enterprises in which there is the involvement of women in the ownership of the business are more likely to witness competition from informal and unregistered providers and more likely to view informal competitors as a major obstacle.

Multivariate Analysis of the World Bank Enterprise Survey (WBES)

To determine whether these associations are statistically significant when other characteristics are taken into account and held constant, Table 4.8 reports the results of a multivariate probit regression analysis. Model 1 shows whether any of these characteristics are statistically significant when considering whether entrepreneurs start up unregistered while controlling for other firm-level characteristics. The first important finding relates to the institutional asymmetry theory propagated in this book. There is a statistically significant association between trust in the formal institutions (i.e., in this case trust in the court system) and the likelihood of being unregistered at start-up. The greater the trust in the formal institutions, the less likely they are to have started up unregistered. This, therefore, provides confirmation of the institutional asymmetry thesis discussed in Chapter 2, which asserts that informal entrepreneurship is more likely when the formal and informal institutions are not aligned.

It is also revealed that there is a significant positive association between firm age and starting up unregistered; older firms are significantly more likely to have started operations on an unregistered basis. This might very tentatively suggest some reduction in the number of firms making the transition from informality to formality in recent decades. Model 1 also reveals results associated with exporting and foreign ownership that are consistent with the descriptive statistics already discussed. Exporting and foreign-owned firms are significantly more likely to have been registered at the start of their operations. However, there are few significant correlations between formal firms that started up unregistered and current workforce characteristics. The only exception is that formal firms that started up unregistered are less likely to employ full-time permanent workers, intimating that the 'standard employment relationship' (against which worker rights and protection tends to be attached) is more likely to be found in firms that started up on a registered basis rather than those formal firms that started up unregistered. Firms now with quality certifications are also less likely to have started up unregistered, as are those that use external auditors and that use modern technology such emails and websites for communication with clients and

Table 4.8 Probit Model of the Firm-Level Determinants of Informality, WBES 2006–2014

Variables	% of formal enterprises that started up unregistered	% of formal enterprises competing against unregistered or informal firms	% of formal enterprises identifying competitors in informal sector as a major obstacle
	Model 1	Model 2	Model 3
Trust	−0.067*** (0.016)	−0.117*** (0.011)	−0.192*** (0.012)
Firm age	0.012*** (0.000)	0.002*** (0.000)	0.002*** (0.000)
Exporter	−0.001*** (0.000)	−0.002*** (0.000)	−0.002*** (0.000)
Foreign ownership	−0.244*** (0.032)	−0.216*** (0.020)	−0.088*** (0.020)
Workforce characteristics			
Top manager experience	0.001 (0.001)	0.003*** (0.001)	0.004*** (0.001)
Temporary worker	0.000 (0.000)	−0.000 (0.000)	0.000 (0.000)
Permanent full-time	−0.000** (0.000)	−0.000*** (0.000)	−0.000*** (0.000)
Female full-time	−0.000 (0.000)	−0.002*** (0.000)	−0.000 (0.000)
Female share in ownership	0.000 (0.000)	0.000 (0.000)	0.000*** (0.000)
Innovation			
Quality certification	−0.001*** (0.000)	−0.000** (0.000)	−0.001*** (0.000)
External auditor	−0.001*** (0.000)	0.000 (0.000)	0.000 (0.000)
Website	−0.001*** (0.000)	0.000*** (0.000)	−0.000** (0.000)
Email	−0.002*** (0.000)	0.000 (0.000)	0.000* (0.000)
Firm size (R.C. small)			
Medium	−0.044** (0.018)	−0.071*** (0.013)	−0.039*** (0.013)
Large	−0.057* (0.031)	−0.159*** (0.020)	−0.132*** (0.022)

Variables	% of formal enterprises that started up unregistered	% of formal enterprises competing against unregistered or informal firms	% of formal enterprises identifying competitors in informal sector as a major obstacle
Legal status (R.C.: Open shareholding)			
Closed sharcholding	−0.279*** (0.034)	0.012 (0.025)	0.099*** (0.026)
Sole proprietor	0.049 (0.036)	0.164*** (0.027)	0.065** (0.028)
Partnership	−0.049 (0.043)	0.062* (0.032)	0.091*** (0.034)
Limited partnership	−0.157*** (0.043)	0.064** (0.031)	0.011 (0.034)
Other form	−0.093 (0.060)	0.023 (0.046)	0.118*** (0.045)
Sector dummies	Yes	Yes	Yes
Year dummies	Yes	Yes	Yes
Region dummies	Yes	Yes	Yes
Constant	−1.238*** (0.061)	−6.182 (86.956)	−0.204*** (0.045)
Pseudo R-squared	0.10	0.16	0.07
N	67,515	67,515	67,515

N.B.: Absolute value of z statistics in parentheses:
* significant at 10%
** significant at 5%
*** significant at 1%
Source: author's own calculations from the WBES data set

suppliers. So too are medium and large formal enterprises significantly less likely to have started up unregistered than smaller firms, as are those whose legal status is a limited partnership or closed shareholding.

Turning to the association between whether firms are competing against unregistered or informal firms and whether informal competitors are a major obstacle to their operations, the finding in Models 2 and 3 is that there is a positive significant association between trust in the formal institutions and the likelihood of suffering competition from informal competitors and this being a major obstacle. Those suffering such competition have less trust in the formal institutions. This again provides reinforcement for the institutional asymmetry thesis, displaying that there is a significant association between the lack of trust in institutions and the prevalence of informality.

Older firms, moreover, are significantly more likely to state that they suffer from competition from unregistered or informal firms and to view informal competitors as a major obstacle to their operations, as do domestic-owned and non-exporting firms. There is also a statistically significant correlation with some workforce characteristics. Formal firms more likely to be suffering competition from informal and unregistered firms, and more likely to view this as a major obstacle to their operations, are significantly less likely to employ full-time permanent workers and for the top manager to have prior experience in the sector, suggesting that informality reduces the existence of the 'standard employment relationship' (against which worker rights and protection are attached) in formal firms competing with them, and that top manager experience in this sector appears to be a way of mitigating the need for formal firms to compete with informal firms, as is involving women in the ownership structure of the firm. Formal firms are also more likely to be suffering competition from informal and unregistered firms and more likely to view this as a major obstacle to their operations that have no quality certification scheme in place and do not have a website, as are smaller firms significantly more likely than medium and larger firms to suffer from competition from the informal sector and for this to be a major obstacle. With respect to the legal status of firms, sole proprietors and partnership arrangements are significantly more likely to both suffer competition from informal and unregistered firms as well as for this to be a major obstacle, compared with open shareholding firms.

Conclusions

This chapter has reviewed the prevalence of informal entrepreneurship from a global perspective. It has revealed that whether the GEM, ILO or WBES data set is used, informal entrepreneurship is not some minor activity existing in a few marginal enclaves of the world economy. Rather, it is an omnipresent endeavour that constitutes a significant share of all entrepreneurship and enterprise and employs a large share of the global workforce. The ILO data set on 38 countries for example reveals that one-quarter (25.3 per cent) of the non-agricultural workforce engage in informal entrepreneurship as their main job and that 40.6 per cent of the workforce across these 38 countries are either informal sector entrepreneurs or are employed in their main job in informal sector enterprises. The WBES across a much wider range of countries reveals not only that one in five (19.9 per cent) formal enterprises started up unregistered operating in the informal sector, but also that 41.9 per cent of formal businesses identify themselves as competing against unregistered or formal firms, and that over one-quarter (26.9 per cent) of all formal enterprises globally identify that competitors in the informal sector are a major obstacle. Whatever measure is used to evaluate the scale of informal entrepreneurship, therefore, its scale is far from minor.

However, it is not evenly distributed across all global regions. Whether the ILO or WBES data are used, and whatever the measurement indicator, the finding is the same. Informal entrepreneurship is more prevalent in the developing world, especially sub-Saharan Africa and South Asia, and far less prevalent in the developed world, such as the OECD nations, Europe and Central Asia. There are also some significant sectoral variations in terms of the prevalence of informal enterprises. One-half of all formal enterprises surveyed by the WBES in the wood and furniture sector, and the whole-sale and retail trade, asserts that they are competing against unregistered or informal firms but less than one-third of formal enterprises surveyed in the chemicals and pharmaceutical industry and in the electronics sector.

There are also statistically significant associations between whether a formal business started up unregistered and not only their level of trust in formal institutions (i.e., the greater the trust, the less likely they are to have started up unregistered), which provides some support for the institutional asymmetry thesis, but also with firm age (i.e., older firms are more likely to have started up unregistered), whether they are exporting and foreign owned (i.e., non-exporting and domestic-owned firms are more likely to have started up unregistered), workforce characteristics (i.e., formal firms that started up unregistered are less likely to employ full-time permanent workers, intimating that the 'standard employment relationship' against which worker rights and protection are attached is more likely to be found in firms that started up registered), technology and innovation (i.e., firms with quality certifications, who use external auditors and with websites and email are less likely to have started up unregistered), firm size (i.e., medium and large formal firms are significantly less likely to have started up unregistered) and legal status (i.e., a limited partnership or closed shareholding is less likely to have started unregistered).

Turning to whether formal firms compete against unregistered or informal firms and whether these informal or unregistered enterprises are a major constraint on their operations, the finding is that this is significantly more prevalent when trust in the formal institutions is low, among older, domestic-owned and non-exporting firms, those less likely to employ full-time permanent workers (suggesting that informality reduces the existence of the 'standard employment relationship'), with less top manager experience (intimating that this is a way of reducing competition with informal firms), without women's involvement in the ownership structure and with fewer innovative practices (without quality certification and a website) and, among smaller firms, sole proprietors and partnership arrangements.

With this global perspective on the scale and distribution of informal entrepreneurship in hand, the next chapter turns to understanding the impacts of informal entrepreneurship. Until now, as briefly touched upon in previous chapters, there has been a tendency to cast informal entrepreneurship in a negative light, emphasising largely its deleterious features. Whether this is a valid portrayal will be now put under the spotlight.

References

Autio, E. and Fu, K. (2015). Economic and political institutions and entry into formal and informal entrepreneurship. *Asia Pacific Journal of Management*, 32(1), pp. 67–94.

Bandyopadhyay, R. (2015). The Street Vendors Act and pedestrianism in India: A reading of the archival politics of the Calcutta hawker. In: K. Graaf and N. Ha, Eds., *Street vending in the neo-liberal city: A global perspective on the practices and policies of a marginalized economy*. Oxford: Berghahn, pp. 191–218.

Bhowmik, S.K. (2007). Street vending in urban India: The struggle for recognition. In: J. Cross and A. Morales, Eds., *Street entrepreneurs: People, place and politics in local and global perspective*. London: Routledge, pp. 92–107.

Castells, M. and Portes, A. (1989). World underneath: The origins, dynamics and effects of the informal economy. In: A. Portes, M. Castells and L. Benton, Eds., *The informal economy: Studies in advanced and less developing countries*. Baltimore: John Hopkins University Press, pp. 19–41.

Chepurenko, A. (2016). Informal entrepreneurship and informal entrepreneurial activity in Russia. In: A. Sauka, F. Schneider and C.C. Williams, Eds., *Entrepreneurship and the shadow economy*. Cheltenham: Edward Elgar, pp. 119–150.

Choi, Y.R. and Shepherd, D.A. (2005). Stakeholder perceptions of age and other dimensions of newness. *Journal of Management*, 31(4), pp. 573–596.

Cross, J. and Morales, A. (2007). Introduction: Locating street markets in the modern/postmodern world. In: J. Cross and A. Morales, Eds., *Street entrepreneurs: People, place and politics in local and global perspective*. London: Routledge, pp. 1–14.

Crossa, V. (2015). Creative resistance: The case of Mexico City's street artisans and vendors. In: K. Graaf and N. Ha, Eds., *Street vending in the neo-liberal city: A global perspective on the practices and policies of a marginalized economy*. Oxford: Berghahn, pp. 59–79.

Dana, L.-P. (1995). Entrepreneurship in a remote sub-Arctic community. *Entrepreneurship Theory and Practice*, 20(1), pp. 57–72.

Dana, L.-P. and Ratten, V. (2017). Characteristics and structures of informal entrepreneurship in Botswana. In: C.C. Williams and A. Gurtoo, Eds., *Routledge handbook of entrepreneurship in developing economies*. London: Routledge, pp. 412–423.

Dau, L.A. and Cuervo-Cazurra, A. (2014). To formalize or not to formalize: Entrepreneurship and pro-market institutions. *Journal of Business Venturing*, 29, pp. 668–686.

Delmar, F. and Shane, S. (2004). Legitimating first: Organizing activities and the survival of new ventures. *Journal of Business Venturing*, 19(3), pp. 385–410.

Denisova-Schmidt, E. and Prytula, Y. (2016). The shadow economy and entrepreneurship in Ukraine. In: A. Sauka, F. Schneider and C.C. Williams, Eds., *Entrepreneurship and the shadow economy*. Cheltenham: Edward Elgar, pp. 151–167.

Dunn, K. (2015). Flexible families: Latina/o food vending in Brooklyn, New York. In: K. Graaf and N. Ha, Eds., *Street vending in the neo-liberal city: A global perspective on the practices and policies of a marginalized economy*. Oxford: Berghahn, pp. 19–42.

Etzold, B. (2015). Selling in insecurity, living with violence: Eviction drives against street food vendors in Dhaka and the informal politics of exploitation. In: K. Graaf and N. Ha, Eds., *Street vending in the neo-liberal city: A global perspective on the practices and policies of a marginalized economy*. Oxford: Berghahn, pp. 164–190.

Fajnzylber, P., Maloney, W.F. and Montes Rojas, G.V. (2009). Releasing constraints to growth or pushing on a string? Policies and performance of Mexican microfirms. *Journal of Development Studies*, 45, pp. 1027–1047.

Farrell, D. (2004). The hidden dangers of informal economy. *McKinsey Quarterly*, 3, pp. 27–37.

Gallin, D. (2001). Propositions on trade unions and informal employment in time of globalisation. *Antipode*, 19(4), pp. 531–549.

Godfrey, P.C. and Dyer, G. (2015). Subsistence entrepreneurs and formal institutions: Semi-formal governance among Ghanaian entrepreneurs. In: P.C. Godfrey, Ed., *Management, society, and the informal economy*. London: Routledge, pp. 142–160.

Graaff, K. and Ha, N. (2015). Introduction: Street vending in the neoliberal city: A global perspective on the practices and policies of a marginalized economy. In: K. Graaf and N. Ha, Eds., *Street vending in the neo liberal city: A global perspective on the practices and policies of a marginalized economy*. Oxford: Berghahn, pp. 1–17.

Hussmanns, R. (2005). *Measuring the informal economy: From employment in the informal sector to informal employment*. Geneva: Working Paper no. 53, ILO Bureau of Statistics.

ILO (2007). *The decent work agenda in Africa, 2007–15*. Geneva: ILO.

ILO (2011). *Statistical update on employment in the informal economy*. Geneva: ILO.

ILO (2012). *Statistical update on employment in the informal economy*. Geneva: ILO.

Kettles, G.W. (2007). Legal responses to sidewalk vending: The case of Los Angeles. In: J. Cross and A. Morales, Eds., *Street entrepreneurs: People, place and politics in local and global perspective*. London: Routledge, pp. 58–78.

Khan, E.A. (2017). An investigation of marketing capabilities of informal micro-enterprises: A study of street food vending in Thailand. *International Journal of Sociology and Social Policy*, 37(3/4), pp. 186–202.

Kistruck, G.M., Webb, J.W., Sutter, C.J. and Bailey, A.V.G. (2015). The double-edged sword of legitimacy in base-of-the-pyramid markets. *Journal of Business Venturing*, 30(3), pp. 436–451.

Kuzilwa, J.A. and Nyamsogoro, G.D. (2017). The influence of credit and formalization on the growth of SMEs in Tanzania. In: C.C. Williams and A. Gurtoo, Eds., *Routledge handbook of entrepreneurship in developing economies*. London: Routledge, pp. 424–439.

La Porta, R. and Shleifer, A. (2008). The unofficial economy and economic development. *Brookings Papers on Economic Activity*, 47(1), pp. 123–135.

London, T., Esper, H., Grogan-Kaylor, A. and Kistruck, G.M. (2014). Connecting poverty to purchase in informal markets. *Strategic Entrepreneurship Journal*, 8, pp. 37–55.

Lyon, F. (2007). Institutional perspectives on understanding street retailer behaviour and networks: Cases from Ghana. In: J. Cross and A. Morales, Eds., *Street entrepreneurs: People, place and politics in local and global perspective*. London: Routledge, pp. 164–179.

Mehrotra, S. and Biggeri, M. (2007). Upgrading informal micro- and small enterprises through clusters: Towards a policy agenda. In: S. Mahrotra and M. Biggeri, Eds., *Asian informal workers: Global risks, local protection*. London: Routledge, pp. 361–399.

Palmer, R. (2007). *Skills development, the enabling environment and informal micro-enterprise in Ghana*. Edinburgh: University of Edinburgh.

Staudt, K. (2007). Street vendors at the border: From political spectacle to bureaucratic iron cage? In: J. Cross and A. Morales, Eds., *Street entrepreneurs: People, place and politics in local and global perspective*. London: Routledge, pp. 79–91.

Stinchcombe, A.L. (1965). Social structure and organizations. In: J.G. March, Ed., *Handbook of organizations*. Chicago, IL: Rand McNally, pp. 142–193.

Webb, J.W., Tihanyi, L., Ireland, R.D. and Sirmon, D.G. (2009). You say illegal, I say legitimate: Entrepreneurship in the informal economy. *Academy of Management Review*, 34(3), pp. 492–510.

Wijebandara, C. and Coonay, N.S. (2017). Determinants of participation in the informal sector in Sri Lanka: Evidence from a recently conducted special survey. In: C.C. Williams and A. Gurtoo, Eds., *Routledge handbook of entrepreneurship in developing economies*. London: Routledge, pp. 356–376.

Williams, C.C. (2008). Beyond necessity-driven versus opportunity-driven entrepreneurship: A study of informal entrepreneurs in England, Russia and Ukraine. *International Journal of Entrepreneurship and Innovation*, 9(3), pp. 157–166.

Williams, C.C. (2010). Spatial variations in the hidden enterprise culture: Some lessons from England. *Entrepreneurship and Regional Development*, 22(5), pp. 403–423.

Williams, C.C. and Horodnic, I. (2017). Regulating the sharing economy to prevent the growth of the informal sector in the hospitality industry. *International Journal of Contemporary Hospitality Management*, 29(9), pp. 1–18.

Williams, C.C., Horodnic, I.A. and Windebank, J. (2016). The participation of the self-employed in the shadow economy in the European Union. In: A. Sauka, F. Schneider and C.C. Williams, Eds., *Entrepreneurship and the shadow economy*. Cheltenham: Edward Elgar, pp. 89–117.

Williams, C.C. and Martinez-Perez, A. (2014a). Do small business start-ups test-trade in the informal economy? Evidence from a UK small business survey. *International Journal of Entrepreneurship and Small Business*, 22(1), pp. 1–16.

Williams, C.C. and Martinez-Perez, A. (2014b). Is the informal economy an incubator for new enterprise creation? A gender perspective. *International Journal of Entrepreneurial Behaviour and Research*, 20(1), pp. 4–19.

Williams, C.C. and Thomas, R. (1996). Paid informal work in the Leeds hospitality industry: Regulated or unregulated work? In: G. Haughton and C.C. Williams, Eds., *Corporate City? Partnership, participation and partition in urban development in Leeds*. Aldershot: Avebury, pp. 41–67.

Yu, X. and Bruton, G. (2015). Informal firms in China: What do we know and where does the research go. In: P.C. Godfrey, Ed., *Management, society, and the informal economy*.

Zimmerman, M.A. and Zeitz, G.J. (2002). Beyond survival: Achieving new venture growth by building legitimacy. *Academy of Management Review*, 27(3), pp. 414–431.

5 Impacts of Informal Entrepreneurship

Introduction

For many years, the vast bulk of the scholarship focused upon highlighting the negative impacts of enterprises operating in the informal sector. This ranged from studies drawing attention to the macro-level deleterious impacts of informal entrepreneurship for economic development and growth through those that highlighted the unfair competition on formal enterprises to those that emphasised the negative impacts on informal enterprises and entrepreneurs themselves (Baumol, 1990; Castells and Portes, 1989; Gallin, 2001). Indeed Baumol (1990) termed such endeavour 'unproductive' entrepreneurship, and this captured the widely held view that informal sector entrepreneurship was composed of inefficient, low-productivity and low-performing enterprises unworthy of investment and support (La Porta and Shleifer, 2008, 2014).

However, in recent years scholarship has begun to turn its attention to some potentially positive impacts of informal entrepreneurship, such as how it provides more affordable goods and services for low-income markets, creates employment and acts as a test bed for fledgling enterprises and breeding ground for the microenterprise system (Ketchen *et al.*, 2014; Williams and Martinez-Perez, 2014a,b). This chapter, therefore, begins to re-evaluate the portrayal of informal entrepreneurship as purely a negative phenomenon and seeks to raise the possibility of a more positive representation of informal entrepreneurship by putting under the spotlight the dominant depiction of informal entrepreneurship as 'unproductive' endeavour (Baumol, 1990) and informal enterprises as inefficient, low-productivity and low-performing enterprises unworthy of investment and support. To do this, this chapter focuses upon the impacts of starting up unregistered on future firm performance.

In consequence, the intention is to advance understanding of informal entrepreneurship in three ways. From an empirical viewpoint, this chapter will transcend previous studies which point to the unproductive character of informal enterprise based on a narrow range of countries, small sample sizes and often a misreading of previous studies (La Porta and Shleifer,

2008; Perry *et al.*, 2007) and instead provides a comparative analysis of firm performance across 127 countries by whether they started up registered or unregistered and the length of time they remained unregistered. From a theoretical perspective meanwhile, this chapter contributes to the growing literature advancing a more positive representation of the impacts of informal entrepreneurship. By displaying how formal firms with five or more employees that started up unregistered outperform those that started up registered, questions begin to be raised about the dominant theorisation of informal entrepreneurship as unproductive endeavour. Finally, and from a policy perspective, this chapter begins to show the need to transcend the currently dominant eradication approach that results in one hand of government curbing precisely the enterprise culture and entrepreneurship that other hands of government wish to foster. By displaying that informal entrepreneurship is a breeding ground and incubator for future high-performance enterprises, this will start to set the scene for Part III of the book by providing a strong rationale for paying greater policy attention to smoothing the transition from informal to formal entrepreneurship.

To do this, the first section of this chapter briefly reviews how, despite the slow recognition that informally entrepreneurship can have positive impacts, the conventional negative depiction of this endeavour as unproductive has not so far been put under the spotlight. In the second section, therefore, the shortcomings of the evidence to support the view of informal entrepreneurship as unproductive and deleterious to future firm performance are highlighted, and resulting from this, a series of propositions are then constructed to compare the firm performance of formal firms by whether they started up registered or unregistered and the length of time they remained unregistered. In the third section, the survey data and methods used to evaluate these propositions are introduced, followed in the fourth section by an evaluation of the relationship between informal entrepreneurship and firm performance. The fifth and final section then draws conclusions regarding the impacts of starting up unregistered and the length of time spent unregistered on future firm performance.

Rethinking the Impacts of Informal Entrepreneurship

In recent years, it has been recognised that a large gap exists between the magnitude of informal entrepreneurship globally and the scant amount of research devoted to it (Ketchen *et al.*, 2014). A major reason for this is that for many decades, the widespread belief was that such endeavour was a remnant of an earlier mode of production and would naturally and inevitably disappear with modernisation and economic development. Although as Chapter 3 revealed, this modernisation perspective has been transcended due to the recognition of the prevalence of informal entrepreneurship globally, what has remained intact in much contemporary theory is a negative depiction of informal entrepreneurship.

Firstly, this negative depiction prevails among those who have sought to update the conventional modernisation thesis (La Porta and Shleifer, 2008, 2014). Even if the persistence and magnitude of informality is now recognised, this nonetheless maintains the depiction of two disconnected sectors and a negative representation of the informal realm, portraying informal entrepreneurs as typically uneducated people operating small, unproductive enterprises in separate 'bottom-of-the-pyramid' markets producing low-quality products for low-income consumers using little capital and adding little value (La Porta and Shleifer, 2014).

Secondly, this negative depiction also persists among a second loose grouping of scholars adopting a political economy perspective. Although recognising that the formal and informal sectors are not entirely disconnected, these scholars continue to adopt a view that it has largely negative impacts. The growth of informal entrepreneurship is viewed as an inherent feature and direct outcome of the emergence of a deregulated open world economy where outsourcing and subcontracting have become a primary way in which informal enterprises are integrated into contemporary capitalism to reduce production costs (Castells and Portes, 1989; Davis, 2006; Meagher, 2010; Slavnic, 2010; Taiwo, 2013). Moreover, the resultant withdrawal of state involvement in social protection and economic intervention which has accompanied deregulation are seen to have resulted in those excluded from the formal labour market and social protection being pushed into informal entrepreneurship as a survival strategy (Chen, 2012, 2014; ILO, 2014; Meagher, 2010; Taiwo, 2013).

Hence, although recognising informal entrepreneurship as intertwined with the formal sector, it remains depicted by political economy scholars as having negative impacts. Economies are viewed as losing 'natural' competitiveness because productive formal enterprises suffer unfair competition from unproductive informal enterprises (Leal Ordóñez, 2014; Levy, 2008; Lewis, 2004). Governments are viewed as losing both regulatory control over work conditions (ILO, 2014) and tax revenue (Bajada and Schneider, 2005) and customers as lacking legal recourse and certainty that health and safety regulations have been followed when using informal enterprises (Williams and Martinez-Perez, 2014b). Informal entrepreneurs, meanwhile, are depicted as 'necessity driven' (Castells and Portes, 1989; Gallin, 2001), lacking access to capital, credit and financial services (ILO, 2014), which when combined with a lack of advice and support (Barbour and Llanes, 2013), the need to keep their business small to stay out of the sight of the authorities (Williams *et al.*, 2012) and an inability to secure formal intellectual property rights to process and product innovations (De Beer *et al.*, 2013) mean such entrepreneurs become locked in a 'poverty trap' (McKenzie and Woodruff, 2006).

In recent years however, counter-narratives to this dominant negative depiction have begun to emerge. Economies and governments have been asserted to potentially benefit from the ability of informal entrepreneurs to create jobs (Ketchen *et al.*, 2014; Williams and Gurtoo, 2017), and this sphere has started to be viewed as a breeding ground for the microenterprise system (Barbour and Llanes, 2013). Formal enterprises have been seen as potentially benefiting from cheaper sources of labour and raw materials (Ketchen *et al.*, 2014), potential formal entrepreneurs from the opportunity to use this realm as a test bed for their business ventures (Williams and Martinez-Perez, 2014a), and informal entrepreneurs from having this realm as an escape route from corrupt public sector officials and the regulatory burden in contexts where this stifles business development (Puffer *et al.*, 2010; Tonoyan *et al.*, 2010). Customers, meanwhile, are viewed as potentially benefiting from more affordable goods and services in lower-income markets, especially at the 'bottom of the pyramid' (Ketchen *et al.*, 2014; London *et al.*, 2014; Pisani, 2017).

A principal catalyst for these more positive representations has been the recognition that informal entrepreneurship is not always necessity driven but sometimes a matter of choice (Cross, 2000; Franck, 2012; Gërxhani, 2004; Maloney, 2004; Snyder, 2004). Arising out of this recognition, the resultant agency-oriented theorisations of informal entrepreneurship have been of two broad varieties. On the one hand, a grouping of mostly neo-liberal scholars has portrayed entrepreneurs voluntarily operating informally as rational economic actors who, after weighing up the costs of informality and benefits of formality, decide not to operate in the formal sector. For these scholars, as Chapter 3 showed, it is burdensome regulations and high taxes that lead entrepreneurs to exit the formal sector and to operate in the informal sector (Becker, 2004; De Soto, 1989, 2001; Nwabuzor, 2005).

On the other hand, and drawing inspiration from institutional theory (North, 1990), another agency-oriented group of scholars adopting a more 'social actor' approach, have viewed informal entrepreneurship as illegal but socially legitimate endeavour that arises when there is asymmetry between the codified laws and regulations that constitute the formal institutions and the norms, values and beliefs that constitute the informal institutions (De Castro *et al.*, 2014; Kistruck *et al.*, 2015; Siqueira *et al.*, 2016; Thai and Turkina, 2014; Vu, 2014; Webb *et al.*, 2009, 2013, 2014). When there is symmetry between formal and informal institutions, the argument is that informal entrepreneurship only occurs unintentionally, for example, due to a lack of awareness of the codified laws and regulations. However, and as Chapter 3 argued, when there is institutional asymmetry, the result is more informal entrepreneurship. Indeed the greater the degree of asymmetry, the greater is the level of informal entrepreneurship (Williams and Shahid, 2016).

Until now, the emergence of more positive accounts of informal entrepreneurship has not been on the whole an evidence-driven endeavour, just as the dominant negative accounts of informal entrepreneurship have not been evidence driven. Such accounts have been predominantly normative and theory driven. This is exemplified by the lack of empirical evaluation of many, if not all, of the supposedly positive and negative features of informal entrepreneurship referred to. To advance understanding of informal entrepreneurship, therefore, evidence-based evaluations of each of these purported positive and negative features are required. Indeed this constitutes a major agenda for future research on informal entrepreneurship. Here, and to begin to fill this significant gap in the literature, an evaluation is conducted of one of the key assumptions upon which most negative representations are currently premised, namely, that informal entrepreneurship is poorly performing, unproductive endeavour. Until now, and as will now be shown, few have questioned this premise and the resultant view that informal entrepreneurship is deleterious to economic development and growth.

Informal Entrepreneurship and Firm Performance

For many years, the dominant depiction has been that informal entrepreneurship is poorly performing endeavour relative to formal entrepreneurship (Farrell, 2004; ILO, 2005, 2007; Palmer, 2007; UNCTAD, 2006; Vandenberg, 2005). This poorer performance thesis is prevalent across all three dominant theories of the relationship between informal entrepreneurship and firm performance, summarised by La Porta and Shleifer (2008) in their seminal paper on this subject. Firstly, and mirroring modernisation theory, the 'dual economy' perspective they outline views informal enterprises as hugely inefficient compared with formal enterprises, operating in different 'bottom-of-the-pyramid' markets and unlikely to be capable of charging lower prices for the same products (La Porta and Shleifer, 2008, 2014). Informal firms are consequently viewed as small and unproductive compared even with the small but registered firms, which themselves are much less productive than larger registered firms. Secondly, and mirroring the political economy approach, the 'parasitic' perspective they outline views the informal sector as a refuge where necessity-driven, low-productivity firms, requiring low levels of start-up capital, stay small to avoid detection and lack the scale to produce efficiently, although the cost advantages gained by avoiding taxes and regulations more than offsets their low productivity and small scale (Farrell, 2004; Palmer, 2007). Thirdly and finally, and akin to the wider agency-oriented viewpoint of neo-liberal and institutionalist perspectives, the 'romantic' perspective they outline views informal entrepreneurs as escaping burdensome regulations and/or weak formal institutions (De Soto, 1989; Wunsch-Vincent *et al.*, 2015). Although again viewed as less productive than formal enterprises, there are nevertheless seen to be productivity-employment trade-offs, and informal enterprises are viewed as creating jobs albeit underemployment (ILO, 2005). The consensus across all three perspectives, therefore, is that informal enterprises are worse performing than their formal counterparts.

To support this negative depiction of informal enterprises as poorer performing, most scholarship cites a seminal study by La Porta and Shleifer

(2008: 344), who find 'that high productivity comes from formal firms, and in particular from large formal firms. Productivity is much higher in small formal firms than in informal firms, and it rises rapidly with the size of formal firms'. The evidence base used is World Bank Informal Surveys in 13 countries and Micro-Enterprise Surveys in 14 countries (19 in Africa, 6 in Asia and 2 in Latin America). The average Informal Survey involved 31 registered and 192 unregistered firms, and the average Micro-Enterprise Survey 137 registered and 77 unregistered enterprises (i.e., the total evidence base comprised 2,321 registered and 3,574 unregistered enterprises). The non-representative sampling strategy in each country was that 'World Bank contractors identified neighbourhoods perceived to have a large number of informal firms' (La Porta and Shleifer, 2008: 295).

Examining this small unrepresentative sample, La Porta and Shleifer (2008) find statistically significant differences in the performance of registered and unregistered enterprises in 10 of the 25 countries on value added per employee at the 0.1 level (and 4 countries at the 0.01 level), 17 of the 26 countries on sales per employee at the 0.1 level (and 12 at the 0.01 level), and in 18 of the 26 countries on output per employee at the 0.1 level (12 at the 0.01 level). Significant variations in firm performance between formal and informal enterprises are therefore not universal. Indeed, unregistered enterprises actually performed better than registered enterprises in 6 of the 25 countries on value added per employee, 3 of the 26 countries on sales per employee and 4 of the 26 on output per employee (see La Porta and Shleifer, 2008: Tables 13 and 14). Moreover, and ignored by commentators using this as the evidence base to support the poorer performance thesis, they explicitly state in a footnote that the overall productivity gap disappears and 'unregistered firms are not unusually unproductive once we take into account their expenditure on inputs, the human capital of their top managers, and their small size' (La Porta and Shleifer, 2008: 335).

Neither do other studies provide compelling evidence to support this poorer performance thesis (Fajnzylber *et al.*, 2009; Farrell, 2004; McKinsey Global Institute, 2003). For example, Fajnzylber *et al.* (2009) claim in Mexico that firms paying taxes exhibit between 15 per cent and 60 per cent higher 'productivity' levels, but their measure of productivity is profit levels and self-employment income, and they fail to control for the full range of firm-level determinants influencing firm productivity and performance.

Turning to whether there is evidence of this poorer performance thesis when comparing the firm performance of currently formal enterprises that started up unregistered and registered, the only evaluation available is by Perry *et al.* (2007: 173). They examine World Bank survey data on 355 unregistered start-ups across seven Latin American countries (104 in Colombia, 72 in Argentina, 72 in Bolivia, 66 in Mexico, 20 in Peru, 12 in Uruguay and 9 in Panama). The finding is that unregistered start-ups 'at least initially, exhibit on average, much lower levels of output per worker, after controlling for firm size, time in business, sector and region'. However, this is a small sample; the productivity gap is statistically significant in only four out of the seven countries, and the headline national average figure that unregistered start-ups have 29 per cent lower productivity is heavily skewed by the study in Peru, where the productivity gap is over 50 per cent, which is not statistically significant, and only 20 unregistered start-ups were surveyed. It is not only weak evidence, however, that suggests the need to re-evaluate this poorer performance thesis regarding the impacts of starting up unregistered.

Conventionally, and as reflected in the dual economy, parasitic and romantic perspectives, enterprises starting up unregistered and in the informal sector have been viewed as worse performing than their registered formal sector counterparts. Indeed, as La Porta and Shleifer (2008: 279) assert, 'the differences in productivity between formal and informal firms are so large that it is hard to believe that simply registering unregistered firms would eliminate the gap.' However, recognising that many entrepreneurs operate informally out of choice (Gërxhani, 2004; Maloney, 2004; Perry and Maloney, 2007) and adopting a more agency-oriented perspective, the opposite could be argued; enterprises unregistered when starting up will outperform enterprises registered from the outset. This is because unregistered start-ups at least initially avoid paying taxes, burdensome regulations and the additional costs imposed on formal enterprises by corrupt public sector officials, for example, and thus appear to possess many of the prerequisites to outperform the registered enterprises that suffer such constraints. As La Porta and Shleifer (2014) assert, formal firms have to pay taxes and comply with regulations, so they have a huge costs disadvantage relative to unregistered business start-ups. Operating initially unregistered, therefore, might well enable them to boost their levels of firm performance. To begin to evaluate this proposition that being unregistered at start-up might witness higher future firm performance, the following hypothesis can be therefore tested:

Hypothesis 1: Enterprises starting up unregistered and then registering display higher levels of firm performance than those starting up registered, after controlling for other key determinants of firm performance.

Similarly, competing views exist on whether and how the length of time that an enterprise spends unregistered influences future firm performance. On the one hand, and from the perspective that unregistered enterprises are worse performing, it might be posited that this will further diminish future firm performance. Unable to grow and expand due to limited access to credit and loans, and the need to remain small to avoid the authorities (Farrell, 2004; Palmer, 2007), the longer they remain unregistered, the worse will be the firm performance of an unregistered enterprise relative to enterprises registered at start-up.

On the other hand, however, and from the perspective that being unregistered at start-up improves subsequent firm performance, it could be argued that the longer they spend unregistered before registering, the greater will be their advantage over those registering from the outset. This is because the longer they remain freed from paying taxes, burdensome regulations and corruption in the public sector, for example, the more the advantages that allow them to outperform their counterparts starting up registered are consolidated, and the greater will be the differential. As such, the following hypothesis can be tested:

Hypothesis 2: The longer start-ups spend unregistered before registering, the higher is their future firm performance, after controlling for other key determinants of firm performance.

Is it the case nevertheless that a turning point exists after which it is no longer beneficial in terms of performance for enterprises to remain unregistered? While being unregistered helps firms avoid certain costs, it may also preclude access to certain benefits of formalisation, including greater access to credit, increased opportunities to engage with large firms and government contracts, reduced harassment by police and municipal officials and access to broader training and support programmes. It could be thus proposed that although operating unregistered initially might boost levels of firm performance, a turning point may exist when it becomes more beneficial to operate formally. Indeed examining the returns to physical capital of the formal and informal sectors in Ethiopia, Siba (2015) finds that as the capital stock of informal enterprises gets larger, they are more likely to benefit from registration and working formally. As such, although initially benefiting from non-registration, they may reach a size where it becomes necessary and beneficial to formalise. It is at this point that they do so, having taken advantage of informality to reach this size quicker than would otherwise be the case if they suffered the same constraints as their formal counterparts.

Indeed this view finds tentative support in emergent literature on the benefits of formalisation. Fajnzylber *et al.* (2009) in Mexico and Rand and Torm (2012) in Vietna, both find that formalisation, through access to credit, training, tax payments and participation in business associations has positive effects on firm profits and survival by allowing firms to reach their optimal size. McKenzie and Sakho (2010) in Bolivia and McCulloch *et al.* (2010) in Indonesia also find that registration increases firm profitability and sales growth, respectively, but only for mid-sized firms, suggesting that delaying registration until firms reach a certain size may be optimal. Meanwhile, McKenzie and Woodruff (2006) in Mexico highlight how the added value of formalisation is often viewed as limited by micro-business because they are often operated by individuals who are not entrepreneurs at heart but are waiting for an opportunity to enter salaried jobs or are running microbusinesses in parallel with other employment to supplement income, and for them, business expansion may not be a central motivation and formalisation thus irrelevant and potentially costly.

Therefore, although start-ups may initially benefit from being unregistered and remaining so, it can be proposed that a turning point exists after which this is no longer beneficial due to the apparently long-term costs of informality and benefits of formalisation. As such, the following hypothesis can be tested:

> *Hypothesis 3*: A turning point exists after which it no longer remains beneficial in terms of firm performance for an enterprise to operate on an unregistered basis.

To test these propositions to see if there is a refutation of the poorer performance thesis, in the next section, a brief review of the data, variables and methods is provided. This will then be followed by the results.

Data, Variables and Methods

Data

To evaluate the impacts of starting up unregistered and the length of time spent unregistered before registering on future firm performance, as well as whether there is a turning point when it no longer remains beneficial to be unregistered, WBES data are here analysed from 127 developing economies. The WBES collects data using a stratified random sample of formal private sector businesses with five or more employees in each country surveyed, stratified by firm size, business sector and geographic region. Although 135 countries are currently covered and survey data is available from 2002–2014, the sample here is restricted to the 127 countries that since 2006, have used the harmonised questionnaire and common methodology. This ensures that the data is comparable across countries and over time. The result is a sample of 95,522 surveyed enterprises.

Dependent Variables

To evaluate the relationship between registration status at start-up and future firm performance, the dependent variables are the three key dimensions of firm performance upon which data is collected in the WBES, namely, (1) *real annual sales growth* (using GDP deflators) (%): this is a derived variable in the WBES measuring the change in sales reported in the current fiscal year from a previous period. For most countries the difference between the two fiscal year periods is two years. However, for some countries the interval is three years. Hence, an annualised measure is used. All values for sales are converted to the US dollar (USD) using the exchange rate in the corresponding fiscal year of the survey. Sales are deflated to 2009 using the USD deflator. (2) *Annual employment growth* (%): this is a derived variable in the WBES measuring the annualised growth of permanent full-time workers expressed as a percentage. Annual employment growth is the change in full-time employment reported in the current fiscal year from a previous period. For most countries the difference between the two fiscal year periods is two years. However, for some countries the interval is three years. Hence, an annualised measure is used. And (3) *annual productivity growth* (%): this is a derived variable that measures annualised growth in labour productivity, where labour productivity is real sales (using GDP deflators) divided by full-time permanent workers. Annual productivity growth is the change in labour productivity reported in the current fiscal year from a previous period. For most countries the difference between the two fiscal year periods is two years. However, for some countries the interval is three years. Hence, an annualised measure is used. All values for sales are converted to USD using the exchange rate in the corresponding fiscal year of the survey. Sales are then deflated to 2009 using the USD deflator.

Key Independent Variables

To evaluate the impact of informal entrepreneurship on future firm performance, two indicators are used: (1) *started up unregistered*, which is a firm-level measure regarding whether the business was registered when it started operations. This is a dummy variable with a value of 1, indicating that the firm started operations in the country without formal registration and 0 when the firm was formally registered, and (2) *tears unregistered*, which is a continuous variable counting the number of years the firm operated without formal registration. This variable has a value of 0 for those firms operating formally since start-up. Moreover, to evaluate how informal entrepreneurship may influence future firm performance, we investigate whether its impact is conditional on the age of the firm. We do this through interaction terms between the two indicators of informal entrepreneurship and (3) *firm age*, which is a continuous variable for the number of years since the firm was established. Finally, to allow for a non-linear effect of the firm's age and the number of years the firm operated without formal registration, we introduce quadratic specifications of the two variables which are also used in the interaction models.

Control Variables

To measure whether formal enterprises that started up and spent varying amounts of time unregistered witness better or worse future firm performance than enterprises registered from the outset, it is necessary to control for other key determinants of firm performance. Here, eight significant influences on firm performance are analysed, namely firm size, legal status and ownership structure, sector, access to finance, the level of technological innovation, human capital factors and other business environment factors.

Firm size is viewed as determining firm performance, with larger firms performing better than smaller ones (Hsieh and Olken, 2014; La Porta and Shleifer, 2014; Söderbom and Teal, 2001), not least due to the lower average unit costs in larger firms. However, although surveys find sole traders are less efficient than firms with employees, returns to the scale among the latter are very close to unity and, at best, mildly increasing (Perry *et al.*, 2007). Despite this lack of robust evidence for the economics of scale argument, we nevertheless control for firm size but also evaluate this relationship while controlling for other firm-level determinants. Firm size is a categorical variable with a value of 1 for small firms with less than 20 employees, a value of 2 for medium size firms between 20 and 99 employees, and a value of 3 for large firms with more than 100 employees.

Different types of ownership structure and legal status are often viewed as strongly correlated with firm performance, including whether a firm is state or privately owned, foreign or domestic owned and an open or closed shareholding, partnership or sole proprietorship (Barbera and Moores, 2013; Baghdasaryan and la Cour, 2013). Given that unregistered start-ups may have different ownership structures and legal statuses than registered start-ups, controlling for this is important. Here, legal status is a categorical variable indicating whether the enterprise is an open shareholding, a closed shareholding, a sole proprietorship, a partnership, a limited partnership or any other form. In addition, whether the organisation is foreign or domestic owned is examined using a dummy variable with a value pf 1 indicating if the share of the firm's ownership held by foreign individuals or enterprises is larger than 49 per cent and 0 otherwise. Given that export-oriented firms are viewed as displaying higher levels of firm performance (La Porta and Shleifer, 2008), export orientation is also included as a control using a dummy variable with a value of 1 indicating firms exporting directly at least 1 per cent of sales and 0 for those that sell only domestically.

Firm performance is also viewed as varying across economic sectors (Nabar and Yan, 2013; Siqueira *et al.*, 2016). Given that unregistered start-ups may be heavily concentrated in labour-intensive sectors with fewer returns to scale (Perry *et al.*, 2007), controlling for sector is important. Sector is here a categorical variable indicating the sector of the firm (i.e., textiles, leather, garments, food, metals and machinery, electronics, chemicals and pharmaceuticals, wood and furniture, non-metallic and plastic materials, auto and auto components, other manufacturing, retail and wholesale trade, hotels and restaurants and others).

Access to finance is purported to be strongly correlated with firm performance, and given the burgeoning literature on how unregistered start-ups lack access to finance from formal lenders, this may well impact on future firm performance not only because they scale down operations but also because the high cost of informal loans and the limited financing available lead them to substitute (low-skilled) labour for physical capital (Amaral and Quintin, 2006; Cull *et al.*, 2007). Controlling for whether businesses access bank loans and credit is therefore important when analysing the impacts of registration on future firm performance. Access to bank loans or credit is here a dummy variable with a value of 1 indicating whether the firm has access to bank loans or to a line of credit to finance its activities and 0 otherwise.

Firm performance is also often associated with the level of technological innovation (Mansury and Love, 2008). Given that the vast majority of the literature finds less innovation and adoption of new technologies in informal enterprises and that which does exist is more adaptation and imitation rather than innovation (Grimm *et al.*, 2012; Kabecha, 1998; Wunsch-Vincent *et al.*, 2015), this needs to be controlled for when examining the impact of registration on future firm performance, especially given that some argue that this is the key reason for the productivity gap between developed and developing economies (Farrell, 2004; Palmade, 2005). Here, three rather limited control variables available in the WBES are used: quality certification, a dummy variable with a value of 1 indicating that the firm has an internationally recognised certification and 0 otherwise; presence of a website, a dummy variable with a value of 1 when the firm uses a website for business-related activities and 0 otherwise; and the use of email, a dummy variable with a value pf 1 when the firm uses email to interact with clients and suppliers and 0 otherwise.

Human capital factors, such as the educational level, skills and experience of the owners, managers and the workforce, the level of professionalism and whether there is numerical flexibility in the workforce are asserted to have a significant impact on firm performance (Black and Lynch, 1996; Gennaiolo *et al.*, 2013; La Porta and Shleifer, 2014; Söderbom and Teal, 2001; Van der Sluis *et al.*, 2005). Controlling for human capital factors is therefore important, especially given that informality is associated with less productive workers due to more productive workers self-selecting formal enterprises over informal ones (Amaral and Quintin, 2006; Dimova *et al.*, 2008). Here, six control variables available in the WBES are used: top manager's experience, a continuous variable of the years of experience the top manager has working in the sector; temporary workers, a variable measuring the average number of temporary workers in the firm; permanent full-time workers, a continuous variable of the average number of permanent full-time workers in the firm; female full-time workers, examining the share of permanent full-time workers who are female; female involvement in ownership, a dummy variable with a value of 1 indicating whether women are involved in the ownership of the firm and 0 otherwise; and as a signal of professionalism, whether they use an external auditor, a dummy variable with a value of 1 indicating that the firm has its annual financial statement reviewed by an external auditor and 0 otherwise.

So too does the wider business environment determine firm performance. To control for this, two control variables are used measuring whether various facets of the business environment are a major constraint on the firm's activity, namely: transport, a dummy variable with a value of 1 indicating that transportation is a major constraint for the firm's activity and 0 otherwise, and electricity, a dummy variable with a value of 1 indicating that electricity supply is a major constraint for the firm's activity and 0 otherwise.

Multiple Imputation of Missing Values

The method of multiple imputation of missing values is used to solve the missing data problem in survey data. The objective is to substitute the missing values with the values computed using the observed variables. As cross-country data sets like the WBES suffer from missing information which undermines the representativeness of the sample, this is addressed by applying multiple imputation methods (through a system of chained equations) to the sample used in the estimation. In this data set, the average number of imputed missing values across variables with missing information is 6,611 (with a maximum of 30,122 and a minimum of 231). Based on the classical methodological literature on multiple imputation (Collins *et al.*, 2001; Rubin, 1987; Schafer and Graham, 2002), 10 imputations are employed, that is, 10 data copies with the values computed using the observed variables. This increases the reliability of the imputed data set compared with the original one.

Multilevel Modelling

To evaluate the impact of starting up unregistered and the number of years spent unregistered on firm performance and how these may vary according to the age of the firm across the 127 countries surveyed in the WBES data set for the period 2006–2014, multilevel techniques are applied. Given that the surveyed enterprises in the WBES are clustered across country-year subsamples, multilevel modelling is the optimal technique to elicit unbiased standard errors as well as reliable statistical comparisons.

Here random slope and random constant models are used to estimate the average impact of informal entrepreneurship on firm performance across countries and, as the firm ages, accounting for how the size of the informal sector and firm age varies among countries (Schneider and Williams, 2013). The number of countries in the analysis is not drawn from a random sample to infer regularities in the broader population but represents the universe. This means that there is no need to treat combinations of country-years as the Level 2 units but that the average effect of time can be estimated. That is, Level 2 only considers the clustering of firms at the country level, while the multilevel regressions include year dummies to control for time fixed effects at the firm level. Finally, as is customary in multilevel modelling, to interpret the results all control variables are centred on each country at the aggregate level (group mean centring). While centring independent variables is advisable in random intercept models to interpret the average constant in the model, it is of key importance in the random slope models used here to give a substantive interpretation to the intercept and the random components of the constant (Cebolla, 2013). The only three key explanatory variables not centred around the group mean are the two indicators of informal entrepreneurship, as in both cases the value 0 has a substantive interpretation for the purpose of this chapter (started business registered in one case and spent 0 years unregistered in the other) as well as firm age for the same reason.

Impacts of the Registration Decision on Future Firm Performance

Descriptive Statistics

Of the 95,522 formal private sector businesses with five or more employees surveyed in the WBES between 2006 and 2014, Figure 5.1 displays that those formal enterprises that started up unregistered have different annual levels of sales, employment and productivity growth than those registered at start-up (calculated using multiple imputation bivariate linear regressions with clustered standard errors at the country level and including year fixed

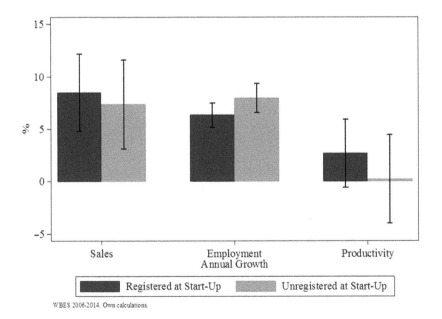

WBES 2006-2014. Own calculations.

Figure 5.1 Cross-Country Average Difference in Performance Between Registered and Unregistered Firms at Start-Up

effects). Enterprises unregistered at start-up have lower average annual sales growth rates than those starting up registered (7.4 per cent compared with 8.5 per cent), and this difference as shown is statistically significant at a 95 per cent confidence interval. Unregistered start-ups also have significantly lower average annual productivity growth rates than registered start-ups (0.2 per cent compared with 2.7 per cent). However, and supportive of the notion of productivity-employment trade-offs (ILO, 2005; Palmer, 2007), unregistered start-ups have a significantly higher annual employment growth rate than registered start-ups (8.0 per cent compared with 6.3 per cent).

The descriptive statistics also suggest that the number of years unregistered influences firm performance (again calculated using multiple imputation bivariate linear regressions with clustered standard errors at the country level and including year fixed effects). As shown by the dashed vertical line in Figure 5.2, the average length of time spent unregistered before registering is just under one year, which explains the considerable widening of the confidence intervals as the years spent unregistered increases due to the relatively small number operating unregistered over long time periods. Examining the influence of length of time spent unregistered on annual sales growth rates, a curvilinear relationship is identified. Average annual sales growth for firms registered from the outset is 8.5 per cent, and this growth rate gradually reduces as the length of time enterprises spent unregistered increases until it reaches 4 per cent for enterprises unregistered for 80 years,

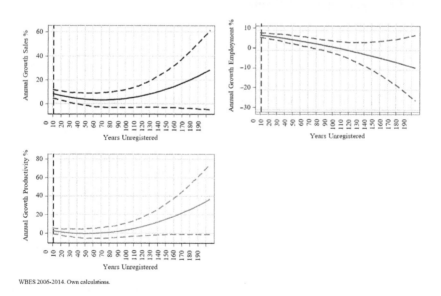

WBES 2006-2014. Own calculations.

Figure 5.2 Cross-Country Average Firm Performance By Number of Years Unregistered

*dashed lines display 95% confidence intervals

after which annual sales growth rates increase again and peak with those reporting to have spent the longest time unregistered in the WBES survey, namely 195 years. Given the very small number unregistered for such a long time period, however, the utmost caution is urged with regard to this eventual upward trend. Indeed it should perhaps be best ignored given the practicality of knowing whether this is the case and the nature of economies in this period in history. Nevertheless it is included here for completeness. The key trajectory, however, is that annual sales growth decreases as the time spent unregistered increases.

The same long-term curvilinear relationship is found for the influence of the length of time spent unregistered on annual productivity growth rates, with enterprises registered from the outset displaying annual productivity growth rates of 2.5 per cent, which decreases as the length of time spent unregistered increases up to 50 years, where the average annual productivity growth is negative (–0.2 per cent), after which it purportedly rises.

A different relationship prevails, however, with regard to how length of time spent unregistered influences average annual employment growth rates. Although annual employment growth is higher in unregistered than registered start-ups, this seems to be due to an initial upwards spike for firms unregistered for 12 months or less since, after that, there is a downwards slope as the number of years spent unregistered increases, reaching zero growth for enterprises operating unregistered for 90 years, and this then turns negative until it reaches –10 per cent for the firms unregistered for the longest time in our sample.

Results From Multilevel Estimations

To analyse whether these descriptive results using bivariate correlations between informal entrepreneurship and firm performance remain valid when other key firm-level determinants of firm performance are introduced and held constant (e.g., firm size, firm age, technology and sector across countries), as well as whether the impact of informal entrepreneurship on firm performance is conditional on the age of the business, Table 5.1 reports the results of the random intercept and random slope multilevel models for the three measures of firm performance analysed. The random intercept specification, to recall, takes into account country-level specific differences on firm performance, whereas the introduction of random slopes for the key independent variables allows for the varying impact of these determinants (informal entrepreneurship and firm age) on firm performance due to country-specific differences.

Evaluating Hypothesis 1 that enterprises starting up unregistered and then registering display higher levels of firm performance than those starting up registered, and in stark contrast to the descriptive results, Model 1 in Table 5.1 reveals that once the influence of other firm-level determinants of firm performance are controlled for, formal enterprises that started up

Table 5.1 Linear Multilevel Regression for the Impact of Starting Up Unregistered on Firm Performance

	Sales		Employment		Productivity
	(1)	(2)	(3)	(4)	(5)
	Model	Model	Model	Model	Model
Started unregistered	1.414*** (0.492)	0.348 (0.823)	1.758*** (0.277)	1.783*** (0.484)	−0.088 (0.471)
Firm age	−0.279*** (0.022)	−0.289*** (0.024)	−0.313*** (0.011)	−0.317*** (0.012)	−0.003 (0.023)
Firm age (squared)	0.002*** (0.000)	0.002*** (0.000)	0.002*** (0.000)	0.002*** (0.000)	0.000 (0.000)
Started unregistered* Firm age		0.078 (0.051)		0.010 (0.027)	
Started unregistered* Firm age (squared)		−0.001 (0.000)		−0.000 (0.000)	
Exporter	−0.182 (0.183)	−0.181 (0.183)	−0.039 (0.062)	−0.038 (0.062)	−0.132 (0.192)
Foreign ownership	0.064 (0.115)	0.064 (0.115)	0.015 (0.039)	0.015 (0.039)	0.067 (0.122)
Workforce					
Top manager's experience	−0.044*** (0.012)	−0.045*** (0.012)	−0.059*** (0.007)	−0.059*** (0.007)	0.009 (0.014)
Temporary workers	0.013*** (0.004)	0.013*** (0.004)	0.005*** (0.002)	0.005*** (0.002)	0.008** (0.004)
Permanent full-time workers	0.005*** (0.001)	0.005*** (0.001)	0.005*** (0.001)	0.005*** (0.000)	0.000 (0.000)
Female full-time workers	−0.013*** (0.004)	−0.013*** (0.004)	−0.033*** (0.002)	−0.033*** (0.002)	0.018*** (0.005)
Female participation in ownership	0.053 (0.067)	0.054 (0.067)	0.001 (0.023)	0.001 (0.023)	0.065 (0.071)
Bank loan/ credit	−0.113 (0.079)	−0.113 (0.079)	0.033 (0.027)	0.033 (0.027)	−0.151* (0.083)
Major constraints					
Transport	0.026 (0.102)	0.027 (0.102)	0.073** (0.035)	0.073** (0.035)	−0.034 (0.107)
Electricity	−0.099* (0.056)	−0.098* (0.056)	−0.022 (0.019)	−0.021 (0.019)	−0.076 (0.059)

(Continued)

Table 5.1 (Continued)

	Sales		Employment		Productivity
	(1)	(2)	(3)	(4)	(5)
	Model	Model	Model	Model	Model
Innovation & technology					
Quality certification	−0.062 (0.111)	−0.061 (0.111)	−0.007 (0.038)	−0.007 (0.038)	−0.061 (0.116)
External auditor	0.009 (0.054)	0.010 (0.054)	−0.004 (0.018)	−0.004 (0.018)	0.002 (0.057)
Website	0.169 (0.109)	0.168 (0.109)	0.023 (0.038)	0.022 (0.038)	0.151 (0.115)
Email	−0.012 (0.102)	−0.013 (0.102)	0.015 (0.034)	0.015 (0.034)	−0.030 (0.107)
Firm size (R.C.: Small)					
Medium	−0.102 (0.170)	−0.103 (0.170)	−0.028 (0.057)	−0.028 (0.057)	−0.078 (0.177)
Large	0.064 (0.167)	0.065 (0.167)	−0.005 (0.057)	−0.005 (0.057)	0.058 (0.174)
Legal status (R.C.: Open shareholding)					
Close shareholding	−0.008 (0.193)	−0.009 (0.193)	0.140** (0.064)	0.139** (0.064)	−0.156 (0.201)
Sole proprietorship	−0.026 (0.191)	−0.027 (0.191)	0.159** (0.064)	0.158** (0.064)	−0.199 (0.199)
Partnership	−0.166 (0.200)	−0.167 (0.200)	0.147** (0.068)	0.146** (0.068)	−0.310 (0.209)
Limited partnership	0.027 (0.192)	0.025 (0.192)	0.115* (0.064)	0.113* (0.064)	−0.108 (0.201)
Industry Sector (R.C.: Textile)					
Other form	−0.604** (0.267)	−0.604** (0.267)	0.059 (0.090)	0.058 (0.090)	−0.682** (0.281)
Leather	−0.000 (0.237)	−0.002 (0.237)	0.064 (0.084)	0.062 (0.084)	−0.085 (0.248)
Garments	0.406 (0.256)	0.405 (0.256)	0.044 (0.087)	0.043 (0.087)	0.336 (0.269)
Food	−0.141 (0.249)	−0.141 (0.249)	−0.063 (0.087)	−0.064 (0.087)	−0.042 (0.260)
Metals & machinery	0.328 (0.294)	0.327 (0.294)	0.120 (0.101)	0.120 (0.101)	0.257 (0.309)
Electronics	0.788 (0.760)	0.780 (0.761)	0.176 (0.252)	0.177 (0.252)	0.679 (0.798)

	Sales		Employment		Productivity
	(1)	(2)	(3)	(4)	(5)
	Model	Model	Model	Model	Model
Chemicals & pharmaceuticals	−0.172 (0.545)	−0.170 (0.545)	0.140 (0.182)	0.136 (0.182)	−0.279 (0.568)
Wood, furniture	−0.025 (0.336)	−0.028 (0.336)	0.230** (0.114)	0.227** (0.113)	−0.256 (0.353)
Non-metallic, plastic materials	−1.443*** (0.371)	−1.441*** (0.372)	−0.227* (0.125)	−0.229* (0.125)	−1.290*** (0.394)
Auto & auto components	2.027 (1.249)	2.014 (1.250)	0.438 (0.419)	0.441 (0.418)	1.593 (1.315)
Other manufacturing	−0.021 (0.226)	−0.023 (0.227)	0.037 (0.078)	0.035 (0.078)	−0.053 (0.237)
Retail & wholesale trade	−0.025 (0.181)	−0.026 (0.181)	−0.012 (0.062)	−0.014 (0.062)	−0.007 (0.189)
Hotels & restaurants	−0.090 (0.287)	−0.092 (0.287)	0.116 (0.099)	0.115 (0.098)	−0.206 (0.301)
Other services	0.188 (0.217)	0.189 (0.217)	0.080 (0.074)	0.079 (0.074)	0.114 (0.228)
Other unclassified	−0.222 (0.208)	−0.224 (0.208)	0.174** (0.073)	0.173** (0.073)	−0.389* (0.219)
Year dummies	YES	YES	YES	YES	YES
Constant (fixed)	11.239*** (0.900)	11.363*** (0.908)	9.603*** (0.302)	9.631*** (0.306)	2.664*** (0.947)
Random disturbance					
Constant	YES	YES	YES	YES	YES
Slope: Started unregistered	YES	YES	YES	YES	YES
Slope: Years unregistered					
Slope: Firm age	YES	YES	YES	YES	YES
Observations	95,522	95,522	95,522	95,522	95,522
Countries	127	127	127	127	127

Significant at p < 0.1*

** p < 0.05

*** p < 0.01, standard errors between parentheses

Source: author's own calculations from the WBES 2006–2014 data set

unregistered have an annual average sales growth rate 1.4 percentage points (i.e., 8.6 per cent compared with 7.2 per cent) and thus 19.4 per cent higher than firms starting up registered; Model 3 that they have an annual average employment growth rate 1.7 percentage points (i.e., 6.6 per cent compared with 4.9 per cent) and thus 34.7 per cent higher than enterprises starting up registered; and Model 5 that starting up unregistered has no significant deleterious impact on their annual productivity growth rate, which is 0.09 percentage points lower than those registered from the outset. For the formal enterprises surveyed in the WBES, and after controlling for other determinants of firm performance, the finding is thus that starting up unregistered significantly boosts average annual sales and employment growth rates and has no effect on annual productivity growth rates.

To explore whether this boost to annual sales and employment growth rates from being unregistered at start-up remains constant over time, Figure 5.3 presents the results based on Models 1 and 3 of a post-estimation exercise performed for a representative enterprise derived using the mean and modal values of the continuous and dummy control variables, respectively, across the countries and years surveyed and sample used. This displays how the better annual sales and employment growth rates of formal enterprises unregistered at start-up compared with those registered indeed remains constant as the firm ages, displayed by the non-significant result of the interaction term between starting up unregistered and firm age in Models 2 and 4. Drawing upon the higher annual sales and employment

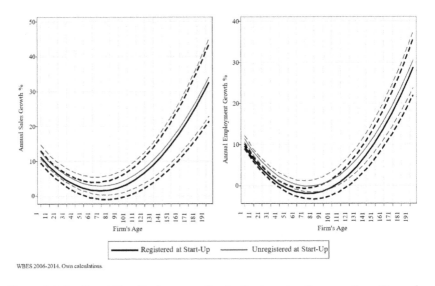

WBES 2006-2014. Own calculations.

Figure 5.3 Predicted Firm Performance By the Registration Status at Start-Up as the Firm Ages

*dashed lines display 95% confidence intervals

growth rates in Models 1 and 3 (1.4 and 1.7 percentage points, respectively), the slope of the predicted performance is estimated by the changing impact of firm age on performance using the significant coefficients of the linear and quadratic specifications of firm age, and not by the impact of registration status at start-up, which does not alter over time. This reveals the sustained benefits of starting up unregistered on annual sales and employment growth rates.

For formal enterprises, firm age has a long-term negative impact on annual sales growth for some 90 years until it reaches 2.3 per cent in registered enterprises, 3.7 per cent in unregistered start-ups and for 80 years in the case of annual employment growth when it reaches –2.0 per cent in registered and –0.2 per cent in unregistered start-ups, after which it again becomes positive. This curvilinear relationship and upwards trend after 80–90 years, however, is perhaps best ignored, although it reflects how in the long term, only the most successful firms survive, independent of whether they started up registered or not. As such, starting up unregistered significantly boosts firm performance in terms of average annual sales and employment growth rates, and this better performance remains constant over time, after controlling for other determinants of firm performance.

Evaluating Hypothesis 2 that the longer start-ups spend unregistered before registering, the higher is their future firm performance, Models 1–5 in Table 5.2 confirm this hypothesis for annual sales and employment growth rates but not for annual productivity growth rates. For each year a firm remains unregistered, annual sales growth rates are 0.149 percentage points higher (in Model 1) and annual employment growth rates are 0.177 percentage points higher (in Model 3) than for firms that started up registered. As Model 5 shows, however, there is no such premium from remaining unregistered for longer for annual productivity growth rates.

Is it the case however, as Hypothesis 3 states, that there is a turning point after which remaining unregistered is no longer beneficial in terms of firm performance, and when is this turning point? Whether such a turning point exists is only relevant to examine for sales and employment growth since there is no significant boost to productivity provided by remaining unregistered. Examining the negative quadratic specification of years unregistered reveals that the gains from remaining unregistered compared with being registered do reach a turning point. However, given that firm age also has a significant negative impact on annual sales and employment growth (i.e., the older is the business, the lower is annual sales and employment growth), as shown in Models 1 and 2 of Table 5.2, it is important to examine the interaction effects between the years spent unregistered and firm age. As Models 2 and 4 in Table 5.2 display, the positive impact of remaining unregistered on annual sales and employment growth reduces over time as revealed by the significant negative interaction of –0.002 percentage points between the linear specifications of time spent unregistered and firm age. That is, for each year the firm spent unregistered, there is a fall in annual

Table 5.2 Linear Multilevel Regression for the Impact of Years Spent Unregistered on Firm Performance

	Sales		Employment		Productivity
	(1)	*(2)*	*(3)*	*(4)*	*(5)*
	Model	*Model*	*Model*	*Model*	*Model*
Years unregistered	0.149*** (0.047)	0.231*** (0.074)	0.177*** (0.022)	0.250*** (0.038)	−0.012 (0.047)
Years unregistered (squared)	−0.001** (0.001)	−0.000 (0.001)	−0.002*** (0.000)	−0.001 (0.001)	0.000 (0.001)
Firm age	−0.279*** (0.019)	−0.285*** (0.020)	−0.321*** (0.009)	−0.327*** (0.010)	0.005 (0.020)
Firm age (squared)	0.002*** (0.000)	0.002*** (0.000)	0.002*** (0.000)	0.002*** (0.000)	0.000 (0.000)
Years unregistered* Firm age		−0.002** (0.001)		−0.002*** (0.001)	−0.000 (0.001)
Years unregistered (squared) *Firm age (squared)		0.000 (0.000)		0.000 (0.000)	0.000 (0.000)
Exporter	−0.200 (0.186)	−0.198 (0.186)	−0.039 (0.057)	−0.038 (0.057)	−0.147 (0.194)
Foreign ownership	0.075 (0.116)	0.074 (0.116)	0.012 (0.036)	0.011 (0.036)	0.076 (0.122)
Workforce					
Top manager's experience	−0.041*** (0.012)	−0.040*** (0.012)	−0.056*** (0.007)	−0.055*** (0.007)	0.009 (0.014)
Temporary workers	0.012*** (0.004)	0.012*** (0.004)	0.005** (0.002)	0.005** (0.002)	0.008** (0.004)
Permanent full-time workers	0.005*** (0.001)	0.005*** (0.001)	0.005*** (0.000)	0.005*** (0.000)	0.001 (0.001)
Female full-time workers	−0.013*** (0.004)	−0.013*** (0.004)	−0.034*** (0.002)	−0.033*** (0.002)	0.018*** (0.005)
Female participation ownership	0.046 (0.068)	0.045 (0.068)	−0.010 (0.021)	−0.011 (0.021)	0.065 (0.071)
Bank loan/ credit	−0.106 (0.080)	−0.106 (0.080)	0.028 (0.025)	0.027 (0.025)	−0.140* (0.083)

	Sales		Employment		Productivity
	(1)	*(2)*	*(3)*	*(4)*	*(5)*
	Model	Model	Model	Model	Model
Major constraints					
Transport	0.016	0.015	0.075**	0.075**	−0.044
	(0.104)	(0.103)	(0.032)	(0.032)	(0.107)
Electricity	−0.088	−0.088	−0.026	−0.026	−0.064
	(0.057)	(0.057)	(0.018)	(0.018)	(0.059)
Innovation & technology					
Quality certification	−0.073	−0.073	−0.000	−0.000	−0.073
	(0.112)	(0.112)	(0.035)	(0.035)	(0.117)
External auditor	0.018	0.018	0.004	0.004	0.004
	(0.055)	(0.055)	(0.016)	(0.016)	(0.057)
Website	0.167	0.166	0.028	0.028	0.145
	(0.110)	(0.110)	(0.035)	(0.035)	(0.115)
Email	−0.026	−0.026	0.001	0.001	−0.032
	(0.103)	(0.103)	(0.031)	(0.031)	(0.108)
Firm size (R.C.: Small)					
Medium	−0.096	−0.096	−0.020	−0.020	−0.079
	(0.171)	(0.171)	(0.052)	(0.052)	(0.178)
Large	0.063	0.063	−0.012	−0.012	0.060
	(0.169)	(0.169)	(0.052)	(0.052)	(0.175)
Legal status (R.C.: Open shareholding)					
Close shareholding	−0.050	−0.050	0.106*	0.106*	−0.167
	(0.194)	(0.194)	(0.059)	(0.059)	(0.202)
Sole proprietorship	−0.055	−0.056	0.139**	0.139**	−0.208
	(0.193)	(0.193)	(0.059)	(0.059)	(0.200)
Partnership	−0.208	−0.208	0.119*	0.119*	−0.323
	(0.202)	(0.202)	(0.062)	(0.062)	(0.210)
Limited partnership	−0.020	−0.020	0.079	0.078	−0.119
	(0.193)	(0.193)	(0.058)	(0.058)	(0.200)
Industry Sector (R.C.: Textile)					
Other form	−0.650**	−0.650**	0.032	0.032	−0.696**
	(0.268)	(0.268)	(0.083)	(0.083)	(0.280)
Leather	−0.005	−0.005	0.065	0.065	−0.092
	(0.241)	(0.241)	(0.076)	(0.076)	(0.250)
Garments	0.413	0.413	0.036	0.037	0.344
	(0.258)	(0.258)	(0.080)	(0.080)	(0.269)
Food	−0.145	−0.145	−0.084	−0.084	−0.030
	(0.252)	(0.252)	(0.078)	(0.078)	(0.261)
Metals & machinery	0.375	0.374	0.084	0.083	0.311
	(0.298)	(0.298)	(0.092)	(0.092)	(0.310)

Table 5.2 (Continued)

	Sales		Employment		Productivity
	(1)	*(2)*	*(3)*	*(4)*	*(5)*
	Model	*Model*	*Model*	*Model*	*Model*
Electronics	0.690 (0.771)	0.692 (0.771)	0.173 (0.232)	0.175 (0.232)	0.602 (0.801)
Chemicals & pharmaceuticals	−0.101 (0.553)	−0.103 (0.553)	0.216 (0.169)	0.215 (0.168)	−0.280 (0.572)
Wood, furniture	−0.064 (0.341)	−0.065 (0.341)	0.220** (0.105)	0.220** (0.105)	−0.283 (0.355)
Non-metallic, plastic materials	−1.412*** (0.380)	−1.413*** (0.380)	−0.185 (0.115)	−0.186 (0.115)	−1.286*** (0.397)
Auto & auto components	2.030 (1.259)	2.037 (1.258)	0.569 (0.386)	0.576 (0.386)	1.501 (1.313)
Other manufacturing	−0.017 (0.229)	−0.019 (0.229)	0.022 (0.071)	0.021 (0.071)	−0.043 (0.237)
Retail & wholesale trade	−0.020 (0.183)	−0.019 (0.183)	−0.012 (0.056)	−0.011 (0.056)	−0.005 (0.190)
Hotels & restaurants	−0.128 (0.291)	−0.128 (0.291)	0.120 (0.090)	0.120 (0.090)	−0.243 (0.302)
Other services	0.179 (0.219)	0.178 (0.219)	0.059 (0.068)	0.058 (0.068)	0.116 (0.228)
Other unclassified	−0.214 (0.210)	−0.215 (0.210)	0.165** (0.066)	0.164** (0.066)	−0.378* (0.219)
Year dummies	YES	YES	YES	YES	YES
Constant (fixed)	11.408*** (0.918)	11.437*** (0.918)	9.816*** (0.290)	9.846*** (0.290)	2.632*** (0.957)
Random disturbance					
Constant	YES	YES	YES	YES	YES
Slope: Started unregistered					
Slope: Years unregistered	YES	YES	YES	YES	YES
Slope: Firm age	YES	YES	YES	YES	YES
Observations	95,522	95,522	95,522	95,522	95,522
Countries	127	127	127	127	127

Significant at $p < 0.1$*
** $p < 0.05$
*** $p < 0.01$, standard errors between parentheses
Source: author's own calculations from the WBES 2006–2014 data set

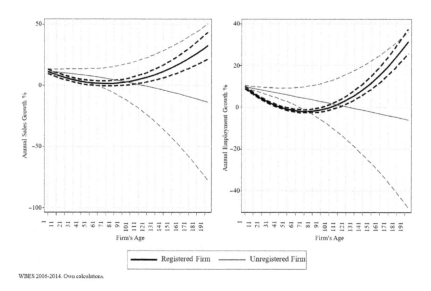

WBES 2006-2014. Own calculations.

Figure 5.4 Predicted Firm Performance By Number of Years Spent Unregistered
*dashed lines display 95% confidence intervals

sales and employment growth equal to that amount. Overall, however, this small figure suggests long-lasting positive effects on sales and employment growth from elongating the time spent unregistered, even if these effects gradually weaken over time.

To graphically portray this weakening and identify the turning point, Figure 5.4 presents the results of a post-estimation exercise for a representative enterprise which investigates the changing impact of the years spent unregistered on annual sales and employment growth as the firm ages. To see this impact, the changing annual sales and employment growth rates are analysed for a representative enterprise, firstly, that has been registered from the outset and has remained registered and, secondly, that continuously operates unregistered as it ages (i.e., the years unregistered and firm age are the same). This shows that if enterprises are unregistered for a long time period, the beneficial premium of non-registration on annual sales and employment growth disappears.

For annual sales growth, however, the turning point where spending any longer unregistered fails to have any premium is 90 years, although this is only statistically significant up to 60 years, as displayed by the 95 per cent dashed-line confidence intervals, not least because the number of firms reporting to have operated unregistered for this length of time decreases and the confidence intervals widen. While enterprises registered from the outset witness a dip in annual sales growth rates and then improvements in longer surviving registered firms, firms remaining unregistered witness a constant decline in annual sales growth rates, which is not perhaps surprising since their opportunities for growth may remain constrained by for example the need to remain small enough to avoid the authorities and their greater difficulties accessing finance and inability to bid for government contracts, to name but a few constraining factors.

Comparing how the length of time unregistered influences annual employment growth rates, similar patterns are found. Those remaining unregistered outperform those starting up registered for up to 100 years (1.9 and –0.4 per cent for unregistered and registered firms, respectively), although this is statistically significant only up to 80 years, not least because the number of firms operating unregistered for this length of time decreases and the confidence intervals widen. After this, those starting up registered outperform those that have remained unregistered. The important finding is thus that remaining unregistered on a long-term basis benefits annual sales and employment growth rates for many decades, and the turning point at which remaining unregistered ceases to be beneficial is more than 60 years for annual sales growth rates and 80 years for annual employment growth rates.

Conclusions

This chapter has thus begun to question the view that informal entrepreneurship has largely negative impacts. To do this, it has not only outlined some of the potentially positive impacts of informal sector enterprise but also has put under the spotlight one of the core tenets of those who depict informal entrepreneurship as a negative phenomenon, namely, the poorer performance thesis. This views enterprises starting up unregistered and in the informal sector as worse performing than their registered formal sector counterparts.

Evaluating the WBES data, this chapter has shown that unregistered start-ups which make the transition to formality outperform their counterparts that started up registered and continue to do so for a considerable number of decades. Formal enterprises that started up unregistered witness 19.4 per cent higher average annual sales growth than enterprises starting up registered (i.e., 8.6 per cent compared with 7.2 per cent) and 34.7 per cent higher annual employment growth than enterprises registered at start-up (i.e., 6.6 per cent compared with 4.9 per cent), and this better performance is sustained and compounded as the firm ages. Moreover, the longer start-ups spend unregistered before registering, the better are their annual sales and employment growth rates, and this is again not only sustained but also compounded as firms age. For each year a firm remains unregistered, annual sales growth rates are 0.149 percentage points higher and annual employment growth rates 0.177 percentage points higher than for registered start-ups, and the turning point after which it is no longer beneficial in terms of firm performance to remain unregistered is more than

60 years for annual sales growth rates and 80 years for annual employment growth rates. Contrary to previous assertions, furthermore, no significant differences exist in future annual productivity growth rates of formal enterprises starting up registered and unregistered.

These findings have four important theoretical implications for the conceptualisation of informal entrepreneurship. Firstly, and contrary to the dominant lower firm performance thesis, formal enterprises starting up unregistered, and also those remaining unregistered for long periods, have higher annual sales and employment growth rates than registered start-ups, and there are no deleterious impacts on their productivity growth rates. This necessitates a fundamental re-conceptualisation of informal entrepreneurship as having negative impacts on firm performance.

Secondly, the higher firm performance that results from being unregistered and remaining unregistered is not short-lived but very long-lasting. The turning point at which it becomes advantageous in terms of firm performance to register and formalise is not reached for many decades, strongly intimating that the benefits of formalisation remain insufficient to outweigh the benefits of informality for many decades for the majority of unregistered start-ups in the developing world.

Thirdly, the finding that enterprises which started up unregistered and later register witness higher firm performance than registered start-ups strongly suggests the need for a broader evaluation of firm performance of informal enterprises compared with formal enterprises. Until now, the dominant view has been that 'informal firms stay permanently informal . . . they are extremely unproductive, and they are unlikely to benefit much from becoming formal' (La Porta and Shleifer, 2014: 124). What now needs investigating is whether those that remain unregistered, akin to those that later register, also display higher levels of firm performance than formal enterprises. This is particularly necessary given the current weak evidence to support the poorer performance thesis of informal enterprises (e.g., La Porta and Shleifer, 2008),and the fact that similar to unregistered start-ups that later register, they operate under the same conditions that boost firm performance, including being able to avoid taxes, burdensome regulations and corrupt public sector officials.

And fourthly and finally in terms of theoretical implications, these findings provide a strong rationale for a more rigorous evaluation of the other normatively driven views regarding the negative impacts of informal entrepreneurship. So too does it suggest that the other potentially positive impacts require an evidence-based evaluation, such as that customers benefit from more affordable goods and services. Until these costs and benefits of informal entrepreneurship are evaluated, the overall net impact of informal entrepreneurship will not be known.

In sum, formal enterprises which start up unregistered and a spend longer time unregistered have been shown to outperform those that start up registered. This suggests that questions need to be asked about the policy approaches towards informal entrepreneurship. Until now, that is, and based on a negative representation of informal entrepreneurship, it has been common for state authorities to adopt a policy approach that seeks to stifle and eradicate such entrepreneurial endeavour in the informal sector. By revealing the positive impacts on future firm performance of being unregistered at start-up, this chapter intimates that perhaps a different approach is required. This will be the focus of Part III of this book. Before discussing the policy approaches towards informal entrepreneurship, however, it is first necessary to complete this evaluation of the prevalence, impacts and causes of informal entrepreneurship by examining the final issue, namely, what determines the prevalence of informal entrepreneurship.

References

Amaral, P.S. and Quintin, E. (2006). A competitive model of the informal sector. *Journal of Monetary Economics*, 53, pp. 1541–1553.

Baghdasaryan, D. and la Cour, L. (2013). Competition, ownership and productivity: A panel analysis of Czech firms. *Journal of Economics and Business*, 69, pp. 86–100.

Bajada, C. and Schneider, F. (2005). Introduction. In: C. Bajada and F. Schneider, Eds., *Size, causes and consequences of the underground economy: An international perspective*. Aldershot: Ashgate, pp. 1–14.

Barbera, F. and Moores, K. (2013). Firm ownership and productivity: A study of family and non-family SMEs. *Small Business Economics*, 40, pp. 953–976.

Barbour, A. and Llanes, M. (2013). *Supporting people to legitimise their informal businesses*. York: Joseph Rowntree Foundation.

Baumol, W.J. (1990). Entrepreneurship: Productive, unproductive and destructive. *Journal of Political Economy*, 98, pp. 893–921.

Becker, K.F. (2004). *The informal economy*. Stockholm: Swedish International Development Agency.

Black, S.E. and Lynch, L.M. (1996). Human-capital investments and productivity. *The American Economic Review*, 25, pp. 263–267.

Castells, M. and Portes, A. (1989). World underneath: The origins, dynamics and effects of the informal economy. In: A. Portes, M. Castells and L. Benton, Eds., *The informal economy: Studies in advanced and less developing countries*. Baltimore: John Hopkins University Press, pp. 1–19.

Cebolla, H. (2013). *Introducción al análisis multinivel*. Madrid: Centro de Investigaciones Sociológicas.

Chen, M. (2012). *The informal economy: Definitions, theories and policies*. Manchester: Women in Informal Employment Global and Organising.

Chen, M. (2014). Informal employment and development: Patterns of inclusion and exclusion. *European Journal of Development Research*, 26(4), pp. 397–418.

Collins, L.M., Schafer, J.L. and Kam, C.M. (2001). A comparison of inclusive and restrictive strategies in modern missing data procedures. *Psychological Methods*, 6(4), pp. 330–351.

Cross, J.C. (2000). Street vendors, modernity and postmodernity: Conflict and compromise in the global economy. *International Journal of Sociology and Social Policy*, 20(1), pp. 29–51.

Cull, R., McKenzie, D. and Woodruff, C. (2007). *Experimental evidence on returns to capital and access to finance in Mexico*. Washington, DC: World Bank.

Davis, M. (2006). *Planet of slums*. London: Verso.

De Beer, J., Fu, K. and Wunsch-Vincent, S. (2013). *The informal economy, innovation and intellectual property: Concepts, metrics and policy considerations.* Geneva: Economic Research Working Paper no. 10, World Intellectual Property Organization.

De Castro, J.O., Khavul, S. and Bruton, G.D. (2014). Shades of grey: How do informal firms navigate between macro and meso institutional environments? *Strategic Entrepreneurship Journal*, 8(1), pp. 75–94.

De Soto, H. (1989). *The other path: The economic answer to terrorism.* London: Harper and Row.

De Soto, H. (2001). *The mystery of capital: Why capitalism triumphs in the West and fails everywhere else.* London: Black Swan.

Dimova, R., Nordman, C.J. and Roubaud, F. (2008). *Allocation of labour in urban West Africa: Implication for development policies.* Bonn: IZA Discussion Paper no. 3558, IZA.

Fajnzylber, P., Maloney, W. and Montes Rojas, G. (2009). Releasing constraints to growth or pushing on a string? Policies and performance of Mexican microfirms. *Journal of Development Studies*, 45, pp. 1027–1047.

Farrell, D. (2004). The hidden dangers of informal economy. *McKinsey Quarterly*, 3, pp. 27–37.

Franck, A.K. (2012). Factors motivating women's informal micro-entrepreneurship: Experiences from Penang, Malaysia. *International Journal of Gender and Entrepreneurship*, 4(1), pp. 65–78.

Gallin, D. (2001). Propositions on trade unions and informal employment in time of globalization. *Antipode*, 19(4), pp. 531–549.

Gennaiolo, N., La Porta, R., Lopez-de-Silanes, F. and Shleifer, A. (2013). Human capital and regional development. *Quarterly Journal of Economics*, 128(1), pp. 105–164.

Gërxhani, K. (2004). The informal sector in developed and less developed countries: A literature survey. *Public Choice*, 120(3/4), pp. 267–300.

Grimm, M., Knorringa, P. and Lay, J. (2012). Constrained gazelles: High potentials in West Africa's informal economy. *World Development*, 40(7), pp. 1352–1368.

Hsieh, C.-T. and Olken, B. (2014). The missing 'missing middle'. *Journal of Economic Perspectives*, 28(3), pp. 89–108.

ILO (2005). *World employment report 2004–05: Employment, productivity and poverty reduction.* Geneva: ILO.

ILO (2007). *The decent work agenda in Africa, 2007–15.* Geneva: ILO.

ILO (2014). *Transitioning from the informal to the formal economy.* Report V (1), International Labour Conference, 103rd Session (2014). Geneva: ILO.

Kabecha, W.W. (1998). Technological capability of the micro-enterprises in Kenya's informal sector. *Technovation*, 19(2), pp. 117–126.

Ketchen, D.J., Ireland, R.D. and Webb, J.W. (2014). Towards a research agenda for the informal economy: A survey of the Strategic Entrepreneurship Journal's Editorial Board. *Strategic Entrepreneurship Journal*, 8, pp. 95–100.

Kistruck, G.M., Webb, J.W., Sutter, C.J. and Bailey, A.V.G. (2015). The double-edged sword of legitimacy in base-of-the-pyramid markets. *Journal of Business Venturing*, 30(3), pp. 436–451.

La Porta, R. and Shleifer, A. (2008). The unofficial economy and economic development. *Brookings Papers on Economic Activity*, 47(1), pp. 123–135.

La Porta, R. and Shleifer, A. (2014). Informality and development. *Journal of Economic Perspectives*, 28(3), pp. 109–126.

Leal Ordóñez, J.C. (2014). Tax collection, the informal sector and productivity. *Review of Economic Dynamics*, 17, pp. 262–286.

Levy, S. (2008). *Good intentions, bad outcomes: Social policy, informality and economic growth in Mexico.* Washington, DC: Brookings Institution.

Lewis, W.W. (2004). *The power of productivity: Wealth, poverty, and the threat to global stability.* Chicago: University of Chicago Press.

London, T., Esper, H., Grogan-Kaylor, A. and Kistruck, G.M. (2014). Connecting poverty to purchase in informal markets. *Strategic Entrepreneurship Journal,* 8(1), pp. 37–55.

Maloney, W.F. (2004). Informality revisited. *World Development,* 32(7), pp. 1159–1178.

Mansury, M.A. and Love, J.H. (2008). Innovation, productivity and growth in US business services: A firm-level analysis. *Technovation,* 28(1/2), pp. 52–62.

McCulloch, N., Schulze, G. and Voss, J. (2010). *What determines firms' decisions to formalize?* Frieburg: Discussion Paper Series, no. 13, University of Frieburg Department of International Economic Policy.

McKenzie, D. and Sakho, Y.S. (2010). Does it pay firms to register for taxes? The impact of formality on firm profitability. *Journal of Development Economics,* 91(1), pp. 15–24.

McKenzie, D. and Woodruff, C. (2006). Do entry costs provide an empirical basis for poverty traps? Evidence from microenterprises. *Economic Development and Cultural Change,* 55(1), pp. 3–42.

McKinsey Global Institute. (2003). *Turkey: Making the productivity and growth breakthrough.* New York: McKinsey.

Meagher, K. (2010). *Identity economics: Social networks and the informal economy in Nigeria.* New York: James Currey.

Nabar, M. and Yan, K. (2013). *Sector-level productivity, structural change and rebalancing in China.* Washington, DC: IMF Working Paper no. 240, IMF.

North, D.C. (1990). *Institutions, institutional change and economic performance.* Cambridge: Cambridge University Press.

Nwabuzor, A. (2005). Corruption and development: New initiatives in economic openness and strengthened rule of law. *Journal of Business Ethics,* 59(1/2), pp. 121–138.

Palmade, V. (2005). *Rising informality.* Washington, DC: Viewpoint Series note 298, Private Sector Development, World Bank.

Palmer, R. (2007). *Skills development, the enabling environment and informal micro-enterprise in Ghana.* Edinburgh: University of Edinburgh.

Perry, G.E. and Maloney, W.F. (2007). Overview: Informality: Exit and exclusion. In: G.E. Perry, W.F. Maloney, O.S. Arias, P. Fajnzylber, A.D. Mason and J. Saavedra-Chanduvi, Eds., *Informality: Exit and exclusion.* Washington, DC: World Bank, pp. 1–20.

Perry, G.E., Maloney, W.F., Arias, O.S., Fajnzylber, R., Mason, A.D. and Saavedra-Chanduvi, J. (2007). Eds., *Informality: Exit and exclusion.* Washington, DC: World Bank.

Pisani, M. (2017). Entrepreneurship at the base of the pyramid: The case of Nicaragua. In: C.C. Williams and A. Gurtoo, Eds., *Routledge handbook of entrepreneurship in developing economies.* London: Routledge, pp. 343–355.

Puffer, S.M., McCarthy, D.J. and Boisot, M. (2010). Entrepreneurship in Russia and China: The impact of formal institutional voids. *Entrepreneurship Theory and Practice,* 34(3), pp. 441–467.

Rand, J. and Torm, N. (2012). The benefits of formalization: Evidence from Vietnamese manufacturing. *Small Business Economics,* 29, pp. 1–13.

Rubin, D. (1987). *Multiple imputation for nonresponse in surveys.* New York: Wiley.

Schafer, J. and Graham, J. (2002). Missing data: Our view of the state of the art. *Psychological Methods,* 7(2), pp. 1–47.

Schneider, F. and Williams, C.C. (2013). *The shadow economy.* London: Institute of Economic Affairs.

Siba, E. (2015). Returns to physical capital in Ethiopia: Comparative analysis of formal and informal firms. *World Development,* 68, pp. 215–229.

Siqueira, A.C.O., Webb, J.W. and Bruton, G.D. (2016). Informal entrepreneurship and industry conditions. *Entrepreneurship Theory and Practice*, 40(1), pp. 177–200.

Slavnic, Z. (2010). Political economy of informalisation. *European Societies*, 12(1), pp. 3–23.

Snyder, K.A. (2004). Routes to the informal economy in New York's East village: Crisis, economics and identity. *Sociological Perspectives*, 47(2), pp. 215–240.

Söderbom, M. and Teal, F. (2001). *Firm size and human capital as determinants of productivity and earnings*. Geneva: United Nations Industrial Development Organization.

Taiwo, O. (2013). Employment choice and mobility in multi-sector labour markets: Theoretical model and evidence from Ghana. *International Labour Review*, 152(3/4), pp. 469–492.

Thai, M.T.T. and Turkina, E. (2014). Macro-level determinants of formal entrepreneurship versus informal entrepreneurship. *Journal of Business Venturing*, 29(4), pp. 490–510.

Tonoyan, V., Strohmeyer, R., Habib, M. and Perlitz, M. (2010). Corruption and entrepreneurship: How formal and informal institutions shape small firm behaviour in transition and mature market economies. *Entrepreneurship Theory and Practice*, 34(5), pp. 803–831.

United Nations Conference on Trade and Development (UNCTAD) (2006). *The least developed countries report 2006: Developing productive capacities*. Geneva: UNCTAD.

Vandenberg, P. (2005). *Productivity, decent employment and poverty: Conceptual and practical issues related to small enterprises*. Geneva: ILO.

Van der Sluis, J., Van Praag, M. and Vijverberg, W. (2005). Entrepreneurship selection and performance: A meta-analysis of the impact of education in developing economies. *The World Bank Economic Review*, 19(2), pp. 225–261.

Vu, T.T. (2014). *Institutional incongruence and the informal economy: An empirical analysis*. Paper presented at the European Public Choice Society Meeting, Cambridge. Available at: www.econ.cam.ac.uk/epcs2014/openconf/modules/request.php?module=oc_program&action=summary.php&id=54 (last accessed 6 January 2017).

Webb, J.W., Bruton, G.D., Tihanyi, L. and Ireland, R.D. (2013). Research on entrepreneurship in the informal economy: Framing a research agenda. *Journal of Business Venturing*, 28, pp. 598–614.

Webb, J.W., Ireland, R.D. and Ketchen, D.J. (2014). Towards a greater understanding of entrepreneurship and strategy in the informal economy. *Strategic Entrepreneurship Journal*, 8(1), pp. 1–15.

Webb, J.W., Tihanyi, L., Ireland, R.D. and Sirmon, D.G. (2009). You say illegal, I say legitimate: Entrepreneurship in the informal economy. *Academy of Management Review*, 34(3), pp. 492–510.

Williams, C.C. and Gurtoo, A. (2017). Informal entrepreneurship in developing countries. In: C.C. Williams and A. Gurtoo, Eds., *Routledge handbook of entrepreneurship in developing economies*. London: Routledge, pp. 329–342.

Williams, C.C. and Martinez-Perez, A. (2014a). Do small business start-ups test-trade in the informal economy? Evidence from a UK small business survey. *International Journal of Entrepreneurship and Small Business*, 22(1), pp. 1–16.

Williams, C.C. and Martinez-Perez, A. (2014b). Is the informal economy an incubator for new enterprise creation? A gender perspective. *International Journal of Entrepreneurial Behaviour and Research*, 20(1), pp. 4–19.

Williams, C.C., Nadin, S., Barbour, A. and Llanes, M. (2012). *Enabling enterprise: Tackling the barriers to formalisation*. London: Community Links.

Williams, C.C. and Shahid, M. (2016). Informal entrepreneurship and institutional theory: Explaining the varying degrees of (in)formalisation of entrepreneurs in Pakistan. *Entrepreneurship and Regional Development*, 28(1/2), pp. 1–25.

Wunsch-Vincent, S., de Beer, J. and Fu, K. (2015). What we know and do not know about innovation in the informal economy. In: E. Kraemer-Mbula and S. Wunsch-Vincent, Eds., *The informal economy in developing nations: Hidden engine of innovation? New economic insights and policies.* Cambridge: Cambridge University Press. pp. 142–160.

6 Reasons for Informal Entrepreneurship

Introduction

Having outlined the prevalence and impacts of informal entrepreneurship, this chapter turns its attention to the reasons for informal entrepreneurship and in particular how to explain the cross-national variations in informal entrepreneurship reported in Chapter 4. As Part I of the book highlighted, recent years have seen the emergence of an institutional theory approach which asserts that informal entrepreneurship is more prevalent when formal institutional failures and imperfections result in an asymmetry between the formal and informal institutions (Ostapenko and Williams, 2016; Sallah and Williams, 2016; Sauka *et al.*, 2016; Williams, 2015f,g, 2016; Williams and Shahid, 2016; Williams *et al.*, 2017a,b). This chapter, therefore, firstly evaluates whether there is a significant association between the prevalence of informal entrepreneurship and institutional asymmetry and, secondly, identifies the formal institutional failures that are associated with the greater prevalence of informal entrepreneurship.

To do this, the first section briefly reviews both the emergent institutional theory along with the competing theories regarding which formal institutional failures are associated with higher levels of informal entrepreneurship. The outcome of this will be a set of hypotheses. The second section of the chapter then reports the data and methodology used to test these hypotheses regarding the determinants of informal entrepreneurship, namely WBES data from 142 countries collected between 2006 and 2014 on the extent to which formal firms identify that they are competing with unregistered or informal competitors and the multivariate regression analysis methodology. The third section then reports the results. This will reveal not only the validity of the institutional asymmetry thesis which asserts that the greater the institutional asymmetry, the higher are the levels of informal entrepreneurship, but also displays the formal institutional failures and imperfections that are associated with the greater prevalence of informal entrepreneurship. This will positively confirm the modernisation and political economy explanations and negatively confirm the tenets of the neo-liberal thesis.

Competing Reasons for the Cross-National Variations in Informal Entrepreneurship

In Chapter 4, it was highlighted that there are considerable cross-national variations in informal entrepreneurship. Here, it was identified that 41.9 per cent of formal businesses globally identify themselves as competing against unregistered or formal firms. However, this share varies across global regions, ranging from a high of 52.1 per cent in sub-Saharan Africa to a low of 20.5 per cent in OECD nations. There are also considerable cross-national variations, ranging from 85 per cent in Suriname, 84 per cent in Cameron and 82 per cent in Tonga to 17 per cent in The Gambia, 14 per cent in Venezuela and only 11 per cent in Namibia. How, therefore, can these cross-national variations in the scale of informal sector entrepreneurship be explained?

Institutional Asymmetry Thesis

In Part I of this book, and drawing inspiration from institutional theory (Baumol, 1990; Baumol and Blinder, 2008; North, 1990), it was argued that informal entrepreneurship arises where there are formal institutional failures that result in an asymmetry between the formal institutions that define the formal rules of the game and the norms, values and beliefs of informal institutions (De Castro *et al.*, 2014; Siqueira *et al.*, 2016; Thai and Turkina, 2014; Vu, 2014; Webb *et al.*, 2009, 2013, 2014; Williams and Shahid, 2016). The consequent argument is that cross-national variations in the level of informal entrepreneurship are associated with cross-national variations in the level of institutional asymmetry. The greater is the level of institutional asymmetry, the greater is the prevalence of informal entrepreneurship. As such, this institutional explanation for the cross-national variations in the prevalence of informal entrepreneurship can be evaluated by testing the following proposition:

> *Institutional asymmetry hypothesis (H1)*: The greater the asymmetry between formal and informal institutions, the greater the prevalence of informal entrepreneurship.

What, however, causes the existence of this asymmetry between the laws and regulations, and the norms, values and beliefs of entrepreneurs regarding the acceptability of not adhering to these laws and regulations? Until now, as outlined in Chapter 3, there have been three competing theorisations regarding which formal institutional failures lead to this institutional asymmetry and thus the prevalence of entrepreneurship in the informal sector. These variously explain informal entrepreneurship to be a result of either economic underdevelopment and poor-quality governance (modernisation thesis), high taxes and state interference in the free market which lead entrepreneurs to voluntarily exit the formal sector (neo-liberal thesis) or inadequate state intervention to protect workers from poverty which results in informal entrepreneurship being pursued as a survival tactic by those involuntarily excluded from the formal sector (political economy thesis). Each is here briefly reviewed in turn to formulate hypotheses (see Chapter 3 for a more in-depth review of each theory).

Modernisation Thesis

For most of the twentieth century, a recurring assumption was that the modern formal sector was extensive and growing, while the separate informal sector was small and gradually vanishing. Entrepreneurs operating in the informal sector, such as street hawkers, were consequently represented as a leftover from an earlier pre-modern mode of production and disappearing as they became incorporated into the modern formal sector. The existence of informal entrepreneurs in an economy was thus a sign of 'traditionalism', 'underdevelopment' and 'backwardness' (Geertz, 1963; Gilbert, 1998; Lewis, 1959; Packard, 2007). From this perspective, therefore, informal entrepreneurship is a product of underdevelopment and will disappear with economic advancement. Applying this to explaining the cross-national variations in the extent of informal entrepreneurship, it can be suggested that in less economically developed countries, measured in terms of GDP per capita, and in countries with less modern state bureaucracies, measured by the pervasiveness of public sector corruption (Torgler and Schneider, 2007; Tonoyan *et al.*, 2010), there will be a higher prevalence of informal entrepreneurship. To explore its validity, the following hypotheses can be tested:

> *Modernisation hypothesis (H2)*: The prevalence of informal entrepreneurship will be greater in less developed economies with unmodern state bureaucracies.
> *Hypothesis 2a*: The prevalence of informal sector entrepreneurship will be greater in less developed economies measured in terms of GDP per capita.
> *Hypothesis 2b*: The prevalence of informal sector entrepreneurship will be greater in countries with less modern state bureaucracies, measured in terms of the level of public sector corruption.

Neo-Liberal Thesis

For a neo-liberal school of thought, informal entrepreneurship is a direct product of high taxes and too much state interference in the free market, which leads entrepreneurs to make a rational economic decision to voluntarily exit the formal sector to avoid the costs, time and effort of operating formally (e.g., Becker, 2004; De Soto, 1989, 2001; London and Hart, 2004;

Nwabuzor, 2005; Sauvy, 1984; Small Business Council, 2004). As Becker (2004: 10) puts it, 'informal work arrangements are a rational response by micro-entrepreneurs to over-regulation by government bureaucracies'. For neo-liberals, therefore, informal entrepreneurship is a rational economic response pursued by entrepreneurs whose spirit is stifled by high taxes and state-imposed institutional constraints (De Soto, 1989, 2001; Perry and Maloney, 2007). Informal entrepreneurship is thus an outcome of high taxes, over-regulation and state interference in the free market, and the consequent solution is to pursue tax reductions, deregulation and minimal state intervention. From this perspective, therefore, the extent of informal entrepreneurship should be greater in countries with higher taxes and greater state interference. To explore the validity of this neo-liberal explanation, therefore, the following hypothesis can be tested:

> *Neo-liberal hypothesis (H3)*: The prevalence of informal sector entrepreneurship will be greater in countries with higher tax rates and higher levels of state interference in the free market.
> *Hypothesis H3a*: The prevalence of informal sector entrepreneurship will be greater in countries with higher levels of state interference in the free market, measured by the regulatory burden.
> *Hypothesis H3b*: The prevalence of informal sector entrepreneurship will be greater in countries with higher tax rates, measured by the tax revenue to GDP ratio.
> *Hypothesis 3c*: The prevalence of informal sector entrepreneurship will be greater in countries where the expense of government as a percentage of GDP is higher.

Political Economy Thesis

For a school of political economy thought, in contrast, informal sector entrepreneurship is a direct product of the emergence of a deregulated open world economy in which subcontracting and outsourcing have become a primary means of integrating informal entrepreneurship into contemporary capitalism, causing a further downward pressure on wages and the erosion of incomes, welfare services and benefits and the growth of yet more informal entrepreneurship (Castells and Portes, 1989; Gallin, 2001; Hudson, 2005; Portes, 1994; Sassen, 1996; Slavnic, 2010; Taiwo, 2013). As Meagher (2010: 11) puts it, '[i]nformal economic arrangements . . . have entered into the heart of contemporary economies through processes of subcontracting . . . and diminishing state involvement in popular welfare and employment'. Informal entrepreneurship is thus represented as an unregulated, insecure, low-paid, survival-driven endeavour conducted by populations excluded from the formal labour market (Castells and Portes, 1989; Davis, 2006; Gallin, 2001; Hudson, 2005; Sassen, 1996; Taiwo, 2013). Informal entrepreneurship thus results from a lack of state intervention in work and welfare provision, including social protection and social transfers, and is a direct product of poverty. In consequence, this practice is viewed as more prevalent in countries with inadequate state intervention to protect workers from poverty (Davis, 2006; Gallin, 2001; Slavnic, 2010). To evaluate the validity of this political economy explanation, therefore, the following hypothesis can be tested:

> *Political economy hypothesis (H4)*: The prevalence of informal entrepreneurship will be greater in economies with lower levels of state intervention.
>
> *Hypothesis 4a*: The prevalence of informal sector entrepreneurship will be greater in those countries where the regulatory burden is higher.
>
> *Hypothesis 4b*: The prevalence of informal sector entrepreneurship will be greater in those countries with lower tax-to-GDP ratios.
>
> *Hypothesis 4c*: The prevalence of informal sector entrepreneurship will be greater in those countries where the expense of government as a percentage of GDP is lower.

Data, Variables and Methods

Data

To test these hypotheses, WBES data from 142 countries across the globe are analysed, including both 127 developing countries and 15 developed nations. In each country, the WBES collects data using a stratified random sample of non-agricultural, formal, private sector businesses with five or more employees, which is stratified by firm size, business sector and geographic region. The sampling frame is derived from the universe of eligible firms, normally obtained from the statistical office or another government agency in each country such as the tax or business licensing authorities. To collect data, a harmonised questionnaire is used across all countries, answered by some 1200–1800 business owners and top managers in larger economies, 360 in medium-sized economies and 150 in smaller economies.

Dependent Variable

To evaluate the cross-national variations in the prevalence of entrepreneurship in the informal sector, a WBES question is used that examines responses to the question, 'Does this establishment compete against unregistered or informal firms?'. This is a dummy variable which takes a value of 1 if the firms declare that they are competing against unregistered or informal firms and a value of 0 otherwise. This indicator captures what can be termed the intensity or pervasiveness of informality faced by the registered businesses.

Key Independent Variables

To test the various theories that attempt to explain the main drivers of cross-national variations in the prevalence of informal entrepreneurship, both firm-level and country-level variables are used that capture the tenets of the institutional asymmetry, modernisation, neo-liberal, and political economy perspectives.

To test the institutional asymmetry hypothesis (H1), while holding constant the business-level control variables, the indicator used is the following:

- *trust in the court system*, measured by the percentage of firms believing that the court system is fair, impartial and uncorrupted. This is based on the response to the following question 'I am going to read some statements that describe the court system and how it could affect business. For each statement, please tell me if you strongly disagree, tend to disagree, tend to agree, or strongly agree'. This is a dummy variable with a value of 1 given to those firms who agree and strongly agree that 'the court system is fair, impartial and uncorrupted' and a value of 0 for those who disagree or strongly disagree.

To analyse hypotheses H2–4 regarding the country-level determinants, while holding constant the business-level control variables, variables are analysed used in previous studies, evaluating these hypotheses in relation to the wider informal sector (Eurofound, 2013; Vanderseypen *et al.*, 2013; Williams, 2013a,b, 2014a,b,c, 2015a,b,c,d,e). To evaluate the economic development tenet of the modernisation hypothesis (H2a), the indicator used is the following:

- the current *GDP per capita* of each country expressed as the purchasing power parity in international dollars transformed in natural logs. This was retrieved from IMF World Economic Outlook Database for the relevant years for each country surveyed.

To evaluate the modernisation of governance hypothesis (H2b), meanwhile, a composite index is used which evaluates corruption behaviours available in the WBES, namely:

- *corruption composite index* – a dummy variable which indicates whether the entrepreneur has paid public officials bribes and other payments to 'get things gone' in relation to customs, taxes, licenses, permits, regulations and services. It takes a value of 1 if responding firms reported making any of those payments and 0 otherwise. This is a dummy variable, with value 1 if a firm had paid officials in one or more of such cases and 0 otherwise.

Meanwhile, to test both the tenet of the neo-liberal thesis that state interference increases unregistered business start-ups and the inverse political economy thesis that state intervention reduces informal entrepreneurship, three indicators of the level of state intervention are employed, namely:

- *regulatory burden composite index*, which is captured by their answers to questions about whether they face obstacles in the form of customs, trade and labour regulations. This is a dummy variable defined by giving a value of 1 to those firms that say that customs, trade and labour regulations are obstacles to their operations and 0 otherwise.
- *tax revenue to GDP ratio*, from the IMF World Economic Outlook database.
- *expense of government as a per cent of GDP*, which is a measure of the size of government and therefore a loose proxy of the degree of intervention. The expense of government is the level of cash payments for the operating activities of the government in providing goods and services. It includes compensation of employees (such as wages and salaries), interest and subsidies, grants, social benefits and other expenses such as rent and dividends.

(World Bank, 2017)

Other Control Variables

It is necessary to control for other key explanatory variables that may also affect firms' competition with unregistered and informal competitors. Most of these indicators are firm-level variables defined within the data. These are derived from previous studies which reveal the individual-level variables that influence the likelihood of competing with informal competitors both in a previous analyses of the WBES data (Hudson *et al.*, 2012; Williams *et al.*, 2017a) and other studies of entrepreneurship in the informal sector (Dau and Cuervo-Cazzurra, 2014; Hodosi, 2015; Khan and Quaddus, 2015; Thai and Turkina, 2014; Vu, 2014). These firm-level control variables are the following:

- *firm age* – a continuous variable for the number of years since the firm was established.
- *foreign owned* – a dummy variable with a value of 1 indicating if the share of the firm's ownership held by foreign individuals or enterprises is larger than 49 per cent.
- *export orientation* – a dummy variable with a value of 1 indicating the proportion of firm's sales which are for the export market and 0 for the share of sales for the domestic market.
- *firm size* – a categorical variable with value with a value of 1 for small firms with less than 20 employees, 2 for medium-size firms between 20 and 99 employees, and 3 for large firms with more than 100 employees.

- *legal status* – a categorical variable indicating whether the legal form of the firm is an open shareholding, a closed shareholding, a sole proprietorship, a partnership, a limited partnership or any other form.
- *quality certification* – a dummy variable with a value of 1 indicating the firm has an internationally recognised certification and 0 otherwise.
- *external auditor* – a dummy variable with a value of 1 indicating the firm has its annual financial statement reviewed by an external auditor and 0 otherwise.
- *presence of a website*, a dummy variable with a value of 1 when the firm uses a website for business-related activities and 0 otherwise.
- *use of email* – a dummy variable with a value of 1 when a firm uses email to interact with clients and suppliers and 0 otherwise.
- *top manager's experience* – a continuous variable of the years of experience the top manager has in the sector.
- *temporary workers* – a variable measuring the average number of temporary workers in the firm.
- *permanent full-time workers* – a continuous variable of the average number of permanent full-time workers in the firm.
- *female full-time workers* – examining the share of permanent full-time workers that are female.
- *female involvement in ownership* – a dummy variable with a value of 1 indicating whether women are involved in the ownership of the firm and 0 otherwise.

Methods

To evaluate the country-level determinants of whether formal firms are more likely to state that they compete with unregistered and informal entrepreneurs across the 142 countries, multilevel techniques are used. Given that the surveyed enterprises in the WBES are clustered across country-year subsamples, multilevel modelling is the optimal technique to elicit unbiased standard errors as well as reliable statistical comparisons. The estimating standard probit equation takes the following form:

$$I_i = x'_{1i}\beta_1 + \varepsilon_{1i} \tag{1}$$

Where x_{1i} denotes a vector of exogenous variables capturing firm-level characteristics and I_i represents whether formal firms compete with unregistered and informal firms. The error term ε_{1i} is normally distributed with 0 mean and constant variance.

Findings: Determinants of Cross-National Variations in Informal Entrepreneurship

As shown in Chapter 4, some 41.9 per cent of the formal private sector enterprises with five or more employees surveyed report that they compete with unregistered or informal enterprises. However, there are considerable cross-national variations in the proportion of formal firms competing with unregistered or informal firms, ranging from 85 per cent in Suriname, 84 per cent in Cameron and 82 per cent in Tonga to 17 per cent in The Gambia, 14 per cent in Venezuela and just 11 per cent in Namibia.

How, therefore, can these cross-national variations be explained? Is it indeed the case that cross-national variations in the prevalence of informal entrepreneurship are significantly associated with the cross-national variations in the asymmetry between formal and informal institutions? And what formal institutional failures lead to this institutional asymmetry and the greater prevalence of informal entrepreneurship? Is it the case as the modernisation thesis suggests that cross-national variations in the prevalence of informal entrepreneurship are associated with the level of economic development and the modernisation of governance? Or is it the case as the neo-liberal thesis asserts that these cross-national variations are associated with high taxes and too much state interference in the free market? Or alternatively, are the cross-national variations more associated with inadequate state intervention to protect workers from poverty?

Table 6.1 evaluates the likelihood of a formal firm competing with an unregistered or informal firm across the 142 countries. Model 1 reports the standard probit coefficient estimates of the probability of a formal firm competing with an unregistered or informal firm using only the firm-level variables. The first important finding is that there is a strong significant negative association between trust in formal institutions (measured by whether the court system is viewed as fair, impartial and uncorrupted) and the likelihood of formal firms competing against unregistered and informal enterprises; the lower the trust in formal institutions, the greater is the probability that formal firms will be competing against unregistered or informal enterprises. Importantly, therefore, this confirms H1: the greater the institutional asymmetry, the greater is the prevalence of informal entrepreneurship.

It is also the case that the effect of firm age on informality is positive with older firms being more likely to compete with unregistered or informal enterprises. Meanwhile, firms that export and are foreign owned are significantly less likely to compete with informal and unregistered firms than non-exporting and domestic-owned enterprises, doubtless because they operate in different market segments. Turning to workforce characteristics, top manager's working experience in the sector is positively and significantly associated with competing with informal and unregistered businesses, perhaps indicating that they are in a relatively advantageous position of detecting the competition from unregistered or informal firms. Firms with full-time permanent and female workers, furthermore, are less likely to be competing against informal and unregistered firms, as are firms where women are involved in the ownership of the enterprise. Examining innovation and technology, formal firms with quality certification are less likely to be competing with unregistered and informal firms, but those with a website are more likely to do so. Akin to previous studies (Galiani and Weinschelbaum,

Table 6.1 Probit Model of Determinants of Whether Formal Firms Compete With Unregistered or Informal Enterprises, WBES 2006–2014

Variables	Model 1	Model 2	Model 3	Model 4	Model 5	Model 6
Ln (GDPPC)		−0.109*** (0.007)				
Corruption			0.192*** (0.012)			
Regulatory burden				−0.092*** (0.024)		
Tax revenue-to-GDP ratio					−0.010*** (0.002)	
Expense of government as % of GDP						−0.003*** (0.001)
Trust	−0.117*** (0.011)	−0.115*** (0.011)	−0.051*** (0.011)	−0.115*** (0.011)	−0.091*** (0.017)	−0.069*** (0.015)
Firm characteristics						
Firm age	0.002*** (0.000)	0.002*** (0.000)	0.002*** (0.000)	0.002*** (0.000)	0.002*** (0.001)	0.001** (0.001)
Exporter	−0.002*** (0.000)	−0.002*** (0.000)	−0.002*** (0.000)	−0.002*** (0.000)	−0.002*** (0.000)	−0.003*** (0.000)
Foreign ownership	−0.216*** (0.020)	−0.216*** (0.020)	−0.137*** (0.019)	−0.213*** (0.020)	−0.190*** (0.027)	−0.152*** (0.026)
Workforce						
Top manager experience	0.003*** (0.001)	0.003*** (0.001)	0.003*** (0.001)	0.003*** (0.001)	0.002*** (0.001)	0.002** (0.001)
Temporary worker	−0.000 (0.000)	−0.000 (0.000)	0.000 (0.000)	−0.000 (0.000)	−0.000 (0.000)	−0.000 (0.000)
Permanent full-time	−0.000*** (0.000)	−0.000*** (0.000)	−0.000*** (0.000)	−0.000*** (0.000)	−0.000*** (0.000)	−0.000*** (0.000)
Female full-time	−0.002*** (0.000)	−0.002*** (0.000)	−0.001** (0.000)	−0.002*** (0.000)	−0.001*** (0.000)	−0.001*** (0.000)
Female share in ownership	0.000 (0.000)	0.000 (0.000)	0.000*** (0.000)	0.000 (0.000)	−0.000 (0.000)	0.000 (0.000)
Innovation and technology						
Quality certification	−0.000** (0.000)	−0.000** (0.000)	−0.000 (0.000)	−0.000** (0.000)	−0.001*** (0.000)	−0.001** (0.000)

Variables	Model 1	Model 2	Model 3	Model 4	Model 5	Model 6
External auditor	0.000 (0.000)	0.000 (0.000)	0.000** (0.000)	0.000 (0.000)	−0.000 (0.000)	−0.000 (0.000)
Website	0.000*** (0.000)	0.000** (0.000)	0.000** (0.000)	0.000*** (0.000)	0.000** (0.000)	0.000** (0.000)
Email	0.000 (0.000)	0.000 (0.000)	0.001*** (0.000)	0.000 (0.000)	−0.000 (0.000)	0.000** (0.000)
Firm size (R.C. Small)						
Medium	−0.071*** (0.013)	−0.069*** (0.013)	−0.090*** (0.013)	−0.069*** (0.013)	−0.113*** (0.019)	−0.101*** (0.018)
Large	−0.159*** (0.020)	−0.158*** (0.020)	−0.196*** (0.020)	−0.156*** (0.020)	−0.243*** (0.030)	−0.259*** (0.028)
Legal status (R.C.: Open shareholding)						
Closed shareholding	0.012 (0.025)	0.016 (0.025)	0.035 (0.025)	0.018 (0.025)	0.098*** (0.034)	0.068** (0.032)
Sole proprietor	0.164*** (0.027)	0.169*** (0.027)	0.201*** (0.026)	0.170*** (0.027)	0.122*** (0.038)	0.059* (0.035)
Partnership	0.062* (0.032)	0.068** (0.033)	0.041 (0.032)	0.069** (0.033)	−0.002 (0.048)	−0.116** (0.045)
Limited partnership	0.064** (0.031)	0.068** (0.031)	0.205*** (0.030)	0.069** (0.031)	0.011 (0.051)	−0.050 (0.048)
Other form	0.023 (0.046)	0.026 (0.046)	0.087* (0.046)	0.027 (0.046)	0.141** (0.066)	0.137** (0.064)
Sector dummies	Yes	Yes	Yes	Yes	Yes	Yes
Year dummies	Yes	Yes	Yes	Yes	Yes	Yes
Region dummies	Yes	Yes	Yes	Yes	Yes	Yes
Constant	−6.182 (86.956)	−6.154 (86.889)	−5.666 (124.176)	−6.165 (86.969)	−6.045 (221.551)	(120.580)
Pseudo R-squared	0.16	0.17	0.15	0.17	0.16	0.16
N	67,515	66,588	66,588	66,588	32,393	36,162

N.B.: Absolute value of z statistics in parentheses:

* significant at 10%
** significant at 5%
*** significant at 1%

Source: author's own calculations from WBES

2012; Kanbur, 2015), firm size is negatively associated with the likelihood of competing with informal and unregistered businesses; small firms are more likely to do so than medium-sized and larger enterprises. And finally, and with respect to the legal status of firms, there are positive and significant coefficients of sole proprietor and partnerships, meaning that they are more likely to compete with informal and unregistered enterprises.

Model 2 then adds in the first country-level indicator of the log of GDP per capita and shows a significant negative association. This confirms the first tenet of the modernisation thesis (H2a), namely, that the higher the GDP per capita, the lower is the probability that formal firms will compete with informal and unregistered enterprises. Importantly, the significances and signs of all of the first-level variables in Model 1 remain the same when this country-level variable is added in Model 2. The remaining models then include each of the country-level variables associated with each of the tenets of the different theoretical explanations in a sequential manner to either validate or refute the tenets of each theoretical explanation.

To evaluate the second tenet of the modernisation thesis regarding whether the quality of governance, measured here in terms of the level of corruption, is significantly associated with the likelihood of competing with informal or unregistered firms, Model 3 finds a positive association. The higher is the level of corruption, the higher is the likelihood that formal firms compete with unregistered or informal enterprises. This, therefore, confirms Hypothesis H2b of the modernisation thesis.

Turning to the neo-liberal thesis (H3), the first tenet to be analysed is the regulatory burden hypothesis that the prevalence of informal sector entrepreneurship will be greater in countries with higher levels of state interference in the free market, measured by the regulatory burden. Model 4 reveals that there is a statistically significant association, but the sign is in the opposite direction to that suggested by the neo-liberal thesis. The greater is the level of regulation, the less likely are formal firms to compete with informal or unregistered firms (refuting H3a). This, therefore, is supportive of the political economy explanation; the greater the level of state intervention, the less likely are formal firms to be competing with informal or unregistered enterprises (confirming H4a).

It is similarly the case when Hypothesis H3b is tested, namely, that the prevalence of informal sector entrepreneurship will be greater in countries with higher tax rates, measured by the tax revenue-to-GDP ratio. Contrary to the neo-liberal thesis that higher tax rates result in higher levels of informality, Model 5 reveals that the opposite is again the case. The higher is the level of tax revenue to GDP ratio, the less likely are formal firms to be competing with informal or unregistered enterprises. Again, therefore, this refutes H3b and is supportive of the political economy view that the greater the level of state intervention, measured here by the tax revenue-to-GDP ratio, the less likely are formal firms to be competing with informal or unregistered enterprises (confirming H4b).

Finally, and as a test of whether the prevalence of informal entrepreneurship is due to too much or too little state intervention, the association with the expense of government as a percentage of GDP is evaluated. This refutes the view that the greater the expense of government (as a percentage of GDP), the greater is the prevalence of informal entrepreneurship (refuting H3c). Instead quite the opposite is found to be the case. The greater the expense of government (as a percentage of GDP), the lower is the prevalence of informal entrepreneurship (confirming H4c).

Conclusions

This chapter has sought to explain the cross-national variations in informal entrepreneurship identified in Chapter 4. As Part I highlighted, an institutional theory approach has been adopted which asserts that when formal institutional failures result in an asymmetry between the formal and informal institutions, informal entrepreneurship is more prevalent. This chapter has firstly evaluated whether there is a significant association between the prevalence of informal entrepreneurship and institutional asymmetry, and secondly, has sought to begin to identify the formal institutional failures and imperfections that are associated with the greater prevalence of informal entrepreneurship.

To do this, a brief review has been undertaken of both the emergent institutional theory along with the competing theories regarding which formal institutional failures are associated with higher levels of informal entrepreneurship. This has been followed by an evaluation of WBES data from 142 countries collected between 2006 and 2014 on the extent to which formal firms identify that they are competing with unregistered or informal competitors. Reporting the results of a multivariate regression analysis, this chapter has revealed the validity of the institutional asymmetry thesis, which asserts that the greater the institutional asymmetry, the higher are the levels of informal entrepreneurship. To display the formal institutional failures associated with the greater prevalence of informal entrepreneurship, it has then positively confirmed the modernisation and political economy explanations and negatively confirmed the tenets of the neo-liberal thesis.

The finding is that the institutional asymmetry that leads to the greater prevalence of informal entrepreneurship is determined not only by the level of economic development and lower quality of governance but also lower levels of state intervention. The likelihood of formal firms competing with unregistered or informal enterprises is higher in countries where GDP per capita is lower, there are higher levels of corruption, the level of regulations is lower, the tax revenue-to-GDP ratio is lower and the expense of government as a percentage of GDP is lower. This, therefore, has some significant policy implications for countries seeking to tackle informal entrepreneurship. This will be the focus of attention in Part III of this book.

References

Baumol, W.J. (1990). Entrepreneurship: Productive, unproductive and destructive. *Journal of Political Economy*, 98, pp. 893–921.

Baumol, W.J. and Blinder, A. (2008). *Macroeconomics: Principles and policy.* Cincinnati, OH: South-Western Publishing.

Becker, K.F. (2004). *The informal economy.* Stockholm: Swedish International Development Agency.

Castells, M. and Portes, A. (1989). World underneath: The origins, dynamics and effects of the informal economy. In: A. Portes, M. Castells and L. Benton, Eds., *The informal economy: Studies in advanced and less developing countries.* Baltimore: John Hopkins University Press, pp. 19–41.

Dau, L.A. and Cuervo-Cazurra, A. (2014). To formalize or not to formalize: Entrepreneurship and pro-market institutions. *Journal of Business Venturing*, 29, pp. 668–686.

Davis, M. (2006). *Planet of slums.* London: Verso.

De Castro, J.O., Khavul, S. and Bruton, G.D. (2014). Shades of grey: How do informal firms navigate between macro and meso institutional environments? *Strategic Entrepreneurship Journal*, 8, pp. 75–94.

De Soto, H. (1989). *The other path.* London: Harper and Row.

De Soto, H. (2001). *The mystery of capital: Why capitalism triumphs in the West and fails everywhere else.* London: Black Swan.

Eurofound (2013). *Tackling undeclared work in 27 European Union member states and Norway: Approaches and measures since 2008.* Dublin: Eurofound.

Galiani, S. and Weinschelbaum, F. (2012). Modeling informality formally: Households and firms. *Economic Inquiry*, 50(3), pp. 821–838.

Gallin, D. (2001). Propositions on trade unions and informal employment in time of globalization. *Antipode*, 19(4), pp. 531–549.

Geertz, C. (1963). *Old societies and new states: The quest for modernity in Asia and Africa.* Glencoe, IL: Free Press.

Gilbert, A. (1998). *The Latin American city.* London: Latin American Bureau.

Hodosi, A. (2015). Perceptions of irregular immigrants' participation in undeclared work in the United Kingdom from a social trust perspective. *International Journal of Sociology and Social Policy*, 35(5/6), pp. 375–389.

Hudson, J., Williams, C.C., Orviska, M. and Nadin, S. (2012). Evaluating the impact of the informal economy on businesses in South East Europe: Some lessons from the 2009 World Bank Enterprise Survey. *The South-East European Journal of Economics and Business*, 7(1), pp. 99–110.

Hudson, R. (2005). *Economic geographies: Circuits, flows and spaces.* London: Sage.

Kanbur, R. (2015). *Informality: Causes, consequences and policy responses.* London: Discussion Paper no. 10509, Centre for Economic Policy Research (CEPR).

Khan, E.A. and Quaddus, M. (2015). Examining the influence of business environment on socio-economic performance of informal microenterprises: Content analysis and partial least square approach. *International Journal of Sociology and Social Policy*, 35(3/4), pp. 273–288.

Lewis, A. (1959). *The theory of economic growth.* London: Allen and Unwin.

London, T. and Hart, S.L. (2004). Reinventing strategies for emerging markets: Beyond the transnational model. *Journal of International Business Studies*, 35(3), pp. 350–370.

Meagher, K. (2010). *Identity economics: Social networks and the informal economy in Nigeria.* New York: James Currey.

North, D.C. (1990). *Institutions, institutional change and economic performance.* Cambridge: Cambridge University Press.

Nwabuzor, A. (2005). Corruption and development: New initiatives in economic openness and strengthened rule of law. *Journal of Business Ethics*, 59(1), pp. 121–138.

Ostapenko, N. and Williams, C.C. (2016). Determinants of entrepreneurs' views on the acceptability of tax evasion and the informal economy in Slovakia and Ukraine: An institutional asymmetry approach. *International Journal of Entrepreneurship and Small Business*, 28(2/3), pp. 275–289.

Packard, T. (2007). *Do workers in Chile choose informal employment? A dynamic analysis of sector choice*. Washington, DC: World Bank Latin American and the Caribbean Region Social Projection Unit.

Perry, G.E. and Maloney, W.F. (2007). Overview: Informality: Exit and exclusion. In: G.E. Perry, W.F. Maloney, O.S. Arias, P. Fajnzylber, A.D. Mason and J. Saavedra-Chanduvi, Eds., *Informality: Exit and exclusion*. Washington, DC: World Bank, pp. 1–19.

Portes, A. (1994). The informal economy and its paradoxes. In: N.J. Smelser and R. Swedberg, Eds., *The handbook of economic sociology*. Princeton: Princeton University Press, pp. 142–165.

Sallah, A. and Williams, C.C. (2016). Re-theorizing the role of the informal economy in sub-Saharan Africa: Some lessons from the Gambia. *International Journal of Entrepreneurship and Small Business*, 28(2/3), pp. 195–215.

Sassen, S. (1996). Service employment regimes and the new inequality. In: E. Mingione, Ed., *Urban poverty and the underclass*. Oxford: Basil Blackwell, pp. 142–159.

Sauka, A., Schneider, F. and Williams, C.C. (2016). Eds., *Entrepreneurship and the shadow economy: A European perspective*. Cheltenham: Edward Elgar.

Sauvy, A. (1984). *Le travail noir et l'economie de demain*. Paris: Calmann-Levy.

Siqueira, A.C.O., Webb, J.W. and Bruton, G.D. (2016). Informal entrepreneurship and industry conditions. *Entrepreneurship Theory and Practice*, 40(1), pp. 177–200.

Slavnic, Z. (2010). Political economy of informalisation. *European Societies*, 12(1), pp. 3–23.

Small Business Council (2004). *Small business in the informal economy: Making the transition to the formal economy*. London: Small Business Council.

Taiwo, O. (2013). Employment choice and mobility in multi-sector labour markets: Theoretical model and evidence from Ghana. *International Labour Review*, 152, pp. 469–492.

Thai, M.T.T. and Turkina, E. (2014). Macro-level determinants of formal entrepreneurship versus informal entrepreneurship. *Journal of Business Venturing*, 29(4), pp. 490–510.

Tonoyan, V., Strohmeyer, R., Habib, M. and Perlitz, M. (2010). Corruption and entrepreneurship: How formal and informal institutions shape small firm behaviour in transition and mature market economies. *Entrepreneurship Theory and Practice*, 34(5), pp. 803–831.

Torgler, B. and Schneider, F. (2007). *Shadow economy, tax morale, governance and institutional quality: A panel analysis*. Bonn: IZA Discussion Paper no. 2563, IZA.

Vanderseypen, G., Tchipeva, T., Peschner, J., Renooy, P. and Williams, C.C. (2013). Undeclared work: Recent developments. In: European Commission, Ed., *Employment and social developments in Europe 2013*. Brussels: European Commission, pp. 231–274.

Vu, T.T. (2014). *Institutional incongruence and the informal economy: An empirical analysis*. Paper presented at the European Public Choice Society Meeting, Cambridge. Available at: www.econ.cam.ac.uk/epcs2014/openconf/modules/request.

php?module=oc_program&action=summary.php&id=54 (last accessed 6 January 2017).

Webb, J.W., Bruton, G.D., Tihanyi, L. and Ireland, R.D. (2013). Research on entrepreneurship in the informal economy: Framing a research agenda. *Journal of Business Venturing*, 28(5), pp. 598–614.

Webb, J.W., Ireland, R.D. and Ketchen, D.J. (2014). Toward a greater understanding of entrepreneurship and strategy in the informal economy. *Strategic Entrepreneurship Journal*, 8, pp. 1–15.

Webb, J.W., Tihanyi, L., Ireland, R.D. and Sirmon, D.G. (2009). You say illegal, I say legitimate: Entrepreneurship in the informal economy. *Academy of Management Review*, 34(3), pp. 492–510.

Williams, C.C. (2013a). Beyond the formal economy: Evaluating the level of employment in informal sector enterprises in global perspective. *Journal of Developmental Entrepreneurship*, 18(4), pp. 1–18.

Williams, C.C. (2013b). Tackling Europe's informal economy: A critical evaluation of the neo-liberal de-regulatory perspective. *Journal of Contemporary European Research*, 9(3), pp. 261–279.

Williams, C.C. (2014a). Explaining cross-national variations in the commonality of informal sector entrepreneurship: An exploratory analysis of 38 emerging economies. *Journal of Small Business and Entrepreneurship*, 27(2), pp. 191–212.

Williams, C.C. (2014b). Out of the shadows: A classification of economies by the size and character of their informal sector. *Work, Employment and Society*, 28(5), pp. 735–753.

Williams, C.C. (2014c). Tackling enterprises operating in the informal sector in developing and transition economies: A critical evaluation of the neo-liberal policy approach. *Journal of Global Entrepreneurship Research*, 4(1), pp. 1–17.

Williams, C.C. (2015a). Explaining cross-national variations in the informalisation of employment: Some lessons from Central and Eastern Europe. *European Societies*, 17(4), pp. 492–512.

Williams, C.C. (2015b). Explaining cross-national variations in the scale of informal employment: An exploratory analysis of 41 less developed economies. *International Journal of Manpower*, 36(2), pp. 118–135.

Williams, C.C. (2015c). Explaining the informal economy: An exploratory evaluation of competing perspectives. *Relations Industrielles/Industrial Relations*, 70(4), pp. 741–765.

Williams, C.C. (2015d). Out of the margins: Classifying economies by the prevalence and character of employment in the informal economy. *International Labour Review*, 154(3), pp. 331–352.

Williams, C.C. (2015e). Tackling informal employment in developing and transition economies: A critical evaluation of the neo-liberal approach. *International Journal of Business and Globalisation*, 14(3), pp. 251–270.

Williams, C.C. (2015f). Entrepreneurship in the shadow economy: A review of the alternative policy approaches. *International Journal of Small and Medium Enterprises and Sustainability*, 1(1), pp. 51–82.

Williams, C.C. (2015g). *Informal sector entrepreneurship*. Paris: OECD.

Williams, C.C. (2016). Tackling enterprise in the informal economy: An introductory overview. *International Journal of Entrepreneurship and Small Business*, 28(2/3), pp. 139–153.

Williams, C.C., Martinez-Perez, A. and Kedir, A.M. (2017a). Informal entrepreneurship in developing economies: The impacts of starting-up unregistered on firm performance. *Entrepreneurship Theory and Practice*, doi: 10.1111/etap.12238

Williams, C.C. and Shahid, M. (2016). Informal entrepreneurship and institutional theory: Explaining the varying degrees of (in)formalisation of entrepreneurs in Pakistan. *Entrepreneurship and Regional Development*, 28(1/2), pp. 1–25.

Williams, N., Vorley, T. and Williams, C.C. (2017b). *Entrepreneurship and institutions: The causes and consequences of institutional asymmetry*. London: Rowman and Littlefield.

World Bank (2017). *World development indicators*. Washington, DC: World Bank. Available at: http://data.worldbank.org/data-catalog/world-development-indicators (last accessed 10 January 2017).

Part III
Tackling Informal Sector Entrepreneurship

7 Policy Options and Approaches

Introduction

Having analysed the variations in the prevalence of informal entrepreneurship, the impacts of starting up unregistered in the informal sector, and the range of formal institutional failures that lead to higher levels of informal entrepreneurship, the issue of tackling entrepreneurship in the informal sector is now addressed.

To start to do so, this chapter reviews each of the four possible policy goals available to governments, namely, taking no action, eradicating informal entrepreneurship, deregulating formal entrepreneurship or formalising informal entrepreneurship. In each case, the disadvantages and advantages of these goals of policy are reviewed. This will reveal that so far as the first goal of taking no action is concerned, the disadvantages of doing nothing about informal entrepreneurship appear to far outweigh the advantages. This is because although it might enable entrepreneurs to use the informal sector as a test bed for their ventures, it has significant disadvantages for not only formal businesses (e.g., unfair competition), informal businesses (e.g., the inability to gain access to credit to expand) and customers (e.g., no guarantee that health and safety standards have been followed) but also for governments (e.g., taxes owed are not collected). Secondly, if eradicating informal entrepreneurship is pursued as the goal of policy, the disadvantages again appear to outweigh the advantages. This is because although it gets rid of entrepreneurial endeavour in the informal sector that can be harmful to the formal sector and economic development, it has the significant disadvantage of repressing precisely the enterprise culture and entrepreneurship which governments otherwise wish to foster for the purposes of promoting economic development and growth. Thirdly, and in relation to the goal of deregulating formal entrepreneurship, the disadvantages are again argued to far outweigh the advantages in that the overall outcome is a levelling down rather than up of working conditions and social protection. Instead this chapter will argue that formalising informal entrepreneurship appears to be the most viable policy goal. Indeed this is also the conclusion of most supranational agencies when considering what is to be done about informal entrepreneurship (ILO, 2014; OECD, 2015).

Based on this goal of formalising informal entrepreneurship, the second section of this chapter will briefly introduce the policy approaches and measures available for achieving this objective. This will outline two broad approaches. On the one hand, there is what is here referred to as the conventional 'hard' direct policy approach. This seeks not only to dissuade entrepreneurs from operating in the informal sector but also to incentivise and encourage them to operate in the formal sector. To achieve this, measures are used that directly increase the costs and reduce the benefits of informality and reduce the costs and increase the benefits of operating in the formal sector. In doing so, the intention is to address the formal institutional failure, namely, the powerlessness of formal institutions which results in the greater prevalence of informal entrepreneurship. Using these policy measures alone, however, does not tackle the other formal institutional failures and imperfections that produce institutional asymmetry and thus the greater prevalence of informal entrepreneurship.

On the other hand, therefore, and to address the other formal institutional failures that lead to institutional symmetry and the greater prevalence of informal entrepreneurship, a range of what will be here termed 'soft' indirect macro-level policy approaches and measures are also introduced. These include not only a variety of process innovations across government that develop the perceived level of procedural and redistributive justice and fairness of government to reduce institutional symmetry but also various wider formal institutional failures which Part II revealed are significantly associated with greater institutional asymmetry, such as increasing the level of regulation, tax revenue as a percentage of GDP and the expense of government as a percentage of GDP.

These two broad policy approaches are not either/or choices. They are not mutually exclusive. Given that each policy approach tackles a different set of formal institutional failures and imperfections, both are required to tackle informal entrepreneurship. Indeed in recent years, there has emerged a debate about how these should be combined and sequenced. The concluding section of this chapter will provide an introductory overview of two different views on how this might occur. On the one hand, a responsive regulation approach will be introduced that combines all these approaches but sequences them by starting with the soft indirect policy measures, and if these do not have the desired effect on behaviour, then hard incentives to formalise are used to elicit behaviour change, and as a last resort when all else fails, the hard deterrents are employed to bring about behaviour change. On the other hand, a slippery slope approach will be introduced which argues that compliance is greatest when both the power of authorities (achieved by using a hard direct policy approach and measures) and trust in authorities (achieved using a soft indirect policy approach and measures) are high. If either the power of, or trust in, authorities is low, then governments will find themselves on a slippery slope, and informal entrepreneurship will prevail. Reviewing the evidence base to support this approach, the argument of this chapter is that this latter approach of concurrently combining the hard direct and soft indirect policy approaches is potentially the way forward for those seeking to formalise informal entrepreneurship. This will then set the scene for the next two chapters, which review the hard direct and soft indirect policy approaches in turn to understand what measures can be used to formalise informal entrepreneurship.

Policy Choices: Evaluating the Possible Goals

Reviewing the possible goals of policy which are open to governments, there are logically four possibilities. Policy makers can select to either take no action, eradicate informal entrepreneurship, deregulate formal entrepreneurship or transform informal entrepreneurship into formal entrepreneurship. At first glance, some of these goals may seem a little outlandish. However, all have been advocated by different scholars in recent decades. As such, none can be rejected without seeking to evaluate their advantages and disadvantages.

Take No Action

The first policy goal that needs to be reviewed is that of doing nothing about informal entrepreneurship. Rationales for taking no action might be, as shown in Chapter 5, that informal entrepreneurship it is a seedbed for new venture creation, a breeding ground for the microenterprise system and a test bed for fledgling enterprises. The problem with doing nothing, nevertheless, and as Table 7.1 summarises, is that informal entrepreneurship has significant negative consequences for formal enterprises, informal enterprises, customers and governments along with the wider society and economy.

Until now, entrepreneurship scholarship has not rigorously evaluated whether, and the extent to which, many of these supposed advantages and disadvantages are valid in lived practice in different contexts. This lacuna in scholarship will need be filled in the future, as Chapter 5 concluded. Although such a rigorous evidence base is lacking, the widespread normative consensus is nonetheless that on balance, the disadvantages of taking no action outweigh the advantages. The view is therefore that this is not a valid policy approach. Instead interventions are believed to be required in the realm of informal entrepreneurship. What form of intervention, therefore, is needed?

Eradicate Informal Entrepreneurship

A first form of intervention that could be pursued is to eradicate informal entrepreneurship. If entrepreneurs are represented as 'rational economic actors' who will operate in the informal sector if the payoff is greater than

Table 7.1 Advantages and Disadvantages of Informal Entrepreneurship By Stakeholder Group

Disadvantages	Advantages
For informal sector entrepreneurs:	
Lack of access to capital, credit and financial services to develop and grow, partly due to limited credit history (ILO, 2014)	A source of income to stay out of poverty
Need to keep the business small to stay 'under the radar' of the authorities (Williams *et al.*, 2012)	Flexibility in where, when and how to work (especially important for women who remain responsible for childcare)
Higher barriers of entry to formal markets due to inability to provide employment history to back up their skills (ILO, 2014)	Reduce barriers to entry into work because the majority of informal work starts with close social relations
Cannot secure formal intellectual property rights to process and product innovations (De Beer et al., 2013)	Provide an alternative when the values, norms and beliefs of entrepreneurs do not align with the codified laws and regulations of formal institutions (Webb *et al.*, 2009, 2013)
Lack ability to develop and grow due to the lack of support available compared with formal businesses (ILO, 2014; Karjanen, 2014; Williams *et al.*, 2012)	
For formal entrepreneurs:	
Unfair competitive advantage for informal over formal entrepreneurs (Andrews *et al.*, 2011; Karlinger, 2013)	Provide entrepreneurs with escape route from corrupt public sector officials (Tonoyan *et al.*, 2010)
Deregulatory culture results enticing law-abiding entrepreneurs into a 'race to the bottom' away from regulatory compliance (Gallin, 2001)	Provide an exit strategy in contexts where the regulatory burden stifles business development (De Soto, 1989)
'Hyper-casualisation' as more formal entrepreneurs are driven into the informal entrepreneurship to compete	Cheap source of labour and raw materials for formal firms and reduced production costs through outsourcing and subcontracting to informal enterprises (Ketchen *et al.*, 2014)
For customers:	
Lack legal recourse if a poor job is done, insurance coverage or guarantees in relation to the work conducted and certainty that health and safety regulations have been followed (Small Business Council, 2004; Williams *et al.*, 2012)	More affordable product or service offered to or asked for by customers if payment is made in cash and no receipts change hands (Ketchen *et al.*, 2014)
Hugely inefficient and unlikely to be capable of charging lower prices for the same products and services (La Porta and Shleifer, 2014)	

Disadvantages	Advantages
For governments:	
Cause a loss of revenue for the state in terms of non-payment of taxes owed (Bajada and Schneider, 2005; Müller and Miggelbrink, 2014; Sauka *et al.*, 2016)	Income from informal entrepreneurship spent in formal economy boosts demand for formal goods and services and contributes to 'official' economic growth, and employment (Ketchen *et al.*, 2014)
Reduce state's ability to achieve social cohesion by reducing the money available to governments to pursue social integration and mobility (Andrews *et al.*, 2011)	'On-the-job' training in informal enterprises alleviates pressure on the state and its agencies during times of reduced public spending
Lead to a loss of regulatory control over work conditions and service provision in the economy (ILO, 2014; Williams and Lansky, 2013)	Breeding ground for the microenterprise system (De Soto, 1989; Williams and Martinez-Perez, 2014a)
May encourage a casual attitude towards the law more widely (Dong et al., 2012; Karjanen, 2014; Ojo *et al.*, 2013; Sasunkevich, 2014)	Test bed for fledgling businesses (Williams and Martinez-Perez, 2014a)
Low-productivity informal entrepreneurs stay small to avoid detection and thus lack the scale to produce efficiently, although the substantial cost advantages gained by avoiding taxes and regulations offset their low productivity and small scale, with deleterious consequences for economic development and growth	Challenges the codified laws and regulations of formal institutions (Webb *et al.*, 2013)

the expected cost of being caught and punished (Allingham and Sandmo, 1972), then the way in which eradication of informal entrepreneurship can be achieved is by altering the cost/benefit ratio confronting those entrepreneurs participating or thinking about participating in the informal sector (e.g., Grabiner, 2000; Hasseldine and Li, 1999; Richardson and Sawyer, 2001).

However, whether this is, firstly, achievable and, secondly, appropriate is open to question. On the one hand, the achievement of such a goal is based on the premise that government authorities can be powerful enough to alter this cost/benefit ratio in a manner that is sufficient to eradicate informal entrepreneurship. Whether this is feasible in those areas of world where informal entrepreneurship is most prevalent is open to debate. This is because those areas of the developing world where informal entrepreneurship is most prevalent tend to have weak formal institutional environments. In other words, the enforcement regimes tend to be ineffective. Whether it is possible for the power of authorities to be sufficient to make the eradication of informal entrepreneurship a feasible option, or even its significant reduction, is questionable. Indeed even when advanced economies have attempted to improve detection and/or penalties to increase the power of authorities in order that informal entrepreneurship can be reduced, the evidence that this is effective is by no means clear cut. Some find that increasing the sanctions and risks of detection reduces the informal sector (De Juan *et al.*, 1994; Slemrod *et al.*, 2001), but others identify that it either has no effect on the size of the informal sector or even that the informal sector grows because such an approach might reduce their willingness to comply by reducing their belief in the fairness of the system (Bergman and Nevarez, 2006; Murphy, 2005; Schneider and Enste, 2002).

It can also be questioned whether the eradication of informal entrepreneurship is appropriate. If informal entrepreneurship is recognised as a breeding ground for the microenterprise system and a seedbed for enterprise culture, this sphere is a potential asset that needs to be harnessed and is a driver of economic development (e.g., Williams, 2006). Seeking its eradication will stamp out the entrepreneurship and enterprise culture that governments across the world wish to foster to achieve economic development and growth. The resultant challenge for governments is therefore not so much to eradicate informal entrepreneurship but more to join up their policy approaches towards informal entrepreneurship with their policy goal of nurturing enterprise culture and entrepreneurship as a means of achieving economic development and growth. Indeed given that a multitude of entrepreneurs currently exist but are operating in the informal sector in many developing and developed countries, it seems nonsensical to pursue for example enterprise education to create entrepreneurs and entrepreneurship when so many entrepreneurs already exist in the informal sector and are being deterred from being entrepreneurial. Indeed if governments do not manage to join up their policies on informal entrepreneurship with the wider promotion of entrepreneurship and enterprise culture, then governments will with each new policy initiative to stamp out informal entrepreneurship destroy precisely the entrepreneurship and enterprise culture that they are otherwise seeking to nurture and develop.

Deregulate Formal Entrepreneurship

A third goal open to governments is to deregulate formal entrepreneurship. This in effect shifts formal entrepreneurship into the informal sector, although it is no longer denoted as the informal sector because there are no rules being broken since they have been abandoned. This approach has been advocated by neo-liberal commentators. As an approach, it is based on a belief that informal entrepreneurship is a result of over-regulation of the market and burdensome regulations (Sauvy, 1984; De Soto, 1989, 2001), and therefore the objective is to deregulate the formal sector in order that all activities are performed in a manner akin to what is currently the informal sector, although enterprises would not be engaged in informal entrepreneurship because they would be adhering to the regulations that remain.

This policy approach, nevertheless, suffers from a number of intransigent problems. The assumption is that deregulation reduces informal entrepreneurship. However, there is growing evidence, as shown in the last chapter, that decreasing the level of state intervention in the economy has the opposite effect; it leads to greater levels of informal entrepreneurship (Kus, 2010, 2014; Williams, 2013, 2014a,b). Indeed even if one rejects the evidence presented in this book and assumes for a moment that deregulation does lead to greater formal entrepreneurship, the outcome would be a levelling down rather than up of working conditions (Williams, 2006, 2014a). It would be formality in a context where there were lower levels of social protection and fewer rules and regulations, such as in relation to occupational health and safety, working conditions and customer protection. In sum, even if deregulation were to reduce the magnitude of informal entrepreneurship which by definition is a product of the regulations imposed on formal entrepreneurship, the impact would be probably to widen inequalities and a deterioration of working conditions compared with more regulated states.

Transform Informal Entrepreneurship Into Formal Entrepreneurship

Rather than pursue the goals of taking no action, eradicating informal entrepreneurship or deregulating formal entrepreneurship, a final choice is to adopt the policy goal of transforming informal entrepreneurship into formal entrepreneurship (ILO, 2014; OECD, 2015; Small Business Council, 2004; Williams, 2006; Williams and Nadin, 2012a,b, 2013a,b, 2014). The advantages of formalising informal entrepreneurship vary according to whether one is examining formal entrepreneurs, informal entrepreneurs, customers or the government and wider economy and society.

So far as formal enterprises are concerned, the transforming of informal entrepreneurship into formal entrepreneurship would put a stop to the unfair competitive advantage of informal enterprises over those who abide by the codified laws and regulations (Evans *et al.*, 2006; ILO, 2014; Small Business Council, 2004). This policy approach would also mean that the business community could pursue what can be termed a 'high road' rather than 'low road' approach by adopting higher regulatory standards on working conditions such as health and safety and labour standards and worker protection (Grabiner, 2000; Eurofound, 2013; ILO, 2014; Williams and Gurtoo, 2017; Williams and Windebank, 1998). For informal entrepreneurs, meanwhile, there are multiple benefits to legitimising their endeavour. They would be able to escape the pressure to enter exploitative relationships with the formal sector, which are manifested in the growth of formal businesses subcontracting and outsourcing production to the informal sector to reduce production costs (Gallin, 2001; Williams and Windebank, 1998) and achieve equivalent levels of legal protection as formal enterprises and entrepreneurs (ILO, 2014; Morris and Polese, 2014). Informal entrepreneurs would also be able to secure formal intellectual property rights for their products and processes (De Beer *et al.*, 2013) and transcend the current structural impediments that prevent them from growing their business ventures, such as their lack of access to advice and support as well as capital (ILO, 2014).

For customers, the advantages of formalising informal entrepreneurship and enterprise are that these customers will benefit from legal recourse if a poor job is done, will have access to insurance coverage, can benefit from guarantees with regard to the quality of the work conducted and can have certainty that health and safety regulations have been followed (Williams and Martinez-Perez, 2014a,b). Finally, and for governments, the benefits of formalising informal entrepreneurship are that it improves the level of public revenue via taxes paid, therefore helping governments to pursue higher expenditure on social integration and mobility projects (Williams and Windebank, 1998). This can result in a virtuous cycle in the sense that enterprises and entrepreneurs will then see the benefits of being formal in terms of the additional public goods and services provision, and this will make them more likely to wish to voluntarily comply (assuming of course that they agree with how the public money is being spent). Formalising informal entrepreneurship also enables more formal jobs and thus improves employment participation rates and, importantly, facilitates a joining up of the policy approach towards informal entrepreneurship with the policy approaches towards entrepreneurship and social inclusion (Dekker *et al.*, 2010; European Commission, 2007; Small Business Council, 2004). It also results in a more positive attitude towards the law more widely (Polese, 2014; Sasunkevich, 2014).

In sum, this brief review of the four policy choices reveals that the first option of taking no action would leave intact the current disadvantages for formal entrepreneurs (e.g., unfair competition), informal entrepreneurs (e.g., the inability to gain access to credit to expand), customers (e.g., no guarantee of health and safety standards) and governments (e.g., taxes owed are not collected). Secondly, eradicating informal entrepreneurship would result in governments repressing exactly the entrepreneurship and enterprise culture that they wish to foster, and thirdly, deregulating formal entrepreneurship would level down working conditions rather than up. Transforming informal entrepreneurship into formal entrepreneurship is consequently the most viable policy choice. How, therefore, might this be achieved?

Formalising Informal Entrepreneurship: 'Hard' and 'Soft' Policy Measures

Reviewing the literature on the different policy approaches towards the informal sector, much of the literature identifies two contrasting policy approaches. These are variously termed the 'economic deterrence' approach versus the 'fiscal psychology' approach (Hasseldine and Li, 1999); a 'chauvinistic' versus 'softy' approach (Cullis and Lewis, 1997); a 'deterrence model' versus an 'accommodative model' (Murphy, 2005, 2008); 'regulatory formalism' versus 'responsive regulation' (Braithwaite, 2002); 'market-based' versus 'rights-based' (Vainio, 2012); 'deterrence' versus 'tax morale' (Ahmed and Braithwaite, 2005); 'command and control' versus 'responsive regulation' (Commonwealth Association of Tax Administrators, 2006); a 'sticks' versus 'carrots' approach (Small Business Council, 2004) or a 'deterrence' versus an 'enabling' approach (Williams, 2004a,b).

Much of this literature differentiates in some form between what is here termed a 'hard' direct and a 'soft' indirect policy approach. The hard direct policy approach views informal entrepreneurs as rational economic actors and seeks to change the cost/benefit ratio confronting them by either punishing non-compliant ('bad') behaviour and/or encouraging and rewarding compliant ('good') behaviour. The soft indirect policy approach, meanwhile, views informal entrepreneurs more as social actors who have decided not to comply because specific formal institutional failures and imperfections have led to the situation where there is an incongruence between their own norms, values and beliefs regarding whether it is acceptable to participate in the informal sector and the codified laws and regulations. As such, it seeks to reduce this institutional asymmetry by either changing the norms, values and beliefs of entrepreneurs or the formal institutions so that entrepreneurs have a greater desire to adhere to the codified laws and regulations.

Figure 7.1 provides a summary of these hard direct and soft indirect policy approaches towards tackling informal entrepreneurship. In the hard direct policy approach, as can be seen, the emphasis is on engendering compliance to the rules by treating people as rational economic actors and ensuring that the costs of operating informally are outweighed by the benefits of operating in the formal sector. This is accomplished either by using deterrence measures that increase the costs of non-compliance ('sticks') and/or by making the conduct of work in the formal sector more beneficial and easier ('carrots'). In the soft indirect approach, meanwhile, there is a shift away from using 'sticks' and 'carrots' to elicit behaviour change and enforce compliance. Instead, the focus is upon developing the social contract between the state and its citizens by nurturing a high-trust, high-commitment culture by dealing with the formal institutional failures and imperfections that lead to an asymmetry between a society's formal and informal institutions. Here therefore, each approach is reviewed in turn.

Hard Direct Compliance Approach

To tackle informal entrepreneurship, a first means of doing so is to employ a hard direct compliance approach that treats entrepreneurs as rational economic actors and seeks to change the costs of engaging in informal entrepreneurship and benefits of operating formally. As the OECD (2008: 82) states,

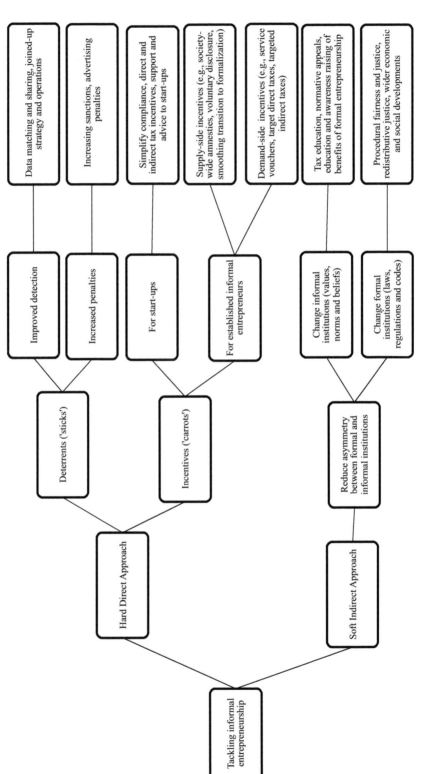

Figure 7.1 Policy Approaches and Measures Towards Tackling Informal Entrepreneurship

'[c]ombating informal employment requires a comprehensive approach to reduce the costs and increase the benefits to business and workers of operating formally'. To outline this hard direct compliance approach therefore, firstly, the measures it uses to detect and punish non-compliant (bad) behaviour are briefly introduced followed, secondly, by its use of 'bribes' or incentives that encourage and reward compliant (good) behaviour.

Hard Direct Approach: Detecting and Punishing Non-Compliance

The conventional reliance on deterrents to engender a formalisation of informal entrepreneurship has its origins in the classical works of both Jeremy Bentham (1788) and Cesare Beccaria (1797). In their classic utilitarian theory of crime, the view is that people are rational actors who act in a way that maximises their expected utility. Put another way, they evaluate the opportunities and risks of being non-compliant with the formal rules and decide to flout the formal rules if the expected penalty and probability of being caught is small relative to the benefits. As Bentham (1788: 399) put it,

> the profit of the crime is the force which urges a man [sic] to delinquency: the pain of the punishment is the force employed to restrain him [sic] from it. If the first . . . be the greater, the crime will be committed.

The belief, therefore, was that the judiciary and governments must deter these rational actors by making the costs outweigh the benefits of non-compliance.

During the late 1960s, this rational actor approach towards criminal activity became popularised by Becker (1968). He argued that governments must change the cost/benefit ratio to make compliant behaviour the rational choice. Interestingly, his treatise placed little emphasis on encouraging and incentivising compliant behaviour. Instead, there was a focus upon increasing the probability of detection and raising the penalties to increase the costs and make non-compliance an irrational behaviour. Prior to the popularising of this rational actor approach by Becker (1968), criminal behaviour had been commonly seen to result from mental illness and/or the social environment, and criminals were thus depicted as victims of their context. Becker's work therefore instigated a paradigm shift in how criminal behaviour was conceptualised.

During the early 1970s, in a seminal paper, Allingham and Sandmo (1972) applied Becker's rational actor approach towards crime to the topic of tax non-compliance. They similarly argued that the non-compliant, such as informal entrepreneurs, make the rational economic decision to operate informally when the payoff is greater than the expected cost of detection and punishment. To deter informality in consequence, what is required is to alter the cost/benefit ratio facing those participating or considering engagement in the informal sector. This view became widely adopted (e.g.,

Grabiner, 2000; Hasseldine and Li, 1999; Job *et al.*, 2007; Richardson and Sawyer, 2001). For most involved in discussing this approach, and similar to the study of crime, the emphasis was on increasing the costs of informality rather than encouraging or incentivising formalisation. Deterrence measures were used that focused upon the cost side of the equation by increasing the actual and perceived risks and sanctions for those engaged in informal entrepreneurship. This was achieved, on the one hand, by raising the perceived or actual likelihood of detection and/or, on the other hand, by increasing the penalties and sanctions for those doing so. This can be therefore seen as what is more widely referred to as a 'negative reinforcement' approach; it changes behaviour by using 'sticks' that punish non-compliant ('bad') behaviour.

This emphasis on deterring informality was perhaps valid and highly appropriate, similar to crime, when the policy goal was eradicating non-compliant behaviour (e.g., informal entrepreneurship). However, with the widespread shift in approach across both supranational institutions, such as the ILO and OECD (ILO, 2014; OECD, 2015), as well as across most national governments (Eurofound, 2013; Williams, 2016, 2017a,b; Williams and Nadin, 2012a), away from eradicating informal entrepreneurship, and towards formalising informal entrepreneurship, questions began to be raised about whether deterrents, although necessary, are sufficient. The result of this shift towards formalising informal entrepreneurship has thus been a raft of new policy measures that seek to encourage and incentivise formal entrepreneurship.

Hard Approach: Compliance Through Incentives

The emphasis on formalising informal entrepreneurship has therefore resulted in a shift away from deterrence measures alone and towards providing incentives to encourage informal entrepreneurs to formalise (Small Business Council, 2004; Williams, 2006). In other words, rather than simply punish non-compliant behaviour, measures have been sought to encourage and reward behaviour that complies with the codified laws and regulations, rather than just take it as given that entrepreneurs will do so. In the realm of tackling informal entrepreneurship, and as displayed in Figure 7.1, these measures take two forms.

On the one hand, a range of measures can be introduced that provide incentives for encouraging entrepreneurs at the business start-up stage to establish their ventures on a registered formal basis. These measures can include the simplification of compliance to make it easier for them to do so, the use of direct and indirect tax incentives that make it beneficial to start up on a formal registered basis and the provision of support and advice to entrepreneurs about how to start up on a registered and formal basis.

On the other hand, a range of measures can be introduced that provide incentives for encouraging those currently operating as informal entrepreneurs to make the transition to formal entrepreneurship. Such measures can take the form of either supply-side measures providing incentives and encouragement to informal entrepreneurs to formalise or demand-side measures targeting their customers and providing them with encouragement and incentives to use formal rather than informal enterprises. Supply-side measures that encourage and incentivise informal entrepreneurs to formalise include society-wide amnesties, voluntary disclosure schemes and the introduction of schemes that facilitate them to undergo a smooth transition to legitimacy. Demand-side measures that incentivise and encourage customers to use formal rather than informal enterprises when sourcing goods and services include the use of service vouchers and targeted direct and indirect tax incentives.

Soft Indirect Commitment Approach

The problem with using a hard compliance approach to change behaviour is that although this helps improve the power of authorities to elicit behaviour change, informal entrepreneurs are not always rational economic actors with perfect information available to them. Many informal entrepreneurs are not able to calculate the costs and benefits of their actions, often misperceive or do not perceive the true costs, have limited self-control and are influenced by their informal institutional environment. Perhaps most importantly, they are motivated not just by self-interest and what is most profitable for them but also by additional motives including redistribution, fairness, reciprocity, social customs, norms and morality (Alm, 2011).

Based on this recognition that informal entrepreneurs are also often as much social actors as rational economic actors, the soft indirect approach moves away from solely using 'sticks' and 'carrots' to change behaviour. Rather, the focus is upon improving the social contract between the state and its citizens by addressing the formal institutional failures and imperfections that result in institutional asymmetry and a low-trust, low-commitment culture. The intention in this social actor approach, therefore, is to bring about willing or voluntary commitment to compliant behaviour to establish a high-trust, high-commitment culture rather than force entrepreneurs to comply using what in effect are threats, harassment and/or bribes.

Here, in consequence, the intention is to encourage a voluntary commitment to acting in a compliant manner (Alm et al., 1995; Andreoni et al., 1998; Torgler, 2003; Weigel et al., 1987; Wenzel, 2002). The origins of this approach lie in the classical work of Georg von Schanz (1890), who over a century ago emphasised the importance of the social (tax) contract between the state and its citizens. Some six decades later, the German 'Cologne school of tax psychology' sought to further develop this approach by undertaking a series of surveys to measure tax morale (see Schmölders, 1952, 1960, 1962; Strümpel, 1969), viewing it as an important and integral attitude that was strongly related to non-compliance (see Schmölders, 1960). Although this body of research, akin to the social environment approach to criminal behaviour, went into abeyance from the 1970s onwards due to the advent of the rational economic actor model, it has begun to resurface since the turn of the millennium (see, e.g., Kirchler, 1997, 1998, 1999, 2007; Torgler, 2003, 2005a,b, 2006a,b, 2007, 2011).

When this soft indirect commitment approach is read through the lens of institutional asymmetry theory, the underlying premise is that informal entrepreneurship arises when the laws and regulations of formal institutions are not aligned with the norms, beliefs and values of informal institutions (i.e., a lack of 'vertical trust'). When the formal and informal institutions are wholly in symmetry, informal entrepreneurship would not exist, except unintentionally, since all entrepreneurs would believe in acting in a compliant manner. However, when the norms, values and beliefs differ to the laws and regulations, resulting in what formal institutions deem to be illegal activities being socially legitimate in terms of the norms, values and beliefs of the society or particular population groups, informal entrepreneurship prevails. To tackle informal entrepreneurship, therefore, there is a need to reduce this institutional asymmetry. Two ways of achieving this exist.

On the one hand, governments can alter the norms, values and beliefs of the population regarding the acceptability of informal entrepreneurship so that these align with the laws, regulations and codes of formal institutions. On the other hand, governments can alter the formal institutions to align better with the norms, values and beliefs of the wider society. By doing so, formal and informal institutions can become more aligned, resulting in a reduction in informal entrepreneurship due to greater self-regulation brought about by an intrinsic social commitment to the formal institutions.

These changes in the formal institutions are of two types. Firstly, changes can be sought in the processes of formal institutions in terms of tax fairness, procedural justice and redistributive justice. Fairness here refers to the extent to which people believe they are paying their fair share compared with others (Wenzel, 2004). Redistributive justice refers to whether they receive the goods and services they believe that they deserve given the taxes that they pay (Richardson and Sawyer, 2001) and procedural justice to the degree to which they believe that the tax authority has treated then in a respectful, impartial and responsible manner (Braithwaite and Reinhart, 2000; Murphy, 2005). Secondly, changes can be sought in the products of formal institutions, by which is meant the wider economic and social conditions discussed in the last chapter in recognition that informal entrepreneurship is in large part a by-product of these macro-level structural conditions.

Combining the Hard and Soft Policy Approaches

To tackle informal entrepreneurship, it is not an either/or choice between using either hard direct or soft indirect policy approaches. Although the focus of most national governments until now when seeking eradication has been upon hard direct controls, especially deterrence measures that increase the costs of participating in informal entrepreneurship by increasing the risks of detection and levels of punishment (see ILO, 2014; OECD, 2015; Williams, 2015), this does not mean that the solution is therefore to use either 'bribes' or soft indirect measures as a replacement when seeking to formalise informal entrepreneurship. The approaches and measures are not mutually exclusive.

Indeed, there has been growing recognition that even if soft indirect measures are a useful and innovative new means of formalising informal entrepreneurship which could be usefully adopted to tackle formal institutional failings (Eurofound, 2013; Williams, 2014a, 2017a,b), these sets of measures, although necessary, might well be insufficient on their own. Hard direct compliance measures are also required. For example, governments may target key country-level macro-economic and social conditions that have a direct influence on the prevalence of informal entrepreneurship, change the culture of government departments, such as tax offices and labour inspectorates, towards a more customer-oriented approach, and introduce public campaigns to encourage a commitment to compliance while simplifying regulatory compliance for business start-ups and introducing incentives for established informal entrepreneurs (e.g., amnesties and tax deductions). However, and at the same time, and in relation to those who fail to comply, they also need sanctions and the ability to detect those operating in the informal sector.

In consequence, the debate is not whether to use either hard direct or soft indirect policy measures. The emergent consensus is that both are required. Instead the major issue is determining which specific policy measures in each approach are most effective and what is the most effective way of putting these measures together in various combinations and sequences to engender effective compliance. For example, measures to improve detection through inspections are currently often combined with campaigns to raise awareness. Tougher sanctions furthermore, often follow amnesties and voluntary disclosure schemes. However, whether these are the most effective combinations and sequences that can be used to foster the formalisation of informal entrepreneurship needs to be evaluated. Nevertheless, two particular approaches have come to the fore in recent years in the scholarly literature that provide ways of combining these hard and soft policy measures in particular sequences, namely, the responsive regulation approach and the slippery slope framework.

Responsive Regulation

Responsive regulation engages entrepreneurs to reflect on their obligations and to take responsibility for operating in a manner consistent with the codified laws and regulations of formal institutions. This approach seeks to win their 'hearts and minds' to bring about a culture of commitment to the formal rules to obviate the need for entrepreneurs to be regulated by external rules. Nevertheless, although this approach gives primacy to the use of soft indirect commitment measures, it does not exclusively limit itself to such measures (see Braithwaite, 2009).

The Australian Tax Office for example has gone some way to adopting this responsive regulation approach. In the first instance soft indirect measures are employed to bring about voluntary adherence to the formal rules, followed by persuasion using incentives and encouragement, and only as a last resort for the small minority still refusing to comply with the formal rules does it use deterrence measures (Braithwaite, 2009; Job *et al.*, 2007). Put another way, the responsive regulation approach is based on a regulatory pyramid. The premise underpinning this approach is that in most cases, an authority does not need to use deterrents to achieve adherence to the formal rules. Instead it can start with soft indirect policy measures, and if these do not result in adherence to the formal rules with some groups, then hard direct incentives can be used on these groups, with hard direct deterrents only employed as a last resort. The level of directness and intrusiveness therefore escalates up the pyramid until it reaches the policy intervention that elicits adherence.

The recognition is that a continuum of attitudes exists towards being compliant and that different policy measures are appropriate for each of these different motivational postures. The result is a temporal sequencing of policy measures, starting with soft indirect policy measures applied to the majority who adopt a positive posture (i.e., commitment), and feel morally committed to follow the formal rules, then hard direct incentives for those with less positive postures (i.e., capitulation or resistance), and only after these fail are hard direct deterrents used for those who are disengaged from the formal institutions (Braithwaite, 2003).

Of course, whether this sequencing is the appropriate combination and temporal sequence is debateable. Until now, no evaluations exist of whether this sequencing is the most appropriate and/or effective means of ensuring commitment to the formal laws and regulations. Although it seems logically to be appropriate and even an effective means of doing so, no evidence base currently exists that this is the case.

Slippery Slope Framework

Another way of combining hard direct and soft indirect measures is to adopt the 'slippery slope framework' (Kirchler *et al.*, 2008). This distinguishes two types of compliance approach, namely, voluntary compliance (achieved using soft indirect measures) and enforced compliance (achieved using hard direct measures). Voluntary compliance is viewed as occurring where there is trust in the authorities. Enforced compliance, meanwhile, is viewed as requiring the authorities to have power (i.e., the ability to get citizens to do what they were before not going to do in the way in which the authorities wish them to do it). When there is neither trust in authorities and authorities have no power, then authorities find themselves on a slippery slope, and informal entrepreneurship will be prevalent.

To formalise informal entrepreneurship, therefore, one can either increase the power of authorities and/or trust in the authorities. The hard direct measures approach, as shown, is used to increase the power of authorities, while the soft indirect measures are used to increase trust in authorities. In practice, however, these are not mutually exclusive approaches. Both can be used together concurrently to formalise informal entrepreneurship. The slippery slope framework accepts that this is the case and seeks to combine both to achieve the formalisation of informal entrepreneurship.

In recent years, there has started to emerge an evidence base that this concurrent combining of voluntary and enforced compliance is the most effective approach. Kogler *et al.* (2013) conducted an experiment to manipulate the power of authorities and citizens' trust in authorities using scenario techniques and to assess intentions to declare taxes honestly in four European countries: Austria, Hungary, Romania and Russia. The aim was to test the impact of power and trust on compliance in countries with different institutional, political, and societal characteristics. In a 2 × 2 design, scenarios described authorities as either trustworthy or untrustworthy and as either powerful or powerless. The finding is that intentions to declare taxes honestly were highest in all countries if the authorities were described as powerful and trustworthy; conversely, evasion was high if both power and trust were at a minimum. In addition, perceptions of high power boosted enforced compliance, whereas high trust was related to strong voluntary cooperation. As in many studies on non-compliance, moreover, and reflecting the finding in Chapter 4, women were found to be more honest than men.

Kogler *et al.* (2015), furthermore, based on a survey of 476 self-employed, show that perceptions of procedural and distributive justice predict voluntary compliance, and trust in authorities mediates this observed relation. In addition, the relation between retributive justice (i.e., the perceived fairness with regard to the sanctioning of self-employed tax evaders) and enforced compliance is mediated by power, which is the relation between perceived deterrence of authorities' enforcement strategies. With regard to both retributive justice and deterrence, a mediational effect of trust on the relation to voluntary compliance was identified. Moreover, voluntary and enforced compliance were related to perceived social norms, but these relations were mediated neither by trust nor power.

In a further extension of the slippery slope framework, Gangl *et al.* (2012) distinguish three climates: a service climate, an antagonistic climate and a confidence climate. They argue that a service climate requires the legitimate power of authorities and that this leads to reason-based trust on the part of citizens and increases voluntary compliance. An antagonistic climate, meanwhile, occurs when the coercive power of authorities prevails, leading to enforced compliance and an atmosphere where authorities and citizens work against each other. A confidence climate, finally, is characterised by an implicit trust between authorities and citizens (an unintentional and automatic form of trust), which results in the perception of compliance as a moral obligation and again voluntary co-operation of citizens.

That power and trust are essential for good governance is also now being seriously considered by authorities in various countries (OECD, 2013). For instance, to improve interactions with their clientele, tax administrators in the Netherlands and Austria have started pilot projects for young entrepreneurs. Duties and service facilities are explained to these inexperienced taxpayers, and co-operation, rather than control, is fostered right from the start of a business. In the 'fair-play' initiative, Austrian tax authorities emphasise differences among taxpayers in their willingness to pay and the importance of reacting with adequate regulation strategies ranging from deterrence to support (Müller, 2012). In 2005, moreover, the Dutch Tax and Customs Administration introduced a pioneering supervisory approach, 'horizontal monitoring', as an alternative to the traditional 'vertical monitoring'. This approach is based on the firm conviction that a positive relationship, based on mutual trust among taxpayers, tax practitioners and tax authorities, reduces unnecessary supervisory costs and burdens, complex discussions about tax designs on the edge of legality and aggressive tax planning with retrospective adjustments (Committee Horizontal Monitoring Tax and Customs Administration, 2012).

In sum, the argument of the slippery slope approach is that entrepreneurs abide by the law either because they fear detection and fines due to the power of authorities (enforced compliance) or because they feel a commitment to be honest because they have trust in the authorities (voluntary co-operation). When there is effective enforced compliance as well as high voluntary co-operation (i.e., both power and trust), informal entrepreneurship is low. When there is ineffective enforced compliance and little voluntary co-operation, informal entrepreneurship is extensive.

Conclusions

This chapter has reviewed how informal entrepreneurship can be addressed. To commence, it has reviewed four policy goals, namely, taking no action, eradicating informal entrepreneurship, deregulating formal entrepreneurship and formalising informal entrepreneurship. This has revealed that taking no action leaves intact the current disadvantages of informal entrepreneurship for formal entrepreneurs (e.g., unfair competition), informal entrepreneurs (e.g., the inability to gain access to credit to expand), consumers (e.g., no guarantee of health and safety standards) and governments and the wider society and economy (e.g., taxes owed are not collected). Eradicating formal entrepreneurship would result in governments deterring precisely the entrepreneurship and enterprise culture that they otherwise wish to foster, while deregulating formal entrepreneurship would level down working conditions rather than up. Formalising informal entrepreneurship is thus revealed as the most viable approach. How, therefore, can this be achieved?

This chapter has revealed that this can be achieved using either a hard direct compliance approach and/or a soft indirect commitment approach, and the range of hard direct measures have been outlined along with the various soft indirect commitment measures that can be used. This reveals that the currently dominant approach of using hard direct compliance measures that improve the probability of detection and increase the punishment for informal entrepreneurship is a rather limited approach and that there is a much larger tool kit available for formalising informal entrepreneurship. These various tools, moreover, are not mutually exclusive.

To show this, the final section of this chapter has outlined various policy approaches that can be adopted which combine hard direct and soft indirect measures when seeking to formalise informal entrepreneurship, namely, a responsive regulation approach and a slippery slope framework. The outcome is that the various policy choices, approaches and measures available to policy makers have been outlined, along with some suggestions regarding how they can be combined.

The conclusion has been that both hard direct compliance measures are required to increase the power of authorities and soft indirect commitment measures to increase trust in authorities. The next two chapters now evaluate how this can be achieved by evaluating each set of measures in turn to set out what can be used to increase the power of, and trust in, authorities.

References

Ahmed, E. and Braithwaite, V. (2005). Understanding small business taxpayers: Issues of deterrence, tax morale, fairness and work practice. *International Small Business Journal*, 23(5), pp. 539–568.

Allingham, M. and Sandmo, A. (1972). Income tax evasion: A theoretical analysis. *Journal of Public Economics*, 1(2), pp. 323–338.

Alm, J. (2011). Designing alternative strategies to reduce tax evasion. In: M. Pickhardt and A. Prinz, Eds., *Tax evasion and the shadow economy*. Cheltenham: Edward Elgar, pp. 13–32.

Alm, J., Sanchez, I. and De Juan, A. (1995). Economic and non-economic factors in tax compliance. *Kyklos*, 48, pp. 3–18.

Andreoni, J., Erard, B. and Fainstein, J. (1998). Tax compliance. *Journal of Economic Literature*, 36(2), pp. 818–860.

Andrews, D., Caldera Sanchez, A. and Johansson, A. (2011). *Towards a better understanding of the informal economy*. Paris: OECD Economics Department.

Bajada, C. and Schneider, F. (2005). Introduction. In: C. Bajada & F. Schneider, Eds., *Size, causes and consequences of the underground economy: An international perspective*. Aldershot: Ashgate, pp. 1–14.

Beccaria, C. (1797) [1986]. *On crimes and punishment*. Indianapolis: Hackett Publishers.

Becker, G.S. (1968). Crime and punishment: An econometric approach. *Journal of Political Economy*, 76(1), pp. 169–217.

Bentham, J. (1788) [1983]. Principles of penal law. In: J.H. Burton, Ed., *The works of Jeremy Bentham*. Philadelphia: Lea and Blanchard, pp. 41–68.

Bergman, M. and Nevarez, N. (2006). Do audits enhance compliance? An empirical assessment of VAT enforcement. *National Tax Journal*, 59(4), pp. 817–832.

Braithwaite, J. (2002). *Restorative justice and responsive regulation*. New York: Oxford University Press.

Braithwaite, V. (2003). Dancing with tax authorities: Motivational postures and non-compliant actions. In: V. Braithwaite, Ed., *Taxing democracy*. Aldershot: Ashgate, pp. 1–11.

Braithwaite, V. (2009). *Defiance in taxation and governance: Resisting and dismissing authority in a democracy*. Cheltenham: Edward Elgar.

Braithwaite, V. and Reinhart, M. (2000). *The taxpayers' charter: Does the Australian Tax Office comply and who benefits*. Canberra: Centre for Tax System Integrity Working Paper no. 1, Australian National University.

Committee Horizontal Monitoring Tax and Customs Administration (2012). *Tax supervision- made to measure: Flexible when possible, strict where necessary*. The Hague, the Netherlands. Available at: www.ifa.nl/Document/Publicaties/Enhanced%20Relationship%20Project/tax_supervision_made_to_measure_tz0151z1fdeng.pdf (last accessed 6 January 2017).

Commonwealth Association of Tax Administrators (2006). *Tax evasion and avoidance: Strategies and initiatives for tax administrators*. London: Commonwealth Association of Tax Administrators.

Cullis, J.G. and Lewis, A. (1997). Why do people pay taxes: From a conventional economic model to a model of social convention. *Journal of Economic Psychology*, 18(2/3), pp. 305–321.

De Beer, J., Fu, K. and Wunsch-Vincent, S. (2013). *The informal economy, innovation and intellectual property: Concepts, metrics and policy considerations*. Geneva: Economic Research Working Paper no. 10, World Intellectual Property Organization.

De Juan, A., Lasheras, M.A. and Mayo, R. (1994). Voluntary tax compliant behavior of Spanish income taxpayers. *Public Finance*, 49, pp. 90–105.

Dekker, H., Oranje, E., Renooy, P., Rosing, F. and Williams, C.C. (2010). *Joining up the fight against undeclared work in the European Union*. Brussels: DG Employment, Social Affairs and Equal Opportunities.

De Soto, H. (1989). *The other path: The economic answer to terrorism*. London: Harper and Row.

De Soto, H. (2001). *The mystery of capital: Why capitalism triumphs in the West and fails everywhere else*. London: Black Swan.

Dong, B., Dulleck, U. and Torgler, B. (2012). Conditional corruption. *Journal of Economic Psychology*, 33, pp. 609–627.

Eurofound (2013). *Tackling undeclared work in 27 European Union member states and Norway: Approaches and measures since 2008*. Dublin: Eurofound.

European Commission (2007). *Stepping up the fight against undeclared work*. Brussels: European Commission.

Evans, M., Syrett, S. and Williams, C.C. (2006). *Informal economic activities and deprived neighbourhoods*. London: Department of Communities and Local Government.

Gallin, D. (2001). Propositions on trade unions and informal employment in time of globalization. *Antipode*, 19(4), pp. 531–549.

Gangl, K., Hofmann, E., Pollai, M. and Kirchler, E. (2012). *The dynamics of power and trust in the 'slippery slope framework' and its impact on the tax climate*. Available at: http://papers/.ssrn.com/sol3/papers.cfm?abstract_id=2024946 (last accessed 11 May 2016).

Grabiner, L. (2000). *The informal economy.* London: HM Treasury.

Hasseldine, J. and Li, Z. (1999). More tax evasion research required in new millennium. *Crime, Law and Social Change,* 31(1), pp. 91–104.

ILO (2014). *Transitioning from the informal to the formal economy.* Report V (1), International Labour Conference, 103rd Session (2014). Geneva: ILO.

Job, J., Stout, A. and Smith, R. (2007). Culture change in three taxation administrations: From command and control to responsive regulation. *Law and Policy,* 29(1), pp. 84–101.

Karjanen, D. (2014). When is an illicit taxi driver more than a taxi driver? Case studies from transit and trucking in post-socialist Slovakia. In: J. Morris and A. Polese, Eds., *The informal post-socialist economy: Embedded practices and livelihoods.* London: Routledge, pp. 102–117.

Karlinger, L. (2013). The 'dark side' of deregulation: How competition affects the size of the shadow economy. *Journal of Public Economic Theory,* 16(2), pp. 283–321.

Ketchen, D.J., Ireland, R.D. and Webb, J.W. (2014). Towards a research agenda for the informal economy: A survey of the Strategic Entrepreneurship Journal's Editorial Board. *Strategic Entrepreneurship Journal,* 8(1), pp. 95–100.

Kirchler, E. (1997). The burden of new taxes: Acceptance of taxes as a function of affectedness and egoistic versus altruistic orientation. *Journal of Socio-Economics,* 26, pp. 421–436.

Kirchler, E. (1998). Differential representations of taxes: Analysis of free associations and judgments of five employment groups. *Journal of Socio-Economics,* 27, pp. 117–131.

Kirchler, E. (1999). Reactance to taxation: Employers' attitudes towards taxes. *Journal of Socio-Economics,* 28, pp. 131–138.

Kirchler, E. (2007). *The economic psychology of tax behaviour.* Cambridge: Cambridge University Press.

Kirchler, E., Hoelzl, E. and Wahl, I. (2008). Enforced versus voluntary tax compliance: The 'slippery slope' framework. *Journal of Economic Psychology,* 29, pp. 210–225.

Kogler, C., Batrancea, L., Nichita, A., Pantya, J., Belianin, A. and Kirchler, E. (2013). Trust and power as determinants of tax compliance: Testing the assumptions of the slippery slope framework in Austria, Hungary, Romania and Russia. *Journal of Economic Psychology,* 34, pp. 169–180.

Kogler, C., Muelbacher, S. and Kirchler, E. (2015). Testing the 'slippery slope framework' among self-employed taxpayers. *Economics of Governance,* 16, pp. 125–141.

Kus, B. (2010). Regulatory governance and the informal economy: Cross-national comparisons. *Socio-Economic Review,* 8(3), pp. 487–510.

Kus, B. (2014). The informal road to markets: Neoliberal reforms, private entrepreneurship and the informal economy in Turkey. *International Journal of Social Economics,* 41(4), pp. 278–293.

La Porta, R. and Shleifer, A. (2014). Informality and development. *Journal of Economic Perspectives,* 28(3), pp. 109–126.

Morris, J. and Polese, A. (2014). Introduction: Informality: Enduring practices, entwined livelihoods. In: J. Morris and A. Polese, Eds., *The informal post-socialist economy: Embedded practices and livelihoods.* London: Routledge, pp. 1–18.

Müller, E. (2012). *Fair play: Fairness zahlt sich aus [Fairness pays].* Lecture presented at the Meeting of the Austrian Science Fund, Vienna, Austria, 6 July.

Müller, K. and Miggelbrink, J. (2014). The glove compartment half full of letters: Informality and cross-border trade at the edge of the Schengen area. In: J. Morris and A. Polese, Eds., _The informal post-socialist economy: Embedded practices and livelihoods._ London: Routledge, pp. 151–164.

Murphy, K. (2005). Regulating more effectively: The relationship between procedural justice, legitimacy and tax non-compliance. _Journal of Law and Society,_ 32(4), pp. 562–589.

Murphy, K. (2008). Enforcing tax compliance: To punish or persuade? _Economic Analysis and Policy,_ 38(1), pp. 113–135.

OECD (2008). _OECD employment outlook._ Paris: OECD.

OECD (2013). _Co-operative compliance: A framework from enhanced relationship to co-operative compliance._ Available at: www.oecd.org/ctp/administration/cooperativecompliance.htm (last accessed 6 July 2016).

OECD (2015). _Informal sector entrepreneurship: A policy briefing._ Paris: OECD.

Ojo, S., Nwankwo, S. and Gbadamosi, A. (2013). Ethnic entrepreneurship: The myths of informal and illegal enterprise in the UK. _Entrepreneurship and Regional Development,_ 25(7/8), pp. 587–611.

Polese, A. (2014). Drinking with Vova: An individual entrepreneur between illegality and informality. In: J. Morris and A. Polese, Eds., _The informal post-socialist economy: Embedded practices and livelihoods._ London: Routledge, pp. 85–101.

Richardson, M. and Sawyer, A. (2001). A taxonomy of the tax compliance literature: Further findings, problems and prospects. _Australian Tax Forum,_ 16(2), pp. 137–320.

Sasunkevich, O. (2014). Business as casual: Shuttle trade on the Belarus-Lithuania border. In: J. Morris and A. Polese, Eds., _The informal post-socialist economy: Embedded practices and livelihoods._ London: Routledge, pp. 135–151.

Sauka, A., Schneider, F. and Williams, C.C. (2016). Eds., _Entrepreneurship and the shadow economy: A European perspective._ Cheltenham: Edward Elgar.

Sauvy, A. (1984). _Le travail noir et l'economie de demain._ Paris: Calmann-Levy.

Schanz, G. von (1890). _Die steuern der schweiz in ihrer entwicklung seit beginn des 19 jahrhunderts, Vol I to V._ Stuttgart: Rowolt.

Schmölders, G. (1952). Finanzpsychologie. _Finanzarchiv,_ 13, pp. 1–36.

Schmölders, G. (1960). _Das irrationale in der öffentlichen finanzwissenschaft._ Hamburg: Rowolt.

Schmölders, G. (1962). _Volkswirtschaftslehre und psychologie._ Berlin: Reinbek.

Schneider, F. and Enste, D. (2002). _Ocultándose en las sombras. El crecimiento de la economía subterránea._ Washington, DC: IMF.

Slemrod, J., Blumenthal, M. and Christian, C.W. (2001). Taxpayer response to an increased probability of audit: Evidence from a controlled experiment in Minnesota. _Journal of Public Economics,_ 79, pp. 455–483.

Small Business Council (2004). _Small business in the informal economy: Making the transition to the formal economy._ London: Small Business Council.

Strümpel, B. (1969). The contribution of survey research to public finance. In: A.T. Peacock, Ed., _Quantitative analysis in public finance._ New York: Praeger Press, pp. 12–32.

Tonoyan, V., Strohmeyer, R., Habib, M. and Perlitz, M. (2010). Corruption and entrepreneurship: How formal and informal institutions shape small firm behaviour in transition and mature market economies. _Entrepreneurship Theory and Practice,_ 34(5), pp. 803–831.

Torgler, B. (2003). To evade taxes or not: That is the question. _Journal of Socio-Economics,_ 32, pp. 283–302.

Torgler, B. (2005a). Tax morale in Latin America. _Public Choice,_ 122, pp. 133–157.

Torgler, B. (2005b). Tax morale and direct democracy. _European Journal of Political Economy,_ 21, pp. 525–531.

Torgler, B. (2006a). *Tax compliance and tax morale: A theoretical and empirical analysis.* Cheltenham: Edward Elgar.

Torgler, B. (2006b). The importance of faith: Tax morale and religiosity. *Journal of Economic Behavior and Organization,* 61(1), pp. 81–109.

Torgler, B. (2007). Tax morale in Central and Eastern European countries. In: N. Hayoz and S. Hug, Eds., *Tax evasion, trust and state capacities: How good is tax morale in Central and Eastern Europe?* Bern: Peter Lang, pp. 155–186.

Torgler, B. (2011). *Tax morale and compliance: Review of evidence and case studies for Europe.* Washington, DC: World Bank Policy Research Working Paper no. 5922, World Bank.

Vainio, A. (2012). *Market-based and rights-based approaches to the informal economy: A comparative analysis of the policy implications.* Oslo: Nordiska Afrijainstitutet.

Webb, J.W., Bruton, G.D., Tihanyi, L. and Ireland, R.D. (2013). Research on entrepreneurship in the informal economy: Framing a research agenda. *Journal of Business Venturing,* 28, pp. 598–614.

Webb, J.W., Tihanyi, L., Ireland, R.D. and Sirmon, D.G. (2009). You say illegal, I say legitimate: Entrepreneurship in the informal economy. *Academy of Management Review,* 34(3), pp. 492–510.

Weigel, R., Hessin, D. and Elffers, H. (1987). Tax evasion research: A critical appraisal and theoretical model. *Journal of Economic Psychology,* 8(2), pp. 215–235.

Wenzel, M. (2002). The impact of outcome orientation and justice concerns on tax compliance: The role of taxpayers' identity. *Journal of Applied Psychology,* 87, pp. 639–645.

Wenzel, M. (2004). An analysis of norm processes in tax compliance. *Journal of Economic Psychology,* 25(2), pp. 213–228.

Williams, C.C. (2004a). Harnessing enterprise and entrepreneurship in the underground economy. *International Journal of Economic Development,* 6(2), pp. 23–54.

Williams, C.C. (2004b). Beyond deterrence: Rethinking the UK public policy approach towards undeclared work. *Public Policy and Administration,* 19(1), pp. 15–30.

Williams, C.C. (2006). What is to be done about undeclared work? An evaluation of the policy options. *Policy and Politics,* 34(1), pp. 91–113.

Williams, C.C. (2013). De-linking entrepreneurship from profit-motivated capitalism: Some lessons from an English locality. *International Journal of Social Entrepreneurship and Innovation,* 2(3), pp. 225–238.

Williams, C.C. (2014a). *Confronting the shadow economy: Evaluating tax compliance and behaviour policies.* Cheltenham: Edward Elgar.

Williams, C.C. (2014b). Public policy approaches towards the undeclared economy in European countries: A critical overview. *European Labour Law Journal,* 5(2), pp. 132–155.

Williams, C.C. (2015). Entrepreneurship in the shadow economy: A review of the alternative policy approaches. *International Journal of Small and Medium Enterprises and Sustainability,* 1(1), pp. 51–82.

Williams, C.C. (2016). *Diagnostic report on undeclared work in Greece.* Geneva: ILO.

Williams, C.C. (2017a). *Dependent self-employment: Trends, challenges and policy responses in the EU.* Geneva: ILO.

Williams, C.C. (2017b). *Developing a holistic approach for tackling undeclared work: A learning resource.* Brussels: European Commission.

Williams, C.C. and Gurtoo, A. (2017). Harnessing entrepreneurship in developing countries: A lived practices approach. In: C.C. Williams and A. Gurtoo, Eds.,

Routledge handbook of entrepreneurship in developing economies. London: Routledge, pp. 547–555.

Williams, C.C. and Lansky, M. (2013). Informal employment in developed and emerging economies: Perspectives and policy responses. *International Labour Review*, 152(3/4), pp. 355–380.

Williams, C.C. and Martinez-Perez, A. (2014a). Entrepreneurship in the informal economy: A product of too much or too little state intervention? *International Journal of Entrepreneurship and Innovation*, 15(4), pp. 227–237.

Williams, C.C. and Martinez-Perez, A. (2014b). Why do consumers purchase goods and services in the informal economy? *Journal of Business Research*, 67(5), pp. 802–806.

Williams, C.C. and Nadin, S. (2012a). Tackling entrepreneurship in the informal economy: Evaluating the policy options. *Journal of Entrepreneurship and Public Policy*, 1(2), pp. 111–124.

Williams, C.C. and Nadin, S. (2012b). Tackling the hidden enterprise culture: Government policies to support the formalization of informal entrepreneurship. *Entrepreneurship and Regional Development*, 24(9/10), pp. 895–915.

Williams, C.C. and Nadin, S. (2013a). Beyond the entrepreneur as a heroic figurehead of capitalism: Re-representing the lived practices of entrepreneurs. *Entrepreneurship and Regional Development*, 25(7/8), pp. 552–568.

Williams, C.C. and Nadin, S. (2013b). Harnessing the hidden enterprise culture: Supporting the formalization of off-the-books business start-ups. *Journal of Small Business and Enterprise Development*, 20(2), pp. 434–447.

Williams, C.C. and Nadin, S. (2014). Facilitating the formalisation of entrepreneurs in the informal economy: Towards a variegated policy approach. *Journal of Entrepreneurship and Public Policy*, 3(1), pp. 33–48.

Williams, C.C., Nadin, S., Barbour, A. and Llanes, M. (2012). *Enabling enterprise: Tackling the barriers to formalisation*. London: Community Links.

Williams, C.C. and Windebank, J. (1998). *Informal employment in the advanced economies: Implications for work and welfare*. London: Routledge.

Woodruff, C., De Mel, S. and Mckenzie, D. (2013). The demand for, and consequences of, formalization among informal firms in Sri Lanka. *Applied Economics*, 5(2), pp. 122–150.

8 Hard Direct Policy Measures

Introduction

Having shown in the last chapter that formalising informal entrepreneurship should be the goal of policy, and having outlined how hard direct and soft indirect policy measures are available for achieving this objective, this chapter reviews the range of hard direct policy measures that can be pursued to not only dissuade entrepreneurs from operating in the informal sector but also to incentivise and encourage entrepreneurs to operate in the formal sector. The point of these measures is to directly increase the costs and reduce the benefits of informality for entrepreneurs and to reduce the costs and increase the benefits of operating in the formal sector. In doing so, they deal with some of the formal institutional failures, especially the weakness of formal institutions, that lead to the greater prevalence of informal entrepreneurship.

To commence this review of the hard direct measures that can be used to formalise informal entrepreneurship, therefore, the first section reviews the deterrence measures that increase the actual or perceived costs of operating informally. On the one hand, this is accomplished by increasing the perceived or actual likelihood of detection and, on the other hand, by raising the penalties for those caught. Firstly, therefore, the various measures used to improve the actual or perceived likelihood of detection and, secondly, the effectiveness of penalties and sanctions as a tool for tackling informal entrepreneurship are evaluated. In the second section, attention then turns towards how incentives can be provided to encourage entrepreneurs to operate in the formal sector. To review how this can be achieved, on the one hand, the supply-side incentive measures are reviewed that focus upon either encouraging entrepreneurs to start up on a formal basis or which encourage informal entrepreneurs to formalise their ventures. This is then followed by a review, on the other hand, of demand-side incentive measures that seek to encourage customers to purchase goods and services on a formal basis rather than in informal sector. If these hard direct measures are pursued, then the net outcome will be to change the cost/benefit ratio confronting entrepreneurs so that they will make the choice to operate in the formal sector.

At the outset, it needs to be stated that these hard direct policy measures will not be applicable everywhere. Improving enforcement regimes requires the resources and political will, as well as the formal institutional infrastructure, which is often lacking in many developed and developing countries across the globe. The discussion that follows, therefore, needs to be seen in that context. It is an ideal type discussion of what might be done, and what good practices exist, so far as hard direct policy measures are concerned, that could be implemented if there was the political will, the resources and the requisite formal institutional infrastructure in place to enable this to happen.

To review the range of hard direct policy measures which can be used to increase the perceived or actual costs of entrepreneurs operating informally, firstly, the range of measures are reviewed that can be used to increase the perceived or actual risks of detection and, secondly, the range of measures that can be used to increase the perceived or actual penalties and sanctions for engaging in informal entrepreneurship.

Deterrence Measures: Increasing the Risks of Detection

One prominent means of deterring participation in informal entrepreneurship is to improve the perceived or actual likelihood of detection. Examining the literature on the effectiveness of improving the risk of detection, it becomes quickly apparent that there is little conclusive evidence about whether this is effective in reducing informality. Some literature finds that increasing the probability of audit and detection reduces informality, at least for some income groups (Alm *et al.*, 1992, 1995; Beron *et al.*, 1992; Dubin and Wilde, 1988; Dubin *et al.*, 1987; Kinsey and Gramsick, 1993; Klepper and Nagin, 1989; Slemrod *et al.*, 2001; Varma and Doob, 1998; Witte and Woodbury, 1985). However, other literature does not. A substantial body of literature displays that increasing the probability of detection does not reduce informality (e.g., Dubin *et al.*, 1987; Dubin and Wilde, 1988; Elffers *et al.*, 1987; Shaw *et al.*, 2008; Webley and Halstead, 1986). Rather, it leads to increased non-compliance, not least due to a breakdown of trust between the state and its citizens (Ayres and Braithwaite, 1992; Blumenthal *et al.*, 1998; Brehm and Brehm, 1981; Kagan and Scholz, 1984; Murphy and Harris, 2007; Tyler *et al.*, 2007). Whether improving the probability of detection, and thus the perceived or actual power of authorities, is effective at reducing informal entrepreneurship, however, depends not only on the context in which this is pursued (e.g., a high- or low-compliance culture) but also on the type of policy measure being evaluated.

Here an evaluation is undertaken of a range of measures available to increase the perceived or actual risk of detection, including workplace inspections, business and payment certification schemes, certified cash registers, deterring cash payments, notification letters, peer-to-peer surveillance and the coordination of strategy, operations and data analysis across government.

Workplace Inspections

One of the most prominent and common measures used to increase the perceived or actual likelihood of detection is the workplace inspection. Many, if not all, countries use this as a core tool for increasing the perceived and actual probability of detection. To improve the effectiveness of workplace inspections as a tool for increasing the perceived or actual risk of detection, initiatives might range from simply increasing the number of inspections conducted through to initiatives that seek to improve the probability of detection, such as by improving the targeting of 'at-risk' or 'suspect' sectors. Announced inspection visits have also been used whereby a locality and/or industrial sector is informed that a visit from the inspection authorities is to occur in the near future.

The evidence that targeted inspections are more effective than non-targeted inspections is not clear cut (see Williams, 2014a,b). Although regular random inspections cannot cease since these have a strong deterrent effect, there are obvious benefits when a more targeted approach is adopted. Given how Part II of this book revealed that globally, informal entrepreneurship is concentrated in particular sectors and types of business, a targeted approach is likely to produce greater dividends than a non-targeted approach. However, this is not always the case. In Hungary, the labour inspectorate in 2012 identified two sectors, namely, the processing sector as well as the private and property security sector, where informality was considered to be more prevalent. No more violations were identified, however, than in random inspections in other sectors (Bakos, 2012a,b).

It is important to note that the ability of governments to undertake workplace inspections is often severely constrained by the number of labour inspectors. The ILO (2006) recommends that there should be one labour inspector per 10,000 employed persons in advanced economies and one inspector per 20,000 employed persons in developing economies. This level, however, is often not achieved. It is not only the number of labour inspectors that hinders the effectiveness of workplace inspections. It is also the quality of information systems. In some developing countries, inspectors do not have real-time employee data available, and if there is no regulation to register workers on or before their first day at work, employers can easily claim that the employee has started work that day. For workplace inspections to be effective, therefore, there is a need for a comprehensive and up-to-date register of employment and also for the legislation to be in place making registration prior to the first day of work mandatory. There is also a need for other forms of mandatory licensing and registration to be up-to-date and for an evidence base to be accessible by inspectors to evaluate whether this is the case, such as trading licenses, registration for taxation and so forth. It is not only improving workplace inspections, therefore, that can increase the perceived or actual likelihood of detection of entrepreneurship in the informal sector.

Business Certification and Payment Certification of Tax and Social Contributions

Another related initiative to deter informal entrepreneurship is therefore to introduce business certification schemes and payment certification of tax and social contributions. In Norway, the Confederation of Norwegian Enterprise (*Næringslivets Hovedorganisasjon*, NHO) created a voluntary certification scheme (*Ren utvikling*) in the cleaning industry where informal work was rife. All participating cleaning businesses provided documentation that their accounts and tax records were in order. User companies were then given a list of enterprises in the cleaning industry whose books conformed in relation to the existing rules and standards on taxes as well as the working environment and workers' rights. In 2008, however, just 27 certified businesses were registered, which was a tiny fraction of all businesses in this sector (Sissel *et al.*, 2011). In 2012 in consequence, a compulsory certification scheme was introduced (*Godkjenningsordningen for renholdsbedrifter*), and it was illegal to purchase cleaning services from companies not approved by the labour inspectorate. Any approved business had to meet the requirements for residence permits for all employees and the registration and reporting obligations on public registers for all employees. The companies also needed to conform on health and safety standards, and all employees had to carry identity cards received from the labour inspectorate. A central register lists the approved companies which customers can employ. In 2012, the government allocated 20 million NOK (€2.69m) to implement this approval scheme (Sissel *et al.*, 2011).

A similar compulsory business registration scheme has been introduced in Norway for temporary work agencies (*Bemanningsforetaksregisteret*). In 2010, workers from Eastern Europe accounted for 22 per cent of those employed in temporary work agencies in Norway, and they had substandard wage and working conditions. This scheme prevented the hiring of workers from temporary work agencies not registered. Breaches are punishable by a fine. In January 2011, 1,362 businesses were on the register. Some 86 per cent of union representatives from businesses that use temporary workers state that their employer checks that the agencies are in the register (Vennesland, 2013).

In most parts of the world, however, it is simply whether a business is registered with one or more of the authorities with which it should be registered that is the issue so far as informal entrepreneurship is concerned. It is therefore perhaps much more about making it easier and simple for entrepreneurs to register their businesses and for it to be not overburdensome or costly, which is the issue. This will be returned to in the following sections.

Use of Certified Cash Registers

In an increasing number of countries, certified cash registers are being introduced. For example, since 2010 in Sweden, businesses selling goods and services in return for cash payments must have a certified cash register. A certified cash register consists of two parts: a cash register with a manufacturer declaration and a special control unit, a black box, connected to the cash register. The black box reads registrations made by the cash register. Only the Swedish Tax Agency can access the data in the black box. The businesses bear the costs of the cash registers, which totals some SEK 15,000 (€1,785). Companies not complying are fined SEK 10,000 (€1,190) by the Swedish Tax Agency. If the company once again fails to comply with the law within a year, a fee of SEK 20,000 (€23,800) is charged. Cash payments also include payment by debit (bank) card, and it is mandatory for the trader to give the customer a receipt. The tax agency then conducts unannounced 'undercover' visits to see if all transactions go through the register and that receipts are given. Failure to issue receipts or register transactions can result in the trader being fined and lead to a full audit.

In 2010 in Poland, the Ministry of Finance introduced a similar scheme making electronic fiscal cash registers mandatory for various professions, including doctors, lawyers, tax advisors, physicians running private practices, funeral homes and translators. Before this, they were allowed not to register each sale and instead were allowed to pay income tax in the form of a lump sum. The decision to register and report each sale made, using a certified cash register, ended controversies regarding the unequal treatment of these groups. Nevertheless, these groups continue to avoid recording sales. For example, physicians only have to use cash registers during official opening hours, even though patients may be seen after hours; they may not record home visits on cash registers, claim the cash register is out of order or negotiate the price with the patient, who is offered a lower fee if no 'paperwork' is involved (Williams and Renooy, 2013). This measure is transferable across both sectors and countries, as displayed by the fact that in taxis, a taximeter can be required to register the fare and print receipts.

In many countries, however, it is not the use of certified cash registers which is the issue but, rather, the use of ordinary cash registers and/or the giving of receipts for transactions. For many developing countries, therefore, it is again perhaps the use of incentives to encourage the use of cash registers and the giving of receipts which is required (e.g., by developing a national lottery based on receipts to encourage customers to ask for a receipt when engaging in a transaction), more than the use of technologically sophisticated certified cash registers. This will be returned to in the following sections.

Deterring Cash Payments

Given that many transactions of informal entrepreneurs can be in cash, deterring cash payments is another policy solution. This has been vigorously pursued by the large global multinational corporations involved in electronic payment systems in recent years, and with considerable success, exemplified by the decision of India in 2016 to significantly curtail the use of cash transactions in what has been widely referred to as the 'demonetisation' of the Indian economy to tackle its large informal sector. Several options exist for countries pursuing this demonetisation approach.

A first option is to introduce mandatory electronic payments. Indeed, countries with high levels of electronic payments have smaller informal economies (Williams, 2017b). A second option is for governments to introduce a ceiling for cash transactions. Again, this has been recently introduced in many countries across the world (Dzhekova and Williams, 2014; Vandersepypen *et al.*, 2013). A third option is to prevent easy access to cash. No-fee automated teller machines (ATMs) provide citizens with access to free cash. By charging withdrawal fees, cash use would reduce. A fourth option is to make point-of-sale (POS) terminals available across all sectors, including bars, restaurants and taxis. A fifth option is for government departments to more fully use electronic payments since they are among the largest initiators and recipients of payments in many economies throughout the world. By paying the salaries of public sector workers into bank accounts, ensuring that taxes and fines are paid online, and that cards or money transfers are used for all public sector purchases, such e-government initiatives, particularly electronic payments for public sector activities, would markedly reduce cash use. In many countries, nevertheless, electronic payments for government services remain an option rather than a requirement or norm. A sixth and final option is to provide incentives to use cards at the point of sale. Many small transactions remain cash based in most nations. Developing incentives for individuals to use cards rather than cash is therefore an option. For example, Argentina offers a 5 per cent value-added tax (VAT) discount on debit card transactions and 3 per cent on credit card purchases. South Korea offers a lump-sum refund if card usage is greater than 20 per cent of individual gross income for credit cards and 25 per cent for debit cards. In the United States, nevertheless, the trend is in the inverse. A US District Court ruling allowed owners of stores in many states to charge purchasers a surcharge of up to 4 per cent for using a credit card. However, past experience on surcharges from Australia show that while few retailers used it in the first instance, about one-third now do, and surcharges have spiralled above card acceptance costs, causing the Reserve Bank of Australia to revisit and relax the rules (see Williams, 2017b).

Given that there is an oligopoly of multinationals through whom the vast majority of global credit and debit card transactions take place, some caution is required by national governments when deciding whether to pursue demonetisation. These corporations have a financial interest in economies shifting from cash-based to card-based transactions, and some care needs to be taken by governments before moving towards greater dependency on such corporations.

Notification Letters

Another method to deter engagement in informal entrepreneurship is to use notification letters. For example, in 2008, the Estonian Tax and Customs Board sent notification letters to companies with low wage levels compared with the average level in the region and the respective business sector. These notification letters informed the employers of the low competitiveness of their wage levels compared with average wage levels. As a result, 46 per cent of the companies receiving these letters adjusted their wage levels and increased their tax payments. After four months, the notification letters had brought an additional EEK 10 million (about €640,000) of tax income, including EEK 8.8 million from notifications sent to enterprises and EEK 1.2 million from those sent to individual employees (Anvelt, 2008; Levit, 2008; Rum, 2008; Tubalkain-Trell, 2008).

This could be more widely applied. Although it is not a substitute for labour or tax inspections, it is a cheap means of deterring engagement in informal entrepreneurship that could be more widely used in many countries to prevent ongoing participation in the informal sector. Indeed notification letters may be particularly useful when used as a follow-up to a data mining exercise to identify entrepreneurs who are found to be 'outliers' on various indicators (e.g., who have higher-than-average expenses, higher ratios of credit card to cash payments compared with other similar businesses or a relatively low number of registered employees for their turnover) that raise suspicions of informality. Indeed in some inspectorates, the use of dynamic benchmarking, where the data determines what is the norm, is being used to identify outliers to whom notification letters are sent. An example is the hotel sector, where turnover to credit card transaction ratios are being used to identify outlier hotels where turnover is closer to the total credit card transactions than is the norm. This dynamic benchmarking of the hotel sector can also occur on an individual city level or for a particular type of accommodation provider. This then enables very targeted notification letters where the evidence can be presented to the entrepreneur. Indeed based on this dynamic benchmarking approach, the UK tax administration authority (HMRC) has used its databases to identify and send 460,000 notification letters to outliers to 'nudge' behaviour towards tax compliance.

Indeed this use of notification letters to 'nudge' changes in behaviour has become ever more popular, especially in the developed world, with Australia, Canada, France, the United States and Switzerland among the countries to have followed the example in the UK, where a 'nudge unit' was established in 2010. However, the evidence of the effectiveness of 'nudge' letters is far from convincing. In Canada, Beeby (2017) reports how 8,000 taxpayers who had been assessed as owing up to $950 in taxes but had not paid were in 2014 targeted. Half received friendly encouragement 'nudge' letters, and half were threatened with punishment. They found that the friendly nudge letters collected 12 per cent more taxes owed than the standard punitive letter. However, in March 2016, a similar campaign involving 6,877 taxpayers failed, with those receiving the punitive notification letter paying more than those receiving the friendly nudge letter. The cost of the 2016 experiment, nevertheless, was low at $17,400. There is a need, therefore, for much more experimentation with the use of notification letters before any firm conclusions can be drawn.

Peer-to-Peer Surveillance

To detect informal entrepreneurship, possible sources of information include audits, data mining of government databases to identify discrepancies and outlier cases, and referrals from other government departments. Recently many governments have additionally encouraged 'whistle-blowing' by asking their populations to directly report instances of informality using peer-to-peer surveillance via telephone hotlines, text messages and online reporting portals. This type of initiative generates a high number of leads that need to be followed up and can be time-consuming and costly to process. Nevertheless it is an option that can be pursued to increase the perceived or actual risk of detection.

In the UK, a telephone hotline and online reporting system was introduced by Her Majesty's Revenue and Customs (HMRC). Some £700,000 per annum is spent on staffing the hotline and £3 million per annum investigating the reports received. At the outset in 2006, to encourage reporting to the hotline, a combination of TV, press and radio campaigns were used, focused upon particular trades such as hairdressers, the home repair and maintenance sector, taxi drivers and motor vehicle repairers. In total, HMRC spent £4.5 million advertising the hotline. In 2006–2007, 120,000 calls and emails were received. The number of reports has averaged 7,000 a month since then. On average, each call costs £6 to handle (National Audit Office, 2008).

One-third of the reports in 2006–2007 lacked relevant information. Of the 76,300 subjected to risk assessment, no further action was taken on 12,400, and 8,400 people were dealt with by offering education and support. HMRC was awaiting the tax returns from 9,800 further cases as no tax was yet due. By 31 March 2007, there had been no decision on the remaining 25,900 cases. Of the 19,800 cases where HMRC had taken investigations further, 3,500 cases had been opened and 2,000 completed, generating additional tax of £2.6 million. This figure of 2,000 compared with a planned target by HMRC to complete 5,500 investigations between April 2006 and March 2007. Their assumptions regarding the resources required proved incorrect since they received three times more calls than expected and needed to use additional resources to evaluate the information received (National Audit Office, 2008).

Again, this use of hotlines could be replicated in many other countries. As can be seen from the example of the UK, however, it is an expensive and resource-intensive process. It also means that by devoting additional resources to follow up on the leads received, labour and tax inspectorates may often find themselves with fewer resources available to engage in either workplace inspections or other preventative activities.

Cross-Government Co-Operation on Data Mining, Operations and Strategy

A further means of improving the risk of detection is to encourage co-operation across government departments on, firstly, data mining, matching and sharing, secondly, operations and finally, strategy towards informal entrepreneurship. Each is here considered in turn.

Data mining refers to the set of automated techniques used to extract buried or previously unknown pieces of information from large databases. Data matching, meanwhile, refers to the large-scale comparison of records or files collected or held for different purposes, with a view to identifying matters of interest. By data matching two or more sets of collected data are compared. Data sharing, meanwhile, is the process of making data available to other users (De Wispelaere and Pacolet, 2017). In recent years, the detection of informal entrepreneurship has turned increasingly to these processes of data mining, data matching and data sharing. The perception is that this is a more effective means of detecting instances of informal entrepreneurship.

This, however, requires significant capital investment in developing data warehouses and keeping up-to-date databases. In the UK, for example, the Connect system of HMRC has 22 billion lines of data, and some 13 million searches have been conducted by the 250 data analysts and 4,000 users. However, it has cost some £90 million to date. Despite this high cost, it is estimated to have generated an additional £3 billion in tax revenues, displaying that despite the high cost, it is an effective tool in identifying tax non-compliance.

To improve the perceived or actual likelihood of detecting informal entrepreneurship, many governments have also pursued joint operations across departments. These, however, largely remain the exception rather than the norm (see, e.g., Dzhekova and Williams, 2014). Such joint operations from an enterprise perspective can be the preferred option. Rather than receive multiple visits from different arms of government (e.g., labour inspectors, health and safety inspectors or tax inspectors), a joined-up approach can be perceived as a business-friendly approach that reduces the perceived burden of government regulation. Of course, this joined-up approach towards operations is only relevant in countries in which there is no one central body responsible for tackling the informal sector and compliance. If one agency was to be responsible, there would be no need for joint operations across departments.

Joining-up strategy is therefore also a means of improving detection. Fully joined-up forms of government are where one agency has responsibility for tackling the informal sector and there are common targets across the sub-sidiary government departments (e.g., France and Germany). A slightly less joined-up form of governance would be where there are a variety of cross-departmental co-operations ranging from initiatives where the co-operating departments have common shared strategic and/or operational objectives, followed by cross-departmental co-operations where each department has separate strategic and/or operational objectives and targets. Finally, and the poorest form of joined-up government, is a departmental 'silos' approach where each government department has its own strategic and/operational targets, and no cross-departmental co-operation takes place. Indeed it is this departmental 'silos' approach which is most common in the majority of countries (Williams *et al.*, 2013). It is also important to consider wider governance and whether this is joined up, in the sense of employer federa-tions, trade unions, private and voluntary sector organisations, as well as local government being involved in decision-making on the informal sector as partners. Across much of the world, the active involvement of such stake-holders in governance with regard to tackling informal entrepreneurship is decidedly lacking (ILO, 2014; Williams *et al.*, 2013).

Finally, there is also joined-up strategy and operations at the supra-national level, exemplified in Europe by the establishment in 2016 of the European Platform Tackling Undeclared Work. This platform brings together national enforcement authorities, such as labour inspectorates, tax and social security authorities, plus the European Commission. European-level social partners (employer and employee organisations), representatives of the European Foundation for the Improvement of Living and Working Conditions (Eurofound), the European Agency for Safety and Health at Work (EU-OSHA) and the ILO participate as observers. A key intention of the platform is to encourage mutual learning to enable the development and sharing of good practice across nations (see Williams, 2017a).

Deterrence Measures: Increasing Penalties

To increase the costs of informal entrepreneurship and make them greater than the benefits, authorities can also increase the sanctions and penalties for informal entrepreneurship. This is not just a case of increasing the actual but also the perceived sanctions. If entrepreneurs perceive the penalties as high, such as a prison sentence or the closure of their business, then they will be less likely to participate in the informal sector. For actual or perceived penalties to be effective, however, they have to be proportionate. If they are perceived as too high, then this will reduce trust in government and thus the level of voluntary compliance. Achieving an appropriate level of penalties, therefore, is a difficult task. It is not simply the case that the higher the level of penalties, the lower is the level of informal entrepreneurship.

Indeed this is perhaps one reason why studies that evaluate the effective-ness of penalties do not always reveal the clear-cut result that increasing penalties reduces informal entrepreneurship. Some evaluations find that increasing fines reduces the size of the informal sector (De Juan *et al.*, 1994; Friedland *et al.*, 1978; Klepper and Nagin, 1989; Schwartz and Orleans, 1967). However, others identify that increasing penalties leads to a growth in the informal sector or has no effect, or only a short-term effect, on compliance (Elffers *et al.*, 1987; Feld and Frey, 2002; Friedland, 1982; Murphy, 2005; Varma and Doob, 1998; Webley and Halstead, 1986). This is because imposing penalties can be counterproductive and undermine trust in authorities (Ayres and Braithwaite, 1992; Blumenthal *et al.*, 1998; Tyler *et al.*, 2007). High penalties can result in the opposite outcome, namely, greater non-compliance (Murphy and Harris, 2007).

Despite caution being required when increasing penalties, there has been a tendency in many countries to do so. In some countries, moreover, new innovative forms of penalty have been introduced. Naming and shaming those caught is one such innovative approach. Shaming can either simply shame the offender, or it can shame them and then offer reintegration. Coricelli *et al.* (2014) show that when cheating is made public and the perpetrator is not successfully reintegrated, the amount of cheating significantly increases compared with when cheating is made public but is followed by reintegration. Until now, however, the former has tended to be used in most countries (e.g., Greece) but without reintegration or rehabilitation measures.

Another innovative sanction is to use either 'blacklists' which exclude businesses from public procurement programmes and contracts that have been non-compliant within a specified time period or 'white lists' that provide a list of businesses that are compliant and can bid for public procurement contracts. Such lists therefore provide an additional sanction in preventing access to a major source of funding for businesses in many countries if they are caught.

Supply-Side Incentives

In the hard direct controls approach, the emphasis has been largely on increasing the costs of informal entrepreneurship in most countries. However, the recognition that the objective is not simply to eradicate informal entrepreneurship, but to shift this endeavour into the formal sector, has resulted in a shift in thinking towards how governments can encourage and reward formal entrepreneurship (OECD, 2016; Williams, 2006a, 2016). Rather than use solely 'sticks' to punish entrepreneurship in the informal sector, an approach has emerged which seeks to reward and encourage formal entrepreneurship rather than taking it as given.

Such a positive reinforcement approach is applied to two different groups of entrepreneurs. Firstly, there are new ventures who need to be facilitated to start up on a legitimate and formal basis. Secondly, there are entrepreneurs already established and operating in the informal sector who need to be encouraged to formalise.

Society-Wide Amnesties

In many countries, a measure used to shift entrepreneurs from the informal into the formal sector has been society-wide amnesties (e.g., Franzoni, 2000; Hasseldine, 1998; LópezLaborda and Rodrigo, 2003; Macho-Stadler *et al.*, 1999; Torgler and Schaltegger, 2005). Baer and LeBorgne (2008: 5) define a tax amnesty as

> a limited-time offer by the government to a specified group of taxpayers to pay a defined amount, in exchange for forgiveness of a tax liability (including interest and penalties) relating to a previous tax period(s), as well as freedom from legal prosecution.

An amnesty therefore enables this specified group (e.g., informal entrepreneurs) who have evaded taxation not to incur the sanctions that the failure to pay on a timely basis would ordinarily incur.

Tax amnesties have a long history. Indeed the first tax amnesty on record, reported on the Rosetta stone, was an amnesty declared by Ptolemy V Epiphanes in Egypt circa 200 BC (Mikesell and Ross, 2012). The continuing issue that has needed to be addressed with amnesties is striking a balance between revenue collection and the perception of fairness. Amnesties enable revenue to be collected that might otherwise be foregone. However, they also raise equity or fairness issues which may impact on the efficiency of the tax collection system in the future. Amnesties can be perceived by legitimate enterprises as providing the evaders with a special deal that violates their views on the fairness of the system. These legitimate enterprises may view themselves as unfairly treated by such special deals provided to informal entrepreneurs, which might harm the future compliance of those who until now have abided by the formal rules of the game. Given the importance of voluntary compliance for the vast majority of tax revenue collected, this is potentially problematic in terms of future compliance. Indeed, this is precisely the reason for many countries being reluctant to use amnesties.

The evidence confirms that it is generally correct for state authorities to be wary of offering amnesties. Luitel and Sobel (2007) find repeated amnesties lead to reductions in state revenue collections, doubtless precisely due to legitimate enterprises viewing governments as violating this principle of equity and fairness. However, Alm *et al.* (1990) find that if there is a one-off amnesty and this is coupled with new tougher enforcement measures for the non-compliant following the amnesty period, such negative impacts are somewhat offset. Overall nevertheless, as Mikesell and Ross (2012) display, the majority of evidence is that amnesties do not increase long-run tax revenues. The general finding is the inverse; amnesties decrease long-run revenues.

However, some types of tax amnesty are more lucrative in terms of short-term revenue and less harmful in terms of harming long-term future tax compliance. As Mikesell and Ross (2012) reveal, at best, amnesties have a zero long-term revenue effect and at worst a negative effect. As such, countries should seek to maximise revenues. To achieve this, they find that the features influencing the level of return are the length of the amnesty period, the quarter in which the amnesty is held, the time since the last amnesty and whether there are accompanying measures. Their finding is that keeping an amnesty open less than 60 days and holding the amnesty in the third quarter of the calendar year increases the gross revenue collected and that states which do not regularly tax sales have low federal audit rates and do not operate a voluntary disclosure scheme have higher revenue rates from amnesties. They importantly find that collections decline with each successive amnesty and increase with the amount of time since the last amnesty, holding constant the other structural features.

The result has been a shift over time in the objectives of holding amnesties. In the 1980s and even 1990s, amnesties were less concerned with increasing short-term revenue and, instead, focused upon combining amnesties with other enforcement initiatives to improve compliance (Parle and Hirlinger, 1986). Since the turn of the new millennium, however, they have become more concerned with short-term revenue generation. Using amnesties also enable an increase in the severity of penalties and sanctions, which might not otherwise be possible and which also helps offset the future negative impacts of amnesties. Amnesties therefore, if offered, must be coupled with an increase in deterrents to ensure that future compliance is not affected.

Simplifying the Formal Regulations

Besides amnesties, governments can also encourage and incentivise entrepreneurs to operate legitimately by simplifying the formal 'rules of the game' and how easy it is to operate in the formal sector. The intention in doing so is to help business start up and operate formally. The importance of pursuing simplification, and the type of measures pursued, depends on whether informal entrepreneurs do not adhere to the formal rules intentionally or unintentionally. Although entrepreneurs often intentionally flout the formal rules, they might also do so unintentionally, for example, by not knowing they are breaking the rules. In both cases, but especially for those unintentionally doing so, better advice on the 'rules of the game' is a way forward. Another possibility is to simplify the formal regulations. Simplification, however, is not the same as deregulation. Simplification might involve deregulation but does not necessarily have to do so. It can also involve simplifying the regulatory framework (e.g., easier registration processes) or increasing the benefits of formalisation (e.g., by providing access to commercial opportunities such as public procurement contracts, more favourable credit markets and greater legal protection).

Simplification, therefore, seeks to reduce both intentional and unintentional informal entrepreneurship. When tackling intentional informal entrepreneurship, simplification might change the legal and administrative requirements, such as registration and licensing procedures, sometimes referred to as the regulatory burden, which can act as a barrier to enterprises starting up and operating formally, especially given that the transaction costs or costs of compliance per worker are higher than in larger firms. This is because smaller enterprises often do not have the resources (i.e., time, money or specialist expertise) to deal with the regulatory burden and cannot spread the costs across large-scale operations (Chittenden *et al.*, 2002; Hansford *et al.*, 2003; Hart *et al.*, 2005; Michaelis *et al.*, 2001; OECD, 2000, 2012). The outcome is that when the costs of administrative compliance are high, informal entrepreneurship may be high (Adams and Webley, 2001; ILO, 2014; Matthews and Lloyd-Williams, 2001). These administrative costs include form filling, inspections (rather than advice), inconsistent application of the rules by different inspectorates or even different inspectors within the same inspectorate, and duplication of information requirements to various inspectorates. Richardson (2006) reveals in an examination of 45 nations that regulatory complexity is the key determinant of non-compliance; the lower the level of regulatory complexity, the lower is the level of tax non-compliance. It should be noted nevertheless, and to repeat, that reducing regulatory complexity (i.e., simplification) is not the same as reducing the regulatory burden (i.e., deregulation).

Often the intention when pursuing simplification is to reduce the costs of formality to increase the formalisation of enterprises. Devas and Kelly (2001) examine a simplified 'single business permit' for small firms in Kenya and report how it led to some degree of formalisation and improved conditions overall for small firms. Sander (2003) reporting a similar pilot project in Entebbe, Uganda, asserts that the reforms reducing the costs of formalisation led to a 43 per cent increase in the registration of enterprises. However, in both Kenya and Uganda, there is little understanding of the long-term impact of these reforms due to a lack of follow-up research. Garcia-Bolivar (2006) report that reducing the costs of formalisation in Bolivia led to a 20 per cent increase in the number of firm registrations and also similar increases in Vietnam. Two experimental studies have examined the impacts of reducing registration costs on formalisation. Jaramillo (2009) reports a field experiment in Lima, Peru. A randomly selected group of entrepreneurs were offered free business licenses and support with registration. Only one in four formalised. This was perhaps due to the recurrent costs of formality, low perceived benefits of formalisation, their limited growth ambitions and the low trust in government. De Mel *et al.* (2012) undertook a similar experiment. A group of entrepreneurs were offered positive financial inducements to formalise. They find that even making a financial offer equivalent to one-half to one month's median profits only resulted in the registration of 20 per cent of the enterprises, and a financial offer equivalent to two months' profits led to 50 per cent registering. Reducing the costs of registration therefore improves formalisation but even offering large cost reductions fails to attract the majority to register. This is doubtless due to the low benefits of formalisation, limited ambitions of the entrepreneurs, mistrust of governments and the fear of the high recurrent costs of formalisation in the medium to long term (Zinnes, 2009). Such experiments therefore clearly reveal that decreasing registration costs alone is insufficient to produce formalisation (see also Altenburg and von Drachenfels, 2006; Arruñada, 2007).

Another simplification option is therefore to reduce administrative complexity, such as by simplifying tax and labour administration for small businesses (e.g., the number of forms and returns and pursuing joint rather than separate inspections) and enhance the provision of support and education to help firms comply. To aid this, compliance cost studies provide a means of evaluating the extent to which the regulatory burden prevents formalisation for different sectors and types of enterprise. However, as Hart *et al.* (2005) reveal, current compliance cost studies have three major weaknesses: they focus upon only the costs easily quantified but exclude other costs (e.g., psychological stress); they often exclude the benefits of regulation to entrepreneurs, and they focus on direct compliance costs rather than indirect costs (e.g., when enterprises decide not to grow or formalise due to the perceived formal regulations).

One solution is to use Regulatory Impact Assessment (RIA) tests for all proposed formal regulations and to even extend this to include an 'informal sector impact assessment' test. However, and as Hart *et al.* (2005) reveal, RIAs vary in the clarity with which the policy objectives are stated; their assessment of the risks; the use of stakeholder engagement; consideration of non-regulatory alternatives; estimates of the expected costs and benefits of the proposed regulations and discussion of the sanctions for non-compliance.

Simplifying the formal regulations can also involve more fundamental regulatory changes. One option in this regard is to simplify the self-assessment tax returns for the self-employed. In many countries, the self-employed complete detailed (often self-assessed) tax returns. These require a significant time commitment and often involve psychological stress. Income must be recorded, receipts kept of all expenditures and calculations made for all tax deductible items so that net profit can be calculated. Elffers and Hessing (1997) propose the introduction of a single standard deduction for expenses (see also Slemrod and Yitzhaki, 1994). This might be a fixed amount or a percentage of gross income. If introduced, this would get rid of the idea of tax deductible items and the need to keep and log receipts from expenditures and significantly simplify the tax system.

The advantage for entrepreneurs of applying this overall deduction, which has operated in the US federal income tax system for many years, is that: it is a safe and certain figure known in advance; it saves time and trouble; there is no need for a tax advisor; and it reduces uncertainty. The higher the standard deduction, the greater is the chance that they will use this rather than operate in the informal sector. Indeed Gross (1990) reports its popularity, revealing that in the United States in 1990, 71 per cent of taxpayers opted for the standard deduction in the form of a fixed amount. From a revenue-to-costs viewpoint, meanwhile, it is wholly ineffective and inefficient for tax administrations to check every deductible item on a self-assessment form. This involves small amounts of money and takes officials much time to check, discuss and correct. In consequence, this measure could considerably reduce the workload of tax administrations, allowing resources to be shifted towards other initiatives to facilitate formalisation. It could also be revenue-neutral. By auditing existing tax returns across various industries and occupations for the mean or median deductions claimed, this standard deduction could be either universally applied (which would be simplest) or applied in the first instance only to those sectors and/or occupations where informal entrepreneurship is rife.

Direct and Indirect Tax and Social Contribution Incentives

A popular assumption is that reducing taxes and social contributions will decrease informal entrepreneurship. However, there is no evidence that this is the case, and the problem with using such general tax reforms to formalise informal entrepreneurship is that they have much broader impacts. For this reason, more targeted measures are required.

Many of those starting up businesses secure their venture capital from informal sources such as family, friends and acquaintances. These loans are frequently relatively informal, and this can result in an attitude being adopted from the outset that informal practices are part of the culture of the business venture being established. To address this, the Netherlands introduced a scheme, *Tante Agaath-Regeling* ('Rich Aunt Agatha Arrangement'), later renamed the Venture and Start-Up Capital tax rules scheme. This provides the lenders with a tax incentive to declare the loan. By exempting lenders from certain taxes, these loans become known to the tax administration, making it less likely that businesses will view themselves as engaged in informal funding arrangements, which might well spill over into their trading practices (Renooy et al., 2004; Williams, 2004b). The loan had to be for a minimum of €2,269 and a maximum of €50,000. No formal evaluations were conducted.

Another example of a tax incentive is the start-up premium (*Gründungszuschuss*, GZ) in Germany. In 2002 the Commission on 'Modern Services in the Labour Market' (known as the Hartz Commission) proposed a new public subsidy for business start-ups (*Existenzgründungszuschuss*). The subsidy, known as the 'Ich-AG', or 'Me PLC' scheme, was criticised for performing the same function as a second existing scheme, the 'bridging grant' (*Überbrückungsgeld*). In August 2006, therefore, the two were fused in the 'start-up premium' (*Gründungszuschuss*) scheme. Available to recipients of unemployment benefits wanting to start up their own business, these entrepreneurs receive in addition to their unemployment benefit a monthly grant of €300 in the first six months. If after six months the recipient can prove intense business activity and initial success, an additional €300 is received for another nine months. Bernhard and Wolff (2011) find that the scheme tends to attract more women than men, while Caliendo *et al.* (2011) also show that GZ participants are older and have higher educational qualifications. As Bernhard and Wolff (2011) note, between 119,000 and 147,000 recipients of unemployment benefits enrolled annually in the GZ scheme between 2007 and 2010. Although there is no evidence regarding whether it reduced informal entrepreneurship, Caliendo *et al.* (2011) reveal a high survival rate of GZ participants' businesses. Some 19 months after start-up, 75–84 per cent of former GZ recipients were still in business. This scheme, therefore, appears to help smooth the transition from unemployment to formal entrepreneurship and to reduce participation in informal entrepreneurship by the unemployed.

It is also possible to use indirect tax incentives, such as reducing VAT on specific goods and services in sectors where informal entrepreneurship is prevalent. This could include the household repair, maintenance and improvement (RMI) sector. Although early research displayed that the introduction of VAT had little effect on the size of the informal sector (Bhattacharyya, 1990; Feige, 1990; Frey and Weck, 1983; Macafee, 1980), many countries have reduced indirect taxes as a means of addressing informal entrepreneurship to encourage consumers to purchase on a formal basis.

Capital Economics Ltd (2003) evaluated one of the few schemes to target entrepreneurs. In the UK in 2003, a short-term one-off incentive scheme was offered to enterprises that should have registered for VAT but had not done so. The forecast was that 6,300 businesses would take advantage of the scheme and raise £11 million in additional VAT and interest. Penalties were waived if enterprises continued to comply for 12 months. This scheme cost £500,000 in advertising costs and an estimated £2.7 million in penalties foregone. When the scheme closed, the tax administration had received 3,000 registrations raising £11.4 million in tax and interest (i.e., an average of £3,800 per case). Around 55 per cent of businesses taking advantage of the scheme subsequently failed to submit a VAT return causing the department to impose £2.5 million in penalties. This had a return-to-cost ratio of 23:1 compared with 4.5:1 overall for all informal sector compliance activity in the UK (National Audit Office, 2008).

An alternative indirect tax scheme to formalise informal entrepreneurship is the use of reverse charges for VAT where the purchaser, rather than seller, must file and pay the VAT. Based on the notion that informal entrepreneurship often occurs further down supply chains due to the use of outsourcing and subcontracting, it has been particularly applied in the construction industry. In Sweden, for example, the government introduced a law on reverse charges for VAT in 2007 whereby a company selling construction services more than on a temporary basis must pay VAT for its subcontractors. If the purchaser is not a construction company, the vendor shall add VAT to the invoice. If the purchaser is a construction company, the vendor shall not add VAT to the invoice. Instead the purchaser will be responsible for reporting the output VAT. Reverse VAT liability does not apply to sales which consist solely of materials. According to a survey by the Swedish Tax Agency (2011), around 39 per cent of the surveyed companies believed that the reverse charge reduced the level of informality in the construction sector. The Swedish Tax Agency (2011) found some evidence of an increase in the reporting of output tax in the construction sector at SEK 700 million (€82.3 million) in 2008.

Again focused on the supply chain, various supply chain responsibility initiatives can be used. These can be either voluntary or mandatory. One such initiative is in Finland. The 2006 Contractor's Obligations and Liability When Work Is Contracted Out Act requires that the enterprise responsible for a construction project to obtain the necessary guarantees that subcontractors fulfil their regulatory obligations. This was amended in 2012 to include accident insurance. The rationale was that long subcontracting chains result in informality, and this legislation placed the responsibility on the users (which tend to be larger businesses) of subcontractors and temporary work agencies that these subcontractors and employment agencies meet their obligations. They must obtain documents that verify registration and payment of taxes. Early evaluations in 2010 reveal that half of the 2,541 contracts examined contained violations (Alvesalo and Hakamo, 2009; *Työ-ja elinkeinoministeriö, 2011*).

Formalisation Support and Advice Services

Another means of encouraging entrepreneurs to start up legitimately, and to formalise informal entrepreneurship, is to provide support and advice services. This might entail the development of Micro-enterprise Development Programmes (MDPs) that provide micro-credit, advice, training and/or support to such ventures (Jurik, 2005). Evaluations reveal that MDPs are effective at promoting business growth, creating jobs and increasing clients' incomes, self-esteem and community involvement (Clark *et al.*, 1999; Edgcomb *et al.*, 1996; Himes and Servon, 1998) as well as helping smooth the transition from unemployment to self-employment (Balkin, 1989). Whether MDPs are effective at helping enterprises start up on a formal basis is not known. By providing formal loans, MDPs might do so, especially if these are complemented with advice, support and training. Until now, however, no evaluations have been undertaken.

What does seem apparent is that bespoke support and advice services are required for informal entrepreneurs seeking to formalise. This has been explored in Italy (e.g., Caianiello and Voltura, 2003; Meldolesi and Ruvolo, 2003), the UK (e.g., Barbour and Llanes, 2013; Evans *et al.*, 2006;

Small Business Council, 2004; Williams, 2004a, 2005, 2006c), Europe more generally (Renooy *et al.*, 2004), the United States (e.g., Jurik, 2005) and Nigeria (Sutter *et al.*, 2017). The rationale for a bespoke support and advice service is that the business advice and support required by those formalising their business ventures differ from that required by start-ups or formal businesses seeking to expand (Caianiello and Voltura, 2003; Copisarow, 2004; Copisarow and Barbour, 2004; ILO, 2002; Meldolesi and Ruvolo, 2003; Williams, 2005). It is also widely acknowledged that support and advice is generally not widely available about how to formalise (Barbour and Llanes, 2013; Copisarow and Barbour, 2004; Small Business Council, 2004; Williams, 2005). In many countries, simple advice about how to formalise a business venture, for example, in the form of flow charts of what needs to be done, is not available. Neither is advice available on how to start up a venture legitimately available again in the form of simple flow charts. Instead entrepreneurs are often confronted with the citation of complex labour and tax codes when approaching labour and tax administrations, which is not at all helpful to entrepreneurs seeking to establish legitimate business ventures.

Viewing such support services through the lens of institutional theory, and drawing upon a case study of a non-governmental organisation which sought to transition 1,800 dairy farmers in rural Nicaragua from the informal to formal sector, Sutter *et al.* (2017) argue that this formalisation of informal entrepreneurs requires them to transfer from one institutional framework (informal markets) to another (formal markets). For these commentators, this requires institutional intermediation using bridging actors to facilitate their shift between institutional frameworks since transitioning from informal to formal markets involves fundamental alterations in the way the business operates.

Demand-Side Incentives

Besides encouraging and incentivising entrepreneurs to operate in the formal sector, many countries have also sought to encourage and incentivise purchasers to acquire goods and services in the formal sector. Such measures include targeted direct tax measures, service voucher schemes and targeted indirect tax incentives. All seek to reduce the demand for goods and services from the informal sector. The rationale is that it is not always entrepreneurs who instigate the idea of the good or service being provided in the informal sector. Often it is consumers, as exemplified by the common statement 'how much for cash?', who are the instigators of transactions in the informal sector (Williams, 2006b, 2008; Williams and Horodnic, 2016; Williams and Martinez-Perez, 2014a,b; Williams *et al.*, 2012). To help formalise informal entrepreneurship, therefore, measures have also targeted consumers to encourage and incentivise them to purchase goods and services on a formal basis.

Direct Tax Incentives for Purchasers

Decreasing tax rates has extensive implications, and there is no evidence that reducing them results in a decline in the size of the informal sector (Vanderseypen *et al.*, 2013; Williams, 2014a). More targeted strategies, however, are an option, such as providing income tax relief, claimed on (self-assessed) tax returns, to customers using formal labour for household repair, maintenance and improvement tasks (e.g., roof maintenance, outside painting and household cleaning). For example, tax rebates on home maintenance expenses have been available in France since 2000, along with tax reductions for house repairs in Italy and Luxembourg. As the European Commission (1998: 14) conclude with regard to such initiatives, 'tax-deductions and subsidies for refurbishing and improvements of houses have . . . had the effect of moving work which might have been done informally to the formal and registered sector'. Meanwhile, similar direct tax schemes for purchasers have been implemented with regard to other domestic services (e.g., household cleaning and gardening) in countries such as Denmark, Finland, France and Germany to formalise informal entrepreneurship in the household cleaning sector and gardening services.

In Sweden since 2008, consumers have been able to deduct from their taxes 50 per cent of the labour cost of work involving renovation, conversion and extension of their homes (ROT) and for household services (RUT), including cleaning, laundry, basic gardening and babysitting. The maximum annual tax deduction an individual consumer can claim is SEK 50,000 (€6,000). It was estimated in 2007 that the RUT deduction would cost SEK1.3 billion per year (€155 million) and in 2009 that the ROT deduction would cost SEK 13.5 billion per year (€416 million) (Swedish Tax Agency, 2011). Entrepreneurs providing such household services charge the customer the cost of the materials and half the labour costs, including VAT. The entrepreneur then requests the outstanding amount from the Swedish Tax Agency. Comparing 2005 and 2011, the Swedish Tax Agency (2011) estimated a 10 per cent decline in the level of informality in the sectors covered by the ROT and RUT deduction. In 2011, moreover, the Swedish Federation of Business Owners (*Företagarna*) undertook a survey of 2,447 construction companies. Some 90 per cent of the construction enterprises surveyed felt that the ROT deduction had a positive impact on reducing the level of informality in the construction sector compared with 78 per cent in 2009. In 2010, 1.1 million consumers acquired services with a RUT or ROT tax deduction, and the Swedish Tax Agency paid out SEK 1.4 billion (€166 million) in RUT deductions and SEK 13.5 billion (€1.6 billion) in ROT deductions. Hence, some 7.6 million hours of ROT services and 53 million hours of ROT were performed using these schemes (Brunk, 2013).

In Denmark since 2011 until the beginning of 2014, it was possible for citizens to deduct from their taxes up to DKK 15,000 (€2,000) to cover the costs of employing craftspeople and domestic helpers under a pilot project called 'Home-Job Plan' (*Bolig-Jobplan*). Hence, while Sweden has a maximum tax deduction of €6,600, the cap is €2,000 in Denmark. The activities covered include cleaning, indoor or outdoor household maintenance, gardening services and babysitting. The cost to the government was estimated to be DKK 1 billion (€134 million) in 2011 and around DKK 1.75 billion (€234 million) in 2012 and 2013. The tax authorities deduct 15 per cent of the amount in the yearly tax or fiscal income of the consumer. Some 270,000 people used this deduction in 2011, mostly for household repair, maintenance and improvement work. Consumers have on average requested tax deductions of DKK 9,800 (€1,315) per person. In total, the deductions reported amount to DKK 2.7 billion (€362 million). The tax value of those deductions is around DKK 900 million (€121 million) (Jørgensen, 2013).

These schemes, therefore, are a means of transforming informal into formal entrepreneurship by targeting the consumers who acquire services in the informal sector and offering them financial incentives to ensure that the work is conducted in the formal sector.

Service Voucher Schemes

Another common initiative widely used in European countries to target purchasers of goods and services in the informal sector with the intention of formalising informal entrepreneurship is the service voucher scheme. In Belgium where it is perhaps most developed, service vouchers are used to pay for everyday personal services. Each voucher costs €9.00 for the first 400 vouchers per person (in 2014) and €10.00 for the next 100. Each individual can buy 500 vouchers per annum or 1,000 vouchers for each family (although single parents or mothers returning to work with young children can buy more). Up to €1,350 per year is tax deductible (at a 30 per cent tax rate). Every voucher pays for one hour of work from certified companies that hire unemployed people to do this work. At first, the company can hire the unemployed person on a part-time temporary contract. After six months, however, the company has to offer the worker a permanent employment contract or at least a 50 per cent full-time contract if the person was previously registered as unemployed. An employee of a certified company can carry out the following activities: housecleaning, washing and ironing, sewing, running errands, preparing meals or accompanying people who are not mobile. The customer pays with the vouchers whose cost price in 2013 was €22.04; the difference is paid by the government. The total cost of the service voucher scheme to the government in 2011 was some €500m. Per employee net costs amounted to €3,520 in 2011 (€2,793 in 2010) (Gerard et al., 2012).

Although early studies found that customers previously sourced some 44 per cent of the work conducted using service vouchers from the informal sector (De Sutter, 2000), recent evaluations find that only 25 per cent reported that they would have purchased these services in the informal sector if they had not used service vouchers. One interpretation is that in its early days, the scheme acted as a tool for formalising informal work but is now becoming more of a means for moving unpaid self-provisioning activities into the formal sector. At the end of 2011, 2,754 businesses were involved, along with 830,000 users; 108,663,966 vouchers were sold and around 150,000 persons employed. Although only 4.6 per cent (10.2 per cent in Brussels) of employees stated they started working in the voucher system to avoid working in the informal sector, this ignores that without it, many customers would doubtless source these services in the informal sector if the service voucher scheme did not exist (Ajzen, 2013).

Variants of this scheme have been pursued in many other countries, although budget constraints are often a limiting factor as is the level of development of the domestic services market. Some countries, that is, have little or no tradition of domestic services being conducted for payment by people outside of the family. The result is that the activities covered by the scheme have been widened to other activities where the informal sector is prevalent in different countries, such as the agricultural sector, and also used to pay suppliers of work rather than consumers in a bid to reduce the supply of labour in the informal sector. Whether it represents value for money relative to other schemes to formalise informal enterprise, however, remains open to question.

Indirect Tax Incentives for Purchasers

Beyond providing consumers with direct tax subsidies, indirect tax subsidies can also be used to formalise informal entrepreneurship. This involves reducing VAT on specific goods and services where informal entrepreneurship is rife, such as home repair, maintenance and improvement. Whether such VAT reductions lead to a transfer of home repair, maintenance and improvement work into formal enterprise and entrepreneurship is open to debate. One of the few studies to evaluate the impacts of reducing VAT on the RMI sector is a study conducted by Capital Economics Ltd (2003) on the UK market. This evaluated the implications of reducing VAT to 5 per cent on the RMI sector. Since a lower VAT rate encourages consumers to purchase in the formal sector, they argue that a reduction could boost VAT revenue. Their argument is that by reducing VAT from 17.5 to 5 per cent, this would reduce the price differential between formal and informal sector prices for customers. They reveal that reducing indirect taxes does not necessarily lead to increased government revenue.

Several other implications also intimate the need for caution with regard to this policy measure of reducing VAT. Reducing taxes may lead to a 'race to the bottom' in that reducing tax in one country encourages others to follow. Although not necessarily the case when an indirect tax reduction targets consumers in home repair, maintenance and improvement work, it remains possible that reducing indirect taxes will then turn attention to reductions in direct taxes. For these reasons, a cautious approach is recommended towards VAT reductions as a policy measure.

Conclusions

This chapter has reviewed a range of hard direct policy measures that firstly seek to increase the costs of informal entrepreneurship and, secondly, seek to encourage and incentivise formal entrepreneurship. This has firstly revealed the range of hard policy measures at the disposal of governments seeking to increase the perceived and/or actual costs of informal entrepreneurship by increasing either the penalties for such endeavour and/or the risks of detection. Secondly, and given that formalising informal entrepreneurship requires that entrepreneurs are not only pushed out of entering or remaining in the informal sector but are also pulled into formal entrepreneurship, a range of measures to encourage and incentivise formal entrepreneurship have been reviewed. On the one hand, supply-side incentives have been reviewed and, on the other hand, demand-side incentives have been evaluated.

To improve the power of authorities, therefore, two changes are required. Firstly, there is a need to directly increase the costs and reduce the benefits of informality for entrepreneurs. This can be achieved by state authorities increasing the risks of detection (using workplace inspections, business certification, cash registers, deterring cash payments, notification letters, peer-to-peer surveillance and cross-government co-operation on data mining, operations and strategy) and the penalties for those caught. Studies until now do not reveal clear-cut results on the effectiveness of this deterrence approach.

Secondly, there is also a need to reduce the costs and increase the benefits of operating in the formal sector. On the one hand, this requires a simplification and reduction in the costs of registration, which studies in Kenya (Devas and Kelly, 2001), Uganda (Sander, 2003), Bolivia (Garcia-Bolivar, 2006) and Peru (Jaramillo, 2009) reveal lead to an increase in registration. On the other hand, the benefits of registration need to be enhanced, although De Mel *et al.* (2012) in Sri Lanka find that even a financial offer equivalent to two months' profits led to only 50 per cent of firms registering. This is perhaps because the mistrust in governments and fear of the high recurrent costs of registration need to be addressed (Maloney, 2004; McKenzie and Woodruff, 2006), along with the provision of higher levels of property rights protection (Marcoullier and Young, 1995; Nwabuzor, 2005; Thomas and Mueller, 2000), improvements in the quality of governance, decreases in public sector corruption and increases in the level of government intervention to resolve the formal institutional voids and weaknesses, such as improved social protection, which have been shown to reduce non-registration and informality (Autio and Fu, 2015; Dau and Cuervo-Cazurra,

2014; Klapper *et al.*, 2007; Thai and Turkina, 2014). It is to these issues, therefore, that attention turns in the next chapter.

In sum, it is important to recognise that the policy measures reviewed in this chapter have been all hard direct controls that either increase the costs and reduce the benefits of informal entrepreneurship or reduce the costs and increase the benefits of formal entrepreneurship. The problem with using such hard direct measures, however, is not only that individuals are not always rational economic actors but also that many countries have limited resources to increase the power of authorities and that these measures only address one particular type of formal institutional failure that leads to informal entrepreneurship, namely, what was referred to in Chapter 2 as formal institutional powerlessness. To address the recognition that entrepreneurs are also social actors, and the issue of trust in authorities, as well as the other formal institutional failures that lead to an asymmetry between formal and informal institutions (i.e., which Chapter 2 identified as formal institutional resource misallocations and inefficiencies, voids and weaknesses, and instability and uncertainty), the next chapter turns its attention to the analysis of the soft indirect measures that can be pursued.

References

Adams, C. and Webley, P. (2001). Small business owners' attitudes on VAT compliance in the UK. *Journal of Economic Psychology*, 22(2), pp. 195–216.

Ajzen, M. (2013). *Service vouchers, Belgium*. Available at: www.eurofound.europa. eu/areas/labourmarket/tackling/cases/be016.htm (last accessed 11 May 2017).

Alm, J., McClelland, G. and Schulze, W. (1992). Why do people pay taxes? *Journal of Public Economics*, 1, pp. 323–338.

Alm, J., Mckee, M. and Beck, W. (1990). Amazing grace: Tax amnesties and compliance. *National Tax Journal*, 43(1), pp. 23–37.

Alm, J., Sanchez, I. and De Juan, A. (1995). Economic and non-economic factors in tax compliance. *Kyklos*, 48, pp. 3–18.

Altenburg, T. and von Drachenfels, C. (2006). The 'new minimalist approach' to private-sector development: A critical assessment. *Development Policy Review*, 24, pp. 387–411.

Alvesalo, A. and Hakamo, T. (2009). Valvontaa ja vastuuta ulkopuolisen työvoiman käyttöön—tutkimus tilaajavastuulain toteutumisesta. *Työ- ja elinkeinoministeriön julkaisuja, Työ ja yrittäjyys*, 51, pp. 1–6.

Anvelt, K. (2008). *Ümbrikupalk röövib riigilt päevas miljoni*. Available at: www.epl. ee/artikkel/432184 (last accessed 11 May 2017).

Arruñada, B. (2007). Pitfalls to avoid when measuring institutions: Is doing business damaging business? *Journal of Comparative Economics*, 35, pp. 729–747.

Autio, E. and Fu, K. (2015). Economic and political institutions and entry into formal and informal entrepreneurship. *Asia Pacific Journal of Management*, 32(1), pp. 67–94.

Ayres, I. and Braithwaite, J. (1992). *Responsive regulation: Transcending the deregulation debate*. New York: Oxford University Press.

Baer, K. and LeBorgne, E. (2008). *Tax amnesties: Theory, trends and some alternatives*. Washington, DC: International Monetary Fund.

Bakos, J. (2012a). *Report of the National Employment Office—Hungarian Labour Inspectorate for the request of the Hungarian NEO correspondents*. Budapest: National Employment Office.

Bakos, J. (2012b). *A nemzeti munkaügyi hivatal munkavédelmi és munkaügyi igazgatóság közleménye a 2012: évre szóló munkaügyi és munkavédelmi ellenőrzési irányelvekről*. Budapest: Nemzetgazdasági Közlöny.

Balkin, S. (1989). *Self-employment for low-income people*. New York: Praeger.

Barbour, A. and Llanes, M. (2013). *Supporting people to legitimise their informal businesses*. York: Joseph Rowntree Foundation.

Beeby, D. (2017). *Underground economy players impervious to CRAs 'nudge' experiment*. Available at: www.cbc.ca/news/politics/nudge-economics-underground-economy-canada-revenue-agency-tax-1.4084932 (last accessed 6 June 2017).

Bernhard, S. and Wolff, J. (2011). *Förderinstrument im SGB III: der gründungszuschuss aus sicht der praxis*. Available at: http://doku.iab.de/kurzber/2011/kb2211.pdf (last accessed 25 April 2017).

Beron, K.J., Tauchen, H.V. and Witte, A.D. (1992). The effect of audits and socioeconomic variables on compliance. In: J. Slemerod, Ed., *Why people pay taxes*. Ann Arbor: University of Michigan Press, pp. 67–89.

Bhattacharyya, D.K. (1990). An econometric method of estimating the hidden economy, United Kingdom (1960–1984): Estimates and tests. *The Economic Journal*, 100, pp. 703–717.

Blumenthal, M., Christian, C. and Slemrod, J. (1998). *The determinants of income tax compliance: Evidence from a controlled experiment in Minnesota*. Massachusetts: National Bureau of Economic Research Working Paper no. 6575.

Brehm, S.S. and Brehm, J.W. (1981). *Psychological reactance: A theory of freedom and control*. New York: Academic Press.

Brunk, T. (2013). *Tax deductions for domestic service work, Sweden*. Available at: www.eurofound.europa.eu/areas/labourmarket/tackling/cases/se015.htm (last accessed 11 May 2017).

Caianiello, D. and Voltura, I. (2003). *Proposal for a service bureau*. Rome: Comitato per l'emersione del lavoro no regolare.

Caliendo, M., Hogenacker, J., Künn, S. and Wießner, F. (2011). *Alte idee, neues programm: der gründungszuschuss als nachfolger von überbrückungsgeld und Ich-AG*. Available at: http://doku.iab.de/discussionpapers/2011/dp2411.pdf (last accessed 25 January 2017).

Capital Economics Ltd (2003). *VAT and the construction industry*. London: Capital Economics Ltd.

Chittenden, F., Kauser, S. and Poutzouris, P. (2002). *Regulatory burdens of small business: A literature review*. London: Small Business Service.

Clark, P., Kays, A. Zandiapour, L., Soto, E. and Doyle, K. (1999). *Microenterprise and the poor: Findings from the self-employment learning project five-year study of microentrepreneurs*. Washington, DC: Aspen Institute.

Copisarow, R. (2004). *Street UK: A micro-finance organisation: Lessons learned from its first three years' operations*. Birmingham: Street UK.

Copisarow, R. and Barbour, A. (2004). *Self-employed people in the informal economy—cheats or contributors?* London: Community Links.

Coricelli, G., Rusconi, E. and Villeval, M.-C. (2014). Tax evasion and emotions: An empirical test of re-integrative shaming theory. *Journal of Economic Psychology*, 40(1), pp. 49–61.

Dau, L.A. and Cuervo-Cazurra, A. (2014). To formalize or not to formalize: Entrepreneurship and pro-market institutions. *Journal of Business Venturing*, 29, pp. 668–686.

De Juan, A., Lasheras, M.A. and Mayo, R. (1994). Voluntary tax compliant behavior of Spanish income taxpayers. *Public Finance*, 49, pp. 90–105.
De Mel, S., McKenzie, D. and Woodruff, C. (2012). *The demand for, and consequences of formalization among informal firms in Sri Lanka*. Washington, DC: Policy Research Working Paper no. 5991, World Bank.
De Sutter, T. (2000). *Het plaatselijk werkgelegenheidsagentschap: regelgeving en praktijk*. Leuven: HIVA.
Devas, N. and Kelly, R. (2001). Regulation or revenue? An analysis of local business licenses, with a case study of the single business permit reform in Kenya. *Public Administration and Development*, 21, pp. 381–191.
De Wispelaere, F. and Pacolet, J. (2017). *Data mining for more efficient enforcement: Discussion paper*. Brussels: European Commission.
Dubin, J., Graetz, M. and Wilde, L. (1987). Are we a nation of tax cheaters? New econometric evidence on tax compliance. *The America Economic Review*, 77, pp. 240–245.
Dubin, J. and Wilde, L. (1988). An empirical analysis of federal income tax auditing and compliance. *National Tax Journal*, 16, pp. 61–74.
Dzhekova, R. and Williams, C.C. (2014). *Tackling the undeclared economy in Bulgaria: A baseline assessment*. Sheffield: GREY Working Paper no. 1, Sheffield University Management School, University of Sheffield.
Edgcomb, E., Klein, J. and Clark, P. (1996). *The practice of microenterprise in the U.S.: Strategies, costs and effectiveness*. Washington, DC: Aspen Institute.
Elffers, H. and Hessing, D.J. (1997). Influencing the prospects of tax evasion. *Journal of Economic Psychology*, 18, pp. 289–304.
Elffers, H., Weigel, R.H. and Hessing, D.J. (1987). The consequences of different strategies for measuring tax evasion behaviour. *Journal of Economic Psychology*, 8, pp. 311–337.
European Commission (1998). *Communication of the commission on undeclared work*. Available at: http://europa.eu.int/comm/employment_social/empl_esf/docs/com98-219_en.pdf (last accessed 11 May 2017).
Evans, M., Syrett, S. and Williams, C.C. (2006). *Informal economic activities and deprived neighbourhoods*. London: Department of Communities and Local Government.
Feige, E.L. (1990). Defining and estimating underground and informal economies. *World Development*, 18(7), pp. 989–1002.
Feld, L.P. and Frey, B. (2002). Trust breeds trust: How taxpayers are treated. *Economics of Government*, 3(2), pp. 87–99.
Franzoni, L.A. (2000). Amnesties, settlements and optimal tax enforcement. *Economica*, 67, pp. 153–176.
Frey, B.S. and Weck, H. (1983). What produces a hidden economy? An international cross-section analysis. *Southern Economic Journal*, 49(4), pp. 822–832.
Friedland, N. (1982). A note on tax evasion as a function of the quality of information about the magnitude and credibility of threatened fines: Some preliminary research. *Journal of Applied Social Psychology*, 12, pp. 54–59.
Friedland, N., Maital, S. and Rutenberg, A. (1978). A simulation study of income tax evasion. *Journal of Public Economics*, 10, pp. 107–116.
Garcia-Bolivar, O. (2006). *Informal economy: Is it a problem, a solution or both? The perspective of the informal business*. Berkeley, CA: Bepress Legal Series.
Gerard, M., Neyens, I. and Valsamis, D. (2012). *Evaluatie van het stelsel van de dienstencheques voor buurtdiensten en—banen 2011*. Brussels: IDEA Consult.
Gross, E.B. (1990). *Individual income tax returns: Preliminary data, 1990*. Washington, DC: SoI Bulletin11, nr 4, Publication 1136, Department of the Treasury, Internal Revenue Service.

Hansford, A., Hasseldine, J. and Howorth, C. (2003). Factors affecting the costs of UK VAT compliance for small and medium-sized enterprises. *Environment and Planning C*, 21(4), pp. 479–492.

Hart, M., Blackburn, R. and Kitching, J. (2005). *The impact of regulation on small business growth: An outline research programme*. London: Small Business Research Centre, Kingston University.

Hasseldine, J. (1998). Tax amnesties: An international review. *Bulletin for International Fiscal Documentation*, 52(7), pp. 303–310.

Himes, C. and Servon, L. (1998). *Measuring client success: An evaluation of ACCION's impact on microenterprises in the U.S.* Washington, DC: ACCION International.

ILO (2002). *Decent work and the informal economy*. Geneva: ILO.

ILO (2006). *Labour inspection*. Geneva: ILO.

ILO (2014). *Transitioning from the informal to the formal economy*. Report V (1), International Labour Conference, 103rd Session (2014). Geneva: ILO.

Jaramillo, M. (2009). *Is there demand for formality among informal firms? Evidence from microfirms in downtown Lima*. Bonn: German Development Institute Discussion Paper no. 12/2009, German Development Institute.

Jørgensen, C. (2013). *Home-job plan, Denmark*. Available at: www.eurofound.europa.eu/areas/labourmarket/tackling/cases/dk015.htm (last accessed 14 May 2017).

Jurik, N.C. (2005). *Bootstrap dreams: U.S. microenterprise development in an era of welfare reform*. Ithaca: Cornell University Press.

Kagan, R.A. and Scholz, J.T. (1984). The criminology of the corporation and regulatory enforcement strategies. In: K. Hawkins and J.M. Thomas, Eds., *Enforcing regulation*. Boston: Klewer-Nijhoff, pp. 62–84.

Kinsey, K. and Gramsick, H. (1993). Did the tax reform act of 1986 improve compliance? Three studies of pre- and post-TRA compliance attitudes. *Law and Policy*, 15, pp. 239–325.

Klapper, L., Amit, R., Guillén, M.F. and Quesada, J.M. (2007). *Entrepreneurship and firm formation across countries*. Washington, DC: World Bank Policy Research Working Paper Series no. 4313.

Klepper, S. and Nagin, D. (1989). Tax compliance and perceptions of the risks of detection and criminal prosecution. *Law and Society Review*, 23, pp. 209–240.

Levit, G. (2008). *More than EEK 330 million of unpaid taxes in half-year*. Available at: http://bbn.ee/Default2.aspx?ArticleID=8de6ee15-be3b-4421-b1a3-5380e0dc446c. (last accessed 16 May 2017).

LópezLaborda, J. and Rodrigo, F. (2003). Tax amnesties and income tax compliance: The case of Spain. *Fiscal Studies*, 24(1), pp. 73–96.

Luitel, H.S. and Sobel, R.S. (2007). The revenue impact of repeated tax amnesties. *Public Budgeting and Finance*, 27(3), pp. 19–38.

Macafee, K. (1980). A glimpse of the hidden economy in the national accounts. *Economic Trends*, 2(1), pp. 81–87.

Macho-Stadler, I., Olivella, P. and Perez-Castrillo, D. (1999). Tax amnesties in a dynamic model of tax evasion. *Journal of Public Economic Theory*, 1(4), pp. 439–463.

Maloney, W.F. (2004). Informality revisited. *World Development*, 32(7), pp. 1159–1178.

Marcoullier, D. and Young, L. (1995). The black hole of graft: The predatory state and the informal economy. *American Economic Review*, 85(3), pp. 630–646.

Matthews, K. and Lloyd-Williams, J. (2001). The VAT evading firm and VAT evasion: An empirical analysis. *International Journal of the Economics of Business*, 6(1), pp. 39–50.

McKenzie, D. and Woodruff, C. (2006). Do entry costs provide an empirical basis for poverty traps? Evidence from microenterprises. *Economic Development and Cultural Change*, 55(1), pp. 3–42.

Meldolesi, L. and Ruvolo, S. (2003). *A project for formalisation*. Rome: Comitato per l'emersione del lavoro no regolare.

Michaelis, C., Smith, K. and Richards, S. (2001). *Regular survey of small businesses' opinions: First survey: Final report*. London: Small Business Service.

Mikesell, J.L. and Ross, J.M. (2012). Fast money? The contributions of state tax amnesties to public revenue systems. *National Tax Journal*, 65(3), pp. 529–562.

Murphy, K. (2005). Regulating more effectively: The relationship between procedural justice, legitimacy and tax non-compliance. *Journal of Law and Society*, 32(4), pp. 562–589.

Murphy, K. and Harris, N. (2007). Shaming, shame and recidivism: A test of re-integrative shaming theory in the white-collar crime context. *British Journal of Criminology*, 47, pp. 900–917.

National Audit Office (2008). *Tackling the hidden economy*. London: National Audit Office.

Nwabuzor, A. (2005). Corruption and development: New initiatives in economic openness and strengthened rule of law. *Journal of Business Ethics*, 59(1/2), pp. 121–138.

OECD (2000). *Tax avoidance and evasion*. Paris: OECD.

OECD (2012). *Reducing opportunities for tax non-compliance in the underground economy*. Paris: OECD.

OECD (2016). *Informal entrepreneurship*. Paris: OECD.

Parle, W.M. and Hirlinger, M.W. (1986). Evaluating the use of tax amnesty by state governments. *Public Administration Review*, 46(3), pp. 246–255.

Renooy, P., Ivarsson, S., van der Wusten-Gritsai, O. and Meijer, R. (2004). *Undeclared work in an enlarged union: An analysis of shadow work: An in-depth study of specific items*. Brussels: European Commission.

Richardson, G. (2006). Determinants of tax evasion: A cross-country investigation. *Journal of International Accounting, Auditing and Taxation*, 15(2), pp. 150–169.

Rum, P. (2008). *Märgukirjade saatmine vähendas ümbrikupalga maksmist* (online). Estonian Tax and Customs Board, 11.06.2008. Available at: www.emta.ee/?id=24233 (last accessed 11 May 2017).

Sander, C. (2003). *Less is more: Better compliance and increased revenues by streamlining business registration in Uganda: A contribution to WDR 2005 on investment climate, growth and poverty*. London: Department for International Development.

Schwartz, R.D. and Orleans, S. (1967). On legal sanctions. *University of Chicago Law Review*, 34, pp. 282–300.

Shaw, J., Slemrod, J. and Whiting, J. (2008). *Administration and compliance*. London: Institute for Fiscal Studies.

Sissel, T., Nergaard, K., Alsos, K., Berge, Ø.M., Bråten, M. and Ødegård, A.M. (2011). *Til renholdets pris*. Oslo: Fafo.

Slemrod, J., Blumenthal, M. and Christian, C.W. (2001). Taxpayer response to an increased probability of audit: Evidence from a controlled experiment in Minnesota. *Journal of Public Economics*, 79, pp. 455–483.

Slemrod, J. and Yitzhaki, S. (1994). Analyzing the standard deduction as a presumptive tax. *International Tax and Public Finance*, 1(1), pp. 25–34.

Small Business Council (2004). Small business in the informal economy: Making the

Scer, M.W. and Lunstedt, S.B. (1976): Understanding tax evasion. *Public Finance*, 31, pp. 295–305.

Sutter, C., Webb, J., Kistruck, G., Ketchen, D.J. and Ireland, R.D. (2017). Transitioning entrepreneurs from informal to formal markets. *Journal of Business Venturing*, http://dx.doi.org/10.1016/j/jbusvent.2017.03.002

Swedish Tax Agency (2011). *Konsumenterna kan skapa schysst konkurrens och minska skattefelet.* Stockholm: Swedish Tax Agency.

Thai, M.T.T. and Turkina, E. (2014). Macro-level determinants of formal entrepreneurship versus informal entrepreneurship. *Journal of Business Venturing*, 29(4), pp. 490–510.

Thomas, A.S. and Mueller, S.I. (2000). A case for comparative entrepreneurship: Assessing the relevance of culture. *Journal of International Business Studies*, 31(2), pp. 287–301.

Torgler, B. and Schaltegger, C.A. (2005). Tax amnesties and political participation. *Public Finance Review*, 33(3), pp. 403–431.

Tubalkain-Trell, M. (2008). *EEK 490 million unpaid taxes in Estonia.* Available at: http://bbn.ee/Default2.aspx?ArticleID=1a549f52-a0d3-4241-ac2d-2f0ca170885f (last accessed 11 May 2014).

Tyler, T.R., Sherman, L., Strang, H., Barnes, G. and Woods, D. (2007). Reintegrative shaming, procedural justice and recidivism: The engagement of offenders' psychological mechanisms in the Canberra RISE drinking and driving experiment. *Law and Society Review*, 41, pp. 533–586.

Työ-ja elinkeinoministeriö. (2011). *Talousrikollisuuden ja harmaan talouden torjuminen rakennus- sekä majoitus- ja ravitsemisalalla -työryhmän mietintö. Työ- ja elinkeinoministeriön julkaisuja, Kilpailukyky.* Available at: www.tem.fi/files/29563/TEM_17_2011_netti.pdf (last accessed 14 May 2017).

Vanderseypen, G., Tchipeva, T., Peschner, J., Renooy, P. and Williams, C.C. (2013). Undeclared work: Recent developments. In: European Commission, Ed., *Employment and social developments in Europe 2013.* Brussels: European Commission, pp. 231–274.

Varma, K. and Doob, A. (1998). Deterring economic crimes: The case of tax evasion. *Canadian Journal of Criminology*, 40, pp. 165–184.

Vennesland, T.E. (2013). *Compulsory registration of temporary work agencies, Norway.* Available at: www.eurofound.europa.eu/areas/labourmarket/tackling/cases/no016.htm (last accessed 14 May 2017).

Webley, P. and Halstead, S. (1986). Tax evasion on the micro: Significant stimulations per expedient experiments. *Journal of Interdisciplinary Economics*, 1, pp. 87–100.

Williams, C.C. (2004a). *Cash-in-hand work: The underground sector and the hidden economy of favours.* Basingstoke: Palgrave Macmillan.

Williams, C.C. (2004b). Beyond deterrence: Rethinking the UK public policy approach towards undeclared work. *Public Policy and Administration*, 19(1), pp. 15–30.

Williams, C.C. (2005). Formalising the informal economy: The case for local initiatives. *Local Government Studies*, 31(3), pp. 337–351.

Williams, C.C. (2006a). *The hidden enterprise culture: Entrepreneurship in the underground economy.* Cheltenham: Edward Elgar.

Williams, C.C. (2006b). Harnessing the hidden enterprise culture: The Street (UK) community development finance initiative. *Local Economy*, 21(1), pp. 13–24.

Williams, C.C. (2006c). How much for cash? Tackling the cash-in-hand ethos in the household services sector. *The Service Industries Journal*, 26(5), pp. 479–492.

Williams, C.C. (2008). Consumers' motives for buying goods and services on an off-the-books basis. *International Review of Retail, Distribution and Consumer Research*, 18(4), pp. 405–421.

Williams, C.C. (2014a). *Confronting the shadow economy: Evaluating tax compliance and behaviour policies*. Cheltenham: Edward Elgar.

Williams, C.C. (2014b). A critical evaluation of the policy options towards the undeclared economy. *Journal of Self-Governance and Management Economics*, 2(4), pp. 7–52.

Williams, C.C. (2016). Tackling enterprise in the informal economy: An introductory overview. *International Journal of Entrepreneurship and Small Business*, 28(2/3), pp. 139–153.

Williams, C.C. (2017a). *Dependent self-employment: Trends, challenges and policy responses in the EU*. Geneva: ILO.

Williams, C.C. (2017b). *Developing a holistic approach for tackling undeclared work: A learning resource*. Brussels: European Commission.

Williams, C.C. and Horodnic, I. (2016). Evaluating the multifarious motives for acquiring goods and services from the informal sector in Central and Eastern Europe. *Journal of Contemporary Central and Eastern Europe*, 24(3), pp. 321–338.

Williams, C.C. and Martinez-Perez, A. (2014a). Why do consumers purchase goods and services in the informal economy? *Journal of Business Research*, 67(5), pp. 802–806.

Williams, C.C. and Martinez-Perez, A. (2014b). Evaluating the cash-in-hand consumer culture in the European Union. *Journal of Contemporary European Studies*, 22(4), pp. 466–482.

Williams, C.C., Nadin, S., Newton, S., Rodgers, P. and Windebank, J. (2013). Explaining off-the-books entrepreneurship: A critical evaluation of competing perspectives. *International Entrepreneurship and Management Journal*, 9(3), pp. 447–463.

Williams, C.C., Nadin, S. and Windebank, J. (2012). How much for cash? Tackling the cash-in-hand culture in the European property and construction sector. *Journal of Financial Management of Property and Construction*, 17(2), pp. 123–134.

Williams, C.C. and Renooy, P. (2013). *Tackling undeclared work in 27 European Union member states and Norway: Approaches and measures since 2008*. Dublin: European Foundation for the Improvement of Living and Working Conditions.

Witte, A.D. and Woodbury, D.F. (1985). The effect of tax laws and tax administration on tax compliance: The case of US individual income tax. *National Tax Journal*, 38, pp. 1–15.

Zinnes, C. (2009). *Business environment reforms and the informal economy*. Available at: www.enterprise-development.org/page/download?id=1489 (last accessed 11 May 2016).

9 Soft Indirect Policy Measures

Introduction

The last chapter reviewed the approach towards formalising informal entrepreneurship that seeks to increase the power of authorities by using hard direct compliance measures to change the cost/benefit ratio confronting entrepreneurs when making the decision on whether to engage in informal entrepreneurship. The problem is that these hard direct policy measures only seek to tackle one aspect of the formal institutional failings that result in the prevalence of informal entrepreneurship, namely, the relative power of the enforcement regime. In this chapter, attention turns to tackling the remaining formal institutional failings that lead to an asymmetry between the formal and informal institutions and thus higher levels of informal entrepreneurship, namely, formal institutional resource misallocations and inefficiencies, voids and weaknesses, and instability and uncertainty.

Across many countries, there has been a focus upon awareness-raising campaigns that have the objective of changing the norms, values and beliefs of entrepreneurs and citizens to align the formal and informal institutions. This chapter, therefore, commences by reviewing these policy measures that begin to address some of the formal institutional instability and uncertainty confronting entrepreneurs. However, the likelihood of these campaigns bringing into symmetry the formal and informal institutions is small, unless the other formal institutional failures and imperfections are solved that have resulted in this institutional asymmetry, namely, the formal institutional resource misallocations and inefficiencies and the formal institutional voids and weaknesses. In the second section of the chapter, therefore, the additional changes required in the formal institutions are addressed. These are of two types. On the one hand, there are a range of process innovations in government which tackle the formal institutional resource misallocations and inefficiencies by developing the perceived level of procedural and redistributive justice and fairness of government to reduce institutional symmetry. On the other hand, there are changes in various economic and social conditions and policies which Part II revealed are significantly associated with greater institutional asymmetry, such as economic underdevelopment and the lack of state intervention in both work and welfare. These tackle the formal institutional voids and weaknesses. Each is now considered in turn.

Changing the Informal Institutions

To tackle the lack of alignment of the formal and informal institutions, one approach is to change the norms, values and beliefs of potential and existing entrepreneurs regarding the acceptability of working in the informal sector so that these are in symmetry with the laws, regulations and codes of formal institutions. This can be achieved by improving understanding of the formal rules using educational and awareness-raising campaigns about the costs of informal entrepreneurship and/or the benefits of formal entrepreneurship and normative appeals.

Improving Understanding of the Formal Rules

Educating entrepreneurs about the formal rules is important if their norms, values and beliefs are to be in symmetry with the codified laws and regulations that constitute the formal institutions. To do this, entrepreneurs require two types of education. Firstly, there is a need to educate entrepreneurs about what the current formal rules require them to do by providing easily consumable information regarding their responsibilities. A significant portion of tax evasion, as well as social insurance and labour law violation, may be unintentional, resulting from a lack of knowledge, misunderstandings and/or a false interpretation of their legal responsibilities (Hasseldine and Li, 1999; Natrah, 2013). In consequence, one way forward is to provide greater information to entrepreneurs in an easily consumable and understood format about their responsibilities (Internal Revenue Service, 2007; Vossler *et al.*, 2011).

At present, this is seldom the case. For example, many tax administrations and labour inspectorates do not provide advice and information on the formal rules in an easily consumable format that entrepreneurs can instantly understand. If one visits the websites of many tax administrations and labour inspectorates around the world, it becomes quickly apparent that this is not the case. Neither do many countries have call centres for entrepreneurs where they can raise queries about their responsibilities and get succinct answers that they can act upon. One 'quick win' for many countries, therefore, is to provide the information required by entrepreneurs to abide by the formal rules in a format that they can easily understand along with an action plan of what they need to do to adhere to these rules. This might be for example as simple as providing an easy-to-understand flow chart of what an entrepreneur needs to do to establish a registered and legitimate business venture.

Secondly, and more broadly, there is also a need for entrepreneurs to be educated about the value and benefits of adhering to the formal rules in order that intentional evasion does not occur. In many countries, for example, entrepreneurs make substantial voluntary donations to private charities but, at the same time, are reticent about paying their taxes, despite these private charities often having parallel goals to the government in terms of the goods or services that they are seeking to provide to the society. This is doubtless because the entrepreneurs think that they know what happens to voluntary charity donations but are less clear regarding what their taxes are spent on (Li *et al.*, 2011). To reduce intentional evasion, therefore, a solution is to educate entrepreneurs about how and on what their taxes are spent and the value of making social insurance contributions and abiding to labour law and regulations. This requires entrepreneurs to be informed about the current and potential public goods and services they receive as a result of paying their taxes and about the benefits of social insurance and labour law (Bird *et al.*, 2006; Saeed and Shah, 2011).

These campaigns can be of different varieties. For example, in the UK, a letter is received by entrepreneurs completing a self-assessment tax return which details how much of their taxes paid in absolute terms has been spent on a variety of public goods and services (e.g., education, the health service, welfare provision and defence). This enables them to see in a very individually tailored manner the exact amount of their taxes that has been spent on specific public goods and services. Other options are to use signals at the point of receipt of public goods and services. For example, signs such as 'your taxes paid for this' could be put on civil construction schemes (e.g., new roads) that convey the clear message of where taxes are being spent. Signs in hospitals, in schools, in medical centres and on ambulances are other obvious options.

In Canada, for example, the Tax System Learning Unit provides information on the tax system and how the government spends the tax dollars collected. It particularly targets junior and high school students to educate them before they join the tax system. Although participation levels have been high, the impact on compliance has not been measured since there has been no evaluation until now that tracks the compliance behaviour of those taking the modules against a control group who have not. Austria has pursued a similar school-level initiative whereby tax officials provide training on future responsibilities for compliance, as has the Internal Revenue Service in the United States (Internal Revenue Service, 2007).

Another strategic option is to pursue an explicit earmarking approach so that entrepreneurs can see where their taxes are being spent. In Sierra Leone, Jibao and Prichard (2013) discuss how Bo City Council developed support for local tax collection by communicating information on revenue and expenditure to the public, which included informally linking revenue increases to specific public expenditures popular with the population. Korsun and Meagher (2004) in Guinea reveal that the collection of market taxes doubled after these taxes were linked explicitly to the development of new market facilities. Earmarking, nevertheless, reduces budget flexibility and leads to the notion that the tax system operates on a fee-for-services basis. Before embarking on an earmarking approach, therefore, caution is required about the long-term consequences of pursuing such a strategy.

Awareness-Raising Campaigns

Besides such educational initiatives about the formal rules, awareness-raising campaigns can be used as a further pro-active approach towards improving understanding of the costs of informal entrepreneurship and/or benefits of formal entrepreneurship. These marketing campaigns can inform entrepreneurs of the costs and risks of operating in the informal sector; potential customers of the risks and costs of purchasing from the informal sector; entrepreneurs of the benefits of operating in the formal sector and/or potential customers of the benefits of using the formal sector.

There is some tentative logic which suggests that marketing campaigns targeted at entrepreneurs will be more effective if they focus upon the benefits of entrepreneurs operating in the formal sector rather than the costs and risks of entrepreneurs participating in the informal sector. Thurman *et al.* (1984) reviewed different ways in which highlighting the adverse impacts of engaging in the informal sector can be negated. Here these are tailored to show how entrepreneurs can use these tactics to neutralise their guilt and negate the effectiveness of campaigns highlighting the costs and risks of operating in the informal sector. Entrepreneurs can do this in the following ways:

- *denial of responsibility* – informal entrepreneurs can view publicity about the negative impacts of informal entrepreneurship to be the result of others, who could even possibly be bigger players than them rather than a result of their own actions.
- *denial of injury* – informal entrepreneurs can deny that their informal economic activity has had negative impacts on others and rationalise their behaviour by asserting that without them participating in transactions in the informal sector, customers would have to pay a higher price or be unable to afford to receive the services provided.
- *denial of victim* – informal entrepreneurs may accept the negative impacts of their informality but believe that the victims deserve it.
- *condemnation of condemners* – informal entrepreneurs may assert that the law, the lawmakers and law enforcers are to blame for an unjust system and believe that the community should not succumb to these formal rules and that this makes operating in the informal sector a socially legitimate activity.
- *appeal to higher loyalties* – informal entrepreneurs may justify their actions in terms of some alternative set of loyalties or social order, believing that this justifies their actions.

- *metaphor of the ledger* – informal entrepreneurs may believe that their actions, although bad, do not reflect their true and good nature as people and regard these actions as temporary deviations from what is otherwise good behaviour.
- *defence of necessity* – informal entrepreneurs may justify their actions to be the outcome of personal circumstances such as that they cannot access formal employment and engage in informal entrepreneurship out of necessity as a survival practice.

Given this, awareness-raising campaigns targeted at informal entrepreneurs perhaps need to focus upon the benefits of formalisation, not the risks and costs of informal entrepreneurship. If they do focus upon the latter, it will be necessary to ensure that these possibilities are not open to informal entrepreneurs to deny their guilt. For example, to prevent a denial of responsibility, it may be that the average level of evasion among the non-compliant should be made public so that informal entrepreneurs do not see themselves as a 'small fish' engaged in minor discrepancies relative to others.

Indeed, the little evidence available seems to show that such marketing campaigns are effective and cost efficient. In the UK, an evaluation of the advertising campaigns run by the tax office reveals that as a result, some 8,300 additional people registered to pay tax who would not have otherwise done so, paying tax of £38 million over three years, providing a return of 19:1 on the expenditure of £2 million. This compares with an overall return of 4.5:1 on the £41 million a year spent on all its compliance work in 2006–2007 (National Audit Office, 2008).

To be effective, however, any campaign has to use tailored advertisements that will vary in terms of the medium used, content and form depending on the specific types of informal entrepreneurship and entrepreneur targeted. The language and media used, wording and slogans that will appeal to one group, such as older informal entrepreneurs, will not be effective for younger entrepreneurs. Similarly the most effective medium to communicate the messages for one group, such as newspaper adverts, will not be for the younger generation, who are more focused upon social media platforms. There are also lessons to be learned from the advertising industry more broadly. Politicians, commercial advertisers and charities for example know that celebrity endorsement can be an effective tool for advertising campaigns. Tax and labour administrations could similarly use celebrities and/or opinion leaders for their own marketing campaigns.

If this use of celebrities and opinion leaders is pursued by tax and labour administrations when mounting marketing campaigns, then as Lessing and Park (1978) identify, three types of campaign need to be distinguished. Firstly, there are information campaigns when entrepreneurs lacking knowledge turn to opinion leaders for information, such as highly respected finance and economics experts via TV commercials, talk shows and newspaper articles. Secondly, there are utilitarian campaigns when entrepreneurs are motivated through hearing about others who are rewarded or punished, such as when names are published of celebrities who pay taxes and/or celebrities who have not and have been punished. Finally, there are value-expressive campaigns when entrepreneurs associate themselves with positive role models who have the values or attributes deemed highly desirable by the aspiring individuals. Given that the entrepreneur is often portrayed as an ideal type heroic figure, as Chapter 1 described, measured by the gap between the subject and the object of desire, value-expressive campaigns using positive role models who act legitimately when addressing informal entrepreneurs is a useful strategy. Such value-expressive campaigns can publicise the formal entrepreneurship of famous entrepreneurs and business tycoons who can act as role models and heroic figureheads for these informal entrepreneurs.

Using Normative Appeals

Normative appeals to entrepreneurs to formalise are another potential way forward. Their effectiveness, however, depends in part on the nature of the appeal made. Chung and Trivedi (2003) examine the impact of normative appeals on a friendly persuasion group who were required to both generate and read a list of reasons why they should comply fully and were compared with a control group not asked to do so. Participants earned $30 by filling in two questionnaires. The friendly persuasion group were required firstly to generate and secondly to read a list of reasons why they should comply fully and were compared with a control group not asked to do so. Participants in both groups were asked to report the income they earned and pay tax on the reported income. The results show a significant difference between the friendly persuasion and control group on income reported. The participants in the friendly persuasion groups report higher earnings than the control group.

Hasseldine *et al.* (2007), meanwhile, examined 7,300 sole proprietors in the UK. Comparing the effect of five different letters ranging from a simple offer of assistance to a letter advising that his/her tax return had been already pre-selected for audit, they find that tax compliance appeals resulted in greater compliance, particularly among those who do not use a paid preparer such as an accountant to prepare their self-assessment tax return. Sanction appeals however, were more effective than normative appeals for both self-preparers as well as paid preparer returns. This, however, is in a context in which there is a widespread belief that the state is a 'big brother' figure that is all-knowing and all seeing. It would perhaps be a different outcome in developing countries where the perception is that the state is weaker, powerless and less all-knowing.

Changing the Formal Institutions

Besides changing the norms, values and beliefs of entrepreneurs to align them with the codes and regulations of the formal institutions, policy can also seek to change the formal institutions. This is particularly important in societies in which there is a lack of trust in government, such as due to public sector corruption (European Commission, 2014), in societies where entrepreneurs do not believe that they receive back from government what they expect or in societies where formal institutional voids and weaknesses reduce the benefits of formalisation. Two types of change are required so far as formal institutions are concerned. Firstly, there is often a need to change internal *processes* in the formal institutions to improve the perception among entrepreneurs that there is procedural and redistributive justice and fairness. Secondly, there is often a need to change the *products* of formal institutions by pursuing wider economic and social developments. Here each is considered in turn starting with the changes required in the internal processes of the formal institutions.

Modernising Governance

To improve the social contract between government and entrepreneurs, and as Part II revealed, entrepreneurs will not formalise if there remains a low level of trust in government and extensive public sector corruption. A modernisation of governance is thus necessary to address what are perceived as formal institutional resource misallocations and inefficiencies. This requires at least three institutional reforms. Firstly, procedural justice must be improved, which here refers to the authorities treating entrepreneurs in a respectful, impartial and responsible manner and thus shifting away from a 'cops and robbers' approach and towards a service-oriented approach. Secondly, procedural fairness must be enhanced, which refers to entrepreneurs believing that they pay their fair share compared with others and, finally, redistributive justice needs improving, which relates to whether entrepreneurs believe that they receive the goods and services they deserve given the taxes they pay. Each is here considered in turn.

Improving Procedural Justice

Procedural justice refers to whether entrepreneurs view the government as dealing with them in a respectful, impartial and responsible manner (Braithwaite and Reinhart, 2000, Murphy, 2005; Taylor, 2005; Tyler, 1997, Wenzel, 2002). This has a significant effect on the level of compliance. If entrepreneurs view tax administration for example as treating them in such a manner, then they have been found to be more likely to engage in compliant behaviour (Hartner *et al.*, 2008; Murphy, 2003; Murphy *et al.*, 2009; Torgler and Schneider, 2007; Wenzel, 2002). Leventhal (1980) formulated the following six rules regarding procedural justice:

- The consistency rule means that procedures should be consistently applied across all people and over time; nobody should be more favoured or disadvantaged compared with others.

- The bias suppression rule points out that egoistic intentions and prejudice on the part of the decision-makers must be avoided.
- The accuracy rule says that all relevant sources of information should be exhausted in order that decisions are based on well-founded evidence and information.
- The correctability rule refers to the possibility that decisions made can be adjusted or revised in the light of evidence.
- The representativeness rule means that the interests and opinions of all stakeholders and individuals involved should be considered.
- The ethicality rule emphasises that procedures should be in accord with the prevailing moral and ethical values.

Leventhal's rules deal primarily with the decision-making process. However, Bies and Moag (1986) emphasise the importance of additionally considering interpersonal interactions. People want respectful and fair treatment, by which is meant interactional fairness with the authorities. As Wenzel (2006) finds, compliance rates are significantly higher among taxpayers who perceived there to be interactional fairness. When entrepreneurs and other taxpayers are treated politely, with respect and dignity, are given a say and have genuine respect shown for their rights and social status, compliance improves (Alm *et al.*, 1993; Feld and Frey, 2002; Gangl *et al.*, 2013; Hartner *et al.*, 2008; Murphy, 2005; Tyler, 1997, 2006; Wenzel, 2002).

However, if entrepreneurs perceive that they are being treated unfairly or unreasonably, such as by inspectors showing disrespect for them, or they believe that taxes are collected and being used to support the interests of powerful private interests who have captured the state, this results in a lack of trust and lower compliance rates (Murphy, 2008). The current prevalence of a 'cops-and-robbers' approach in many tax and labour inspectorates that views entrepreneurs as 'robbers' and the inspectors as 'cops' policing their criminal behaviour, compounds this view of entrepreneurs that little respect is being shown to them (Murphy, 2003, 2005, 2008). There is thus a need to shift from such a 'cops-and-robbers' approach and towards a customer-service-oriented approach which treats entrepreneurs with respect and dignity in their dealings with the state. Examples of this approach can be seen in Australia (Job and Honaker, 2002), Singapore (Alm *et al.*, 2010) and the United States (Rainey and Bozeman, 2000). This treatment of enterprises and entrepreneurs as clients rather than criminals is part of the 'new public management' (Lane, 2000; Osbourne, 1993). This advocates the development of customer-friendly services as part of a market-oriented business strategy and 'good governance' (Bovaird and Löffler, 2003; Gemma-Martinez, 2011; Job and Honaker, 2002; Lane, 2000; Osbourne, 1993). The overarching goal of such an approach is to improve the trust and confidence of entrepreneurs and taxpayers in public administrations, politicians and governance (Bouckeart and van de Walle, 2003; Heintzman and Marson, 2005).

Improving Procedural Fairness

Procedural fairness refers to whether entrepreneurs feel that they are being treated in a fair manner relative to others and that they pay their fair share compared with others (Kinsey and Gramsick, 1993; Wenzel, 2004a,b). Entrepreneurs who perceive that they receive procedurally fair treatment tend to be more likely to trust the authorities and to be more inclined to accept and follow the formal rules (Murphy, 2005). The fairness of the tax system is one of the most important determinants of whether they do so (Bobeck and Hatfield, 2003; Hartner *et al.*, 2008, 2011; Kirchgässner, 2010, 2011; McGee, 2005, 2008; McGee *et al.*, 2008; Molero and Pujol, 2012).

Conversely where there are grievances among entrepreneurs that they are not receiving fair treatment, there is a significant rise in non-compliance (Bird *et al.*, 2006). As Molero and Pujol (2012) find, where there is grievance either in absolute terms (e.g., they feel taxes are too high or public money wasted) or grievances in relative terms (e.g., there is a lack of horizontal trust that others are not cheating), the result is informality. Indeed entrepreneurs can justify their informality using their perceptions of the activities of others. If informal entrepreneurship is viewed as widespread, then this justifies their non-compliant behaviour. This has important implications. If governments publicise that informal entrepreneurship is rife, they create the conditions for widespread grievance and thus even wider participation in informal entrepreneurship by those who might not otherwise have done so.

Similarly if entrepreneurs believe that administrations display disapproval towards them that is stigmatic and displays disrespect, such as labelling them with outcast identities (e.g., thief or tax cheat), the result is continued re-offending since the entrepreneur externalises the blame and feels alienated (Ahmed and Braithwaite, 2004, 2005; Braithwaite and Braithwaite, 2001). Murphy and Harris (2007) analysed 652 offenders and found that those deeming their experience as stigmatising displayed remorse and were more likely to report having evaded tax two years later. Being treated in what is perceived to be a fair manner is thus an important determinant of informal entrepreneurship.

Redistributive Justice

Redistributive justice refers to whether entrepreneurs feel that they receive the goods and services they deserve given the taxes that they pay (Kinsey and Gramsick, 1993; Kinsey *et al.*, 1991; Richardson and Sawyer, 2001; Thurman *et al.*, 1984). Taxes are prices entrepreneurs and citizens pay for the public goods and services that governments provide. The question for the moral evaluation of taxes is whether the price corresponds to the perceived value of these goods and services (i.e., whether it is seen as 'just'), namely, whether there is a 'just price' (Kirchgässner, 2010). Entrepreneurs will be more likely to operate informally and to break the social contract with the state the less they perceive the tax system as just (McGee, 2005). To achieve a high rate of compliance, therefore, the tax system must be seen as just. The result is that governments need to educate entrepreneurs about where their taxes are spent. In situations where entrepreneurs do not know, or do not fully understand what public goods and services are provided with their taxes, then compliance is lower than in situations where citizens are more fully aware of what public goods and services are received and they agree with how their taxes are spent (Lillemets, 2009). There is a need, therefore, for government to explain how taxes are spent and to elicit agreement regarding the public goods and services that are provided by government.

Wider Economic and Social Developments

To formalise informal entrepreneurship, it is also necessary to deal with other formal institutional failures that lead to institutional asymmetry, including the existence of formal institutional voids and weaknesses. This requires wider economic and social developments to be pursued as revealed in Chapter 6. Until now, there have been three theoretical standpoints regarding the specific broader economic and social developments required to formalise informal entrepreneurship. Firstly, the 'modernisation' thesis purports that informal entrepreneurship decreases as economies modernise and develop and therefore that economic development and growth, along with the modernisation of governance, are required to formalise informal entrepreneurship. Secondly, the 'neo-liberal' thesis asserts that the prevalence of informal entrepreneurship is a direct result of high taxes, public sector corruption and state interference in the free market and therefore that tax reductions and reducing the regulatory burden are required (De Soto, 1989, 2001; London and Hart, 2004; Nwabuzor, 2005; Sauvy, 1984; Schneider and Williams, 2013). Finally, the 'political economy' thesis asserts that informal entrepreneurship results from inadequate levels of state intervention in work and welfare and, consequently, that greater social protection, reducing inequality and pursuing labour market interventions to help vulnerable groups are required (Castells and Portes, 1989; Davis, 2006; Gallin, 2001; Slavnic, 2010; Taiwo, 2013).

As shown in Chapter 6 of this book, an evaluation of these competing perspectives reveals that the modernisation and political economy theses are positively confirmed, and the neo-liberal thesis is negatively confirmed. This add further weight to previous studies that have evaluated these competing theses using small data sets (Vanderseypen *et al.*, 2013; Williams, 2013, 2014a,b,c,d; Williams *et al.*, 2013; Windebank and Horodnic, 2016, 2017). Analysing the relationship between cross-national variations in the level of informal entrepreneurship and cross-national variations in the various aspects of the broader economic and social environment deemed important by each of these perspectives, Chapter 6 revealed the need for a synthesis of various tenets of the modernisation and political economy theses. It reveals that informal entrepreneurship is lower in wealthier economies with stable, high-quality government bureaucracies and those with greater levels of state intervention in work and welfare.

Conclusions

This chapter has reviewed a means of tackling informal entrepreneurship that goes beyond the current reliance on a hard direct controls approach, in general, and the use of 'sticks' to ensure that the costs and risks of engaging in informal entrepreneurship outweigh the benefits of doing so. To do this, it has proposed that greater emphasis should be put on soft indirect commitment measures that encourage a social contract to be forged. In many societies, there is an incongruity among the laws, codes and regulations of formal institutions and the norms, beliefs and values of informal institutions. Informal entrepreneurship takes place when the norms, values and beliefs differ to the laws, codes and regulations, resulting in what formal institutions deem to be illegal activities to be legitimate in terms of the norms, values and beliefs of the society or particular population groups. To tackle informal entrepreneurship, therefore, a reduction in this institutional incongruence is required.

On the one hand, this can be achieved by changing the norms, values and beliefs regarding the acceptability of entrepreneurship in the informal sector so that these informal institutions align with the laws, regulations and codes of the formal institutions. The measures reviewed that can achieve this include awareness-raising campaigns about the costs of informal entrepreneurship and benefits of formal entrepreneurship as well as education initiatives and normative appeals. On the other hand, one can change the formal institutions to align with the norms, values and beliefs of the wider society. This can be achieved by changing the processes of government to ensure that entrepreneurs believe that they are paying their fair share compared with others, receive the goods and services they believe that they deserve given what they pay, and believe that the authorities treat them in a respectful, impartial and responsible manner. It can also be achieved, as shown, by developing the broader economic and social conditions in a manner that has been shown to be correlated with reductions in the prevalence of informal entrepreneurship.

In practice, however, these are not mutually exclusive approaches. Changes in formal institutions shape, and are shaped by, changes in informal institutions, and changes in both are required to reduce the level of institutional incongruence. It is not only these two sets of policy measures that need combining if informal entrepreneurship is to be tackled effectively. There is also a need to combine the soft direct controls with measures associated with the hard direct approach to increase not only the power of, but also trust in, authorities.

However, to obtain a fuller understanding of how to combine and sequence the soft and hard measures when tackling informal entrepreneurship, evaluations will be required of which individual policy measures work and which do not, albeit perhaps in conjunction with other measures. Currently few evaluations exist of the effectiveness of even individual policy measures, never mind their effectiveness when used in conjunction with other measures or in different contexts. There is therefore a considerable amount of research required before solutions for specific contexts can be firmly advocated. Hopefully, nevertheless, Part III has begun to detail the range of approaches and measures that might be used to formalise informal entrepreneurship. What can be stated with certainty having reviewed the problem of informal entrepreneurship and its determinants, however, is that hard direct measures which solely focus upon increasing the penalties and risks of detection are not going to result in a formalisation of informal entrepreneurship. There is a need for governments to be much wider ranging in terms of their thinking and policy proposals than has so far been the case.

References

Ahmed, E. and Braithwaite, V. (2004). When tax collectors become collectors for child support and student loans: Jeopardising or protecting the revenue base? *Kyklos*, 3, pp. 303–326.

Ahmed, E. and Braithwaite, V. (2005). Understanding small business taxpayers: Issues of deterrence, tax morale, fairness and work practice. *International Small Business Journal*, 23(5), pp. 539–568.

Alm, J., Cherry, T., Jones, M. and McKee, M. (2010). Taxpayer information assistance services and tax compliance behaviour. *Journal of Economic Psychology*, 31, pp. 577–586.

Alm, J., Jackson, B. and McKee, M. (1993). Fiscal exchange, collective decision institutions and tax compliance. *Journal of Economic Behaviour and Organization*, 22, pp. 285–303.

Bies, R.J. and Moag, J.S. (1986). Interactional fairness. In: R.J. Lewicki, B.M. Sheppard and M.H. Bazerman, Eds., *Research on negotiations in organizations*. Greenwich, CT: Jai, pp. 43–55.

Bird, R., Martinez-Vazquez, J. and Torgler, B. (2006). Societal institutions and tax effort in developing countries. In: J. Alm, J. Martinez-Vazquez and M. Rider, Eds., *The challenges of tax reform in the global economy*. New York: Springer, pp. 283–338.

Bobeck, D.D. and Hatfield, R.C. (2003). An investigation of the theory of planned behaviour and the role of moral obligation in tax compliance. *Behavioural Research in Accounting*, 52(1), pp. 13–38.

Bouckeart, G. and van de Walle, S. (2003). Comparing measures of citizen trust and user satisfaction as indicators of 'good governance': Difficulties in linking trust and satisfaction indicators. *International Review of Administrative Science*, 69(2), pp. 329–343.

Bovaird, T. and Löffler, E. (2003). Evaluating the quality of public governance: Indicators, models and methodologies. *International Review of Administrative Science*, 69, pp. 313–328.

Braithwaite, J. and Braithwaite, V. (2001). Shame, shame management and regulation. In: E. Ahmed, N. Harris. J. Braithwaite and V. Braithwaite, Eds., *Shame management through reintegration*. Cambridge: Cambridge University Press, pp. 101–119.

Braithwaite, V. and Reinhart, M. (2000). *The taxpayers' charter: Does the Australian tax office comply and who benefits*. Canberra: Centre for Tax System Integrity Working Paper no. 1, Australian National University.

Castells, M. and Portes, A. (1989). World underneath: The origins, dynamics, and effects of the informal economy. In: A. Portes, M. Castells and L.A. Benton, Eds., *The informal economy: Studies in advanced and less developed countries*. Baltimore: The Johns Hopkins University Press, pp. 11–37.

Chung, J. and Trivedi, V.U. (2003). The effect of friendly persuasion and gender on tax compliance behaviour. *Journal of Business Ethics*, 47(2), pp. 133–145.

Davis, M. (2006). *Planet of slums*. London: Verso.

De Soto, H. (1989). *The other path*. London: Harper and Row.

De Soto, H. (2001). *The mystery of capital: Why capitalism triumphs in the West and fails everywhere else*. London: Black Swan.

European Commission (2014). *Eurobarometer survey on corruption*. Brussels: European Commission.

Feld, L.P. and Frey, B. (2002). Trust breeds trust: How taxpayers are treated. *Economics of Government*, 3(2), pp. 87–99.

Gallin, D. (2001). Propositions on trade unions and informal employment in time of globalization. *Antipode*, 19(4), pp. 531–549.

Gangl, K., Muehlbacher, S., de Groot, M., Goslinga, S., Hofmann, E., Kogler, C., Antonides, G. and Kirchler, E. (2013). 'How can I help you?': Perceived service orientation of tax authorities and tax compliance. *Public Finance Analysis*, 69(4), pp. 487–510.

Gemma-Martinez, B. (2011). The role of good governance in the tax systems of the European Union. *Bulletin for International Taxation*, 63, pp. 370–379.

Hartner, M., Rechberger, S., Kirchler, E. and Schabmann, A. (2008). Procedural justice and tax compliance. *Economic Analysis and Policy*, 38(1), pp. 137–152.

Hartner, M., Rechberger, S., Kirchler, E. and Wenzel, M. (2011). Perceived distributive fairness of EU transfer payments, outcome favourability, identity and EU-tax compliance. *Law and Policy*, 33(1), pp. 22–31.

Hasseldine, J. and Li, Z. (1999). More tax evasion research required in new millennium. *Crime, Law and Social Change*, 31(1), pp. 91–104.

Hasseldine, J., Hite, P., James, S. and Toumi, M. (2007). Persuasive communications: Tax compliance enforcement strategies for sole proprietors. *Contemporary Accounting Research*, 24(1), pp. 171–194.

Heintzman, R. and Marson, B. (2005). People, service and trust: Is there a public service chain? *International Review of Administrative Science*, 71, pp. 549–575.

Internal Revenue Service (2007). *Understanding taxes*. Available at: www.irs.gov/app/understandingTaxes/jsp/ (last accessed 14 May 2016).

Jibao, S. and Prichard, W. (2013). *Rebuilding local government finances after conflict: The political economy of property taxation in post-conflict Sierra Leone*. Brighton: ICTD Working Paper no. 12, Institute of Development Studies.

Job, J. and Honaker, D. (2002). Short term experience with responsive regulation in the Australian Tax Office. In: V. Braithwaite, Ed., *Taxing democracy: Understanding tax avoidance and tax evasion*. Aldershot: Ashgate, pp. 111–130.

Kinsey, K. and Gramsick, H. (1993). Did the tax reform act of 1986 improve compliance? Three studies of pre- and post-TRA compliance attitudes. *Law and Policy*, 15, pp. 239–325.

Kinsey, K., Gramsick, H. and Smith, K. (1991). Framing justice: Taxpayer evaluations of personal tax burdens. *Law and Society Review*, 25, pp. 845–873.

218   *Tackling Informal Sector Entrepreneurship*

Kirchgässner, G. (2010). *Tax morale, tax evasion and the shadow economy.* St Gallen: Discussion Paper no. 2010–17, Department of Economics, University of St. Gallen.

Kirchgässner, G. (2011). Tax morale, tax evasion and the shadow economy. In: F. Schneider, Ed., *Handbook of the shadow economy.* Cheltenham: Edward Elgar, pp. 347–374.

Korsun, G. and Meagher, P. (2004). Failure by design? Fiscal decentralization in West Africa. In: M. Kimenyi and P. Meagher, Eds., *Devolution and development: Governance prospects in decentralizing states.* Aldershot: Ashgate, pp. 137–195.

Lane, J.-E. (2000). *New public management.* London: Routledge.

Lessing, V.P. and Park, C.W. (1978). Promotional perspectives of reference group influence: Advertising implications. *Journal of Advertising,* 7(2), pp. 41–47.

Leventhal, G.S. (1980). What should be done with equity theory? New approaches to the study of fairness in social relationships. In: K. Gergen, M. Greenberg and R. Willis, Eds., *Social exchange: Advances in theory and research.* New York: Plenum Press, pp. 27–55.

Li, S.X., Eckel, C.C., Grossman, P.J. and Brown, T.L. (2011). Giving to government: Voluntary taxation in the lab. *Journal of Public Economics,* 95, pp. 1190–1201.

Lillemets, K. (2009). *Maksumoraal maksukäitumise kujundajana ja selle peamised isikupõhised mõjutegurid.* Available at: www.riigikogu.ee/rito/index.php?id=14002&op=archive2 (last accessed 11 May 2016).

London, T. and Hart, S.L. (2004). Reinventing strategies for emerging markets: Beyond the transnational model. *Journal of International Business Studies,* 35(5), pp. 350–370.

McGee, R.W. (2005). *The ethics of tax evasion: A survey of international business academics.* Paper presented at the 60th International Atlantic Economic Conference, New York, October 6–9.

McGee, R.W. (2008). *Taxation and public finance in transition and developing countries.* New York: Springer.

McGee, R.W., Alver, J. and Alver, L. (2008). The ethics of tax evasion: A survey of Estonian opinion. In: R.W. McGee, Ed., *Taxation and public finance in transition and developing countries.* Berlin: Springer, pp. 119–136.

Molero, J.C. and Pujol, F. (2012). Walking inside the potential tax evader's mind: Tax morale does matter. *Journal of Business Ethics,* 105, pp. 151–162.

Murphy, K. (2003). Procedural fairness and tax compliance. *Australian Journal of Social Issues,* 38(3), pp. 379–408.

Murphy, K. (2005). Regulating more effectively: The relationship between procedural justice, legitimacy and tax non-compliance. *Journal of Law and Society,* 32(4), pp. 562–589.

Murphy, K. (2008). Enforcing tax compliance: To punish or persuade? *Economic Analysis and Policy,* 38(1), pp. 113–135.

Murphy, K. and Harris, N. (2007). Shaming, shame and recidivism: A test of reintegrative shaming theory in the white-collar crime context. *British Journal of Criminology,* 47, pp. 900–917.

Murphy, K., Tyler, T. and Curtis, A. (2009). Nurturing regulatory compliance: Is procedural fairness effective when people question the legitimacy of the law? *Regulation and Governance,* 3, pp. 1–26.

National Audit Office (2008). *Tackling the hidden economy.* London: National Audit Office.

Natrah, S. (2013). Tax knowledge, tax complexity and tax compliance: Taxpayers' view. *Procedia: Social and Behavioural Sciences,* 109, pp. 1069–1076.

Nwabuzor, A. (2005). Corruption and development: New initiatives in economic openness and strengthened rule of law. *Journal of Business Ethics,* 59(1/2), pp. 121–138.

Osbourne, D. (1993). Reinventing government. *Public Productivity and Management Review*, 16, pp. 349–356.

Rainey, H.G. and Bozeman, B. (2000). Comparing public and private organizations: Empirical research and the power of the a priori. *Journal of Public Administration Research and Theory*, 10, pp. 447–470.

Richardson, M. and Sawyer, A. (2001). A taxonomy of the tax compliance literature: Further findings, problems and prospects. *Australian Tax Forum*, 16(2), pp. 137–320.

Saeed, A. and Shah, A. (2011). Enhancing tax morale with marketing tactics: A review of the literature. *African Journal of Business Management*, 5(35), pp. 13659–13665.

Sauvy, A. (1984). *Le travail noir et l'economie de demain*. Paris: Calmann-Levy.

Schneider, F. and Williams, C.C. (2013). *The shadow economy*. London: Institute of Economic Affairs.

Slavnic, Z. (2010). Political economy of informalisation. *European Societies*, 12(1), pp. 3–23.

Taiwo, O. (2013). Employment choice and mobility in multi-sector labour markets: Theoretical model and evidence from Ghana. *International Labour Review*, 152(3/4), pp. 469–492.

Taylor, N. (2005). Explaining taxpayer noncompliance through reference to taxpayer identities: A social identity perspective. In: C. Bajada and F. Schneider, Eds., *Size, causes and consequences of the underground economy: An international perspective*. Aldershot: Ashgate, pp. 39–54.

Thurman, Q.C., St. John, C. and Riggs, L. (1984). Neutralisation and tax evasion: How effective would a moral appeal be in improving compliance to tax laws? *Law and Policy*, 6(3), pp. 309–327.

Torgler, B. and Schneider, F. (2007). *Shadow economy, tax morale, governance and institutional quality: A panel analysis*. Bonn: IZA Discussion Paper no. 2563, IZA.

Tyler, T.R. (1997). The psychology of legitimacy: A relational perspective on voluntary deference to authorities. *Personality and Social Psychology Review*, 1(4), pp. 323–345.

Tyler, T.R. (2006). *Why people obey the law*. Princeton: Princeton University Press.

Vanderseypen, G., Tchipeva, T., Peschner, J., Renooy, P. and Williams, C.C. (2013). Undeclared work: Recent developments. In: European Commission, Ed., *Employment and social developments in Europe 2013*. Brussels: European Commission, pp. 231–274.

Vossler, C.A., McKee, M. and Jones, M. (2011). *Some effects of tax information services reliability and availability on tax reporting behaviour*. Available at: http://mpra.ub.uni-muenchen.de/38870/ (last accessed 11 May 2016).

Wenzel, M. (2002). The impact of outcome orientation and justice concerns on tax compliance: The role of taxpayers' identity. *Journal of Applied Psychology*, 87, pp. 639–645.

Wenzel, M. (2004a). An analysis of norm processes in tax compliance. *Journal of Economic Psychology*, 25(2), pp. 213–228.

Wenzel, M. (2004b). The social side of sanction: Personal and social norms as moderators of deterrence. *Law and Human Behaviour*, 28, pp. 547–567.

Wenzel, M. (2006). A letter from the tax office: Compliance effects of informational and interpersonal fairness. *Social Fairness Research*, 19, pp. 345–364.

Williams, C.C. (2013). Tackling Europe's informal economy: A critical evaluation of the neo-liberal de-regulatory perspective. *Journal of Contemporary European Research*, 9(3), pp. 261–279.

Williams, C.C. (2014a). Explaining cross-national variations in the commonality of informal sector entrepreneurship: An exploratory analysis of 38 emerging economies. *Journal of Small Business and Entrepreneurship*, 27(2), pp. 191–212.

Williams, C.C. (2014b). Out of the shadows: A classification of economies by the size and character of their informal sector. *Work, Employment and Society*, 28(5), pp. 735–753.

Williams, C.C. (2014c). Public policy approaches towards the undeclared economy in European countries: A critical overview. *European Labour Law Journal*, 5(2), pp. 132–155.

Williams, C.C. (2014d). Tackling enterprises operating in the informal sector in developing and transition economies: A critical evaluation of the neo-liberal policy approach. *Journal of Global Entrepreneurship Research*, 4(1), pp. 1–17.

Williams, C.C., Nadin, S., Newton, S., Rodgers, P. and Windebank, J. (2013). Explaining off-the-books entrepreneurship: A critical evaluation of competing perspectives. *International Entrepreneurship and Management Journal*, 9(3), pp. 447–463.

Windebank, J. and Horodnic, I. (2016). Explaining participation in informal employment: A social contract perspective. *International Journal of Entrepreneurship and Small Business*, 28(2/3), pp. 178–194.

Windebank, J. and Horodnic, I. (2017). Explaining participation in undeclared work in France: Lessons for policy evaluation, *International Journal of Sociology and Social Policy*, 37(5/6).

10 Conclusions

Introduction

In this concluding chapter, the intention is to synthesise the material from the previous chapters and draw conclusions about the way forward both for explaining and tackling informal sector entrepreneurship. To do so, Part I of this book set out the theoretical framework used and how this book has advanced this theoretical approach, namely, an institutional theory of informal entrepreneurship. The argument followed throughout this book has been that formal institutional imperfections and failures produce an asymmetry between formal and informal institutions, and the result is the greater prevalence of entrepreneurship in the informal sector. In the first part of the book, the various formal institutional failures and imperfections were introduced along with the competing views regarding what formal institutional failures and imperfections lead to greater institutional asymmetry and therefore the prevalence of informal entrepreneurship. Part II then reviewed the prevalence, impacts and reasons for informal entrepreneurship in global perspective followed in Part III by a review of the policy options and approaches for tackling informal entrepreneurship. In this chapter, an overview of the findings is presented.

Theorising Entrepreneurship in the Informal Sector

In Part I of this book, the theoretical framework used to understand entrepreneurship in the informal sector was set out along with how this book advances this theoretical lens. To do so, Chapter 2 displayed how scholarship on entrepreneurship in general, and on entrepreneurship in the informal sector in particular, has increasingly adopted the lens of institutional theory to explain entrepreneurial endeavour (Baumol and Blinder, 2008; Helmke and Levitsky, 2004; North, 1990). Seen through this lens, all societies have both formal institutions (i.e., codified laws and regulations) that set out the legal rules of the game as well as informal institutions which are the unwritten socially shared rules expressed in the norms, values and beliefs of entrepreneurs and citizens (Helmke and Levitsky, 2004). Informal entrepreneurship is a form of economic activity that takes place outside of formal institutional prescriptions but within the norms, values and beliefs of informal institutions (Godfrey, 2011; Kistruck *et al.*, 2015; Siqueira *et al.*, 2016; Webb *et al.*, 2009; Welter *et al.*, 2015). In a first wave of institutional theory, informal entrepreneurship was explained as resulting from formal institutional failings and imperfections, including formal institutional voids, inefficiencies, uncertainties and weaknesses. However, in a second wave of institutional theory, it was recognised that focusing upon solely formal institutional failings and imperfections ignores the role played by informal institutions (Godfrey, 2015; North, 1990; Scott, 2008), and informal entrepreneurship was viewed as arising due to the asymmetry between formal and informal institutions (Webb *et al.*, 2009). In this book, a third wave of institutional thought has been introduced. This synthesises the two previous waves of thought by arguing that when formal institutional failures and imperfections result in an asymmetry between formal and informal institutions, the result is a greater likelihood of informal entrepreneurship. These formal institutional failures and imperfections are of four types: formal institutional powerlessness, formal institutional resource misallocations and inefficiencies, formal institutional voids and weaknesses, and formal institutional instability and uncertainty.

To identify the precise nature of these various formal institutional failings and imperfections, Chapter 3 then turned attention to the theoretical explanations that have sought to determine the structural country-level determinants of informal entrepreneurship to set the scene for a theoretically informed evaluation of the formal institutional failings and imperfections that lead to institutional asymmetry and thus the prevalence of entrepreneurship in the informal sector. To do this, the various formal institutional failures identified in three major competing theories of informal entrepreneurship were reviewed, namely, modernisation theory, which pinpoints economic underdevelopment and unmodern systems of governance, manifested in high levels of corruption, as key determinants of informal entrepreneurship; neo-liberal theory, which focuses upon too much government intervention in the form of high taxes and burdensome regulations as key determinants; and political economy theory, which in stark contrast identifies inadequate state intervention and a lack of protection of workers as the key determinants of informal entrepreneurship. This then set the scene for an evaluation of which of these formal institutional failures are significantly associated with the greater prevalence of entrepreneurship in the informal sector in Part II of this book.

Informal Sector Entrepreneurship in Global Perspective

Part II of this book, therefore, provided an empirical evaluation of the prevalence, impacts and determinants of entrepreneurship in the informal sector. In Chapter 4, the findings were reported regarding the variations in the prevalence of informal entrepreneurship. This evaluated the scale and distribution of informal entrepreneurship on a global perspective. It revealed that whether the GEM, ILO or WBES data set is used, informal entrepreneurship is not some minor activity existing in a few marginal enclaves of the world economy. Rather, it is an omnipresent endeavour that constitutes a significant share of all businesses and employs a large share of the global workforce. The ILO data set on 38 developing countries for example reveals that one-quarter (25.3 per cent) of the non-agricultural workforce engages in informal sector entrepreneurship as their main job and that 40.6 per cent of the workforce across these 38 developing countries are either informal sector entrepreneurs or are employed in their main job in informal sector enterprises. The WBES across a much wider range of 142 countries reveals not only that one in five (19.9 per cent) formal enterprises started up unregistered and operate in the informal sector, but also that 41.9 per cent of formal businesses identify themselves as competing against unregistered or formal firms, and over one-quarter (26.9 per cent) of all formal enterprises surveyed identify that competitors in the informal sector are a major constraint. Whatever measure is used to evaluate the scale of informal entrepreneurship, therefore, its scale is far from minor.

However, informal entrepreneurship is not evenly distributed across all global regions. Whether the ILO or WBES data are used, and whatever the measurement indicator, Chapter 4 revealed that the informal entrepreneurship is more prevalent in developing regions, especially sub-Saharan Africa and South Asia, and far less prevalent in developed regions, such as the OECD nations, Europe and Central Asia.

There are also sectoral variations. The proportion of formal enterprises with five or more employees competing against unregistered or informal enterprises ranges at the top end from 51.7 per cent in the wood and furniture sector and 49.3 per cent in the wholesale and retail trade to 32.7 per cent in the chemicals and pharmaceutical industry and 31.3 per cent in the electronics sector. Similarly the share of formal firms identifying competitors in the informal sector as a major obstacle ranges from 35.6 per cent of formal firms in the garment industry and 29.9 per cent in the food industry to 17.6 per cent in the electronics industry. Therefore, there are some marked variations across sectors in the proportion of formal enterprises competing with unregistered or informal competitors and the share viewing informal competitors as a major obstacle.

Moreover, a multivariate probit regression analysis revealed a statistically significant association between whether a formal business started up unregistered and its level of trust in formal institutions (i.e., the greater the trust, the less likely they are to have started up unregistered). This provides support for the institutional asymmetry thesis that the prevalence of informal entrepreneurship is strongly correlated with the level of institutional asymmetry; the greater the lack of alignment between formal and informal institutions, the greater is the prevalence of informal entrepreneurship.

Informal entrepreneurship was also found in Chapter 4 to be significantly associated with firm age (i.e., older firms are more likely to have started up unregistered), whether they are exporting and foreign owned (i.e., non-exporting and domestic-owned firms are more likely to have started up unregistered), workforce characteristics (i.e., formal firms that started up unregistered are less likely to employ full-time permanent workers, intimating that the 'standard employment relationship' against which worker rights and protection are attached is more likely to be found in firms that started up registered), technology and innovation (i.e., firms with quality certifications and who use external auditors, websites and email are less likely to have started up unregistered), firm size (i.e., medium and large formal firms are significantly less likely to have started up unregistered) and legal status (i.e., a limited partnership or closed shareholding is less likely to have started unregistered).

Turning to whether formal firms compete against unregistered or informal firms and if they are a major constraint on their operations, the finding was that this is significantly more prevalent when trust in the formal institutions is low, among older, domestic-owned and non-exporting firms, those less likely to employ full-time permanent workers (suggesting that informality reduces the existence of the 'standard employment relationship'), with less top manager experience (intimating that this is a way of reducing competition with informal firms), without women's involvement in the ownership structure, with fewer innovative practices (without quality certification and a website) and among smaller firms, sole proprietors and partnership arrangements.

With this understanding of the overall scale and distribution of informal entrepreneurship in hand, Chapter 5 then turned to evaluating the impacts of informal entrepreneurship. Until now, there has been a tendency to cast informal entrepreneurship in a negative light, emphasising largely its deleterious features. Whether this is a valid portrayal was put under the spotlight, examining some potentially positive features of informal entrepreneurship, such as how it provides more affordable goods and services for low-income markets, creates employment and acts as a test bed for fledgling enterprises and breeding grounds for the microenterprise system. This more positive representation of informal entrepreneurship was then advanced by putting under the spotlight the dominant depiction of informal entrepreneurship as 'unproductive' endeavour (Baumol, 1990) and informal enterprises as inefficient, low-productivity and low-performing enterprises unworthy of investment and support. To do so, this chapter evaluated the impacts of starting up unregistered on future firm performance. It revealed how enterprises that started up unregistered, and stayed unregistered for longer before registering, display higher levels of future firm performance than those that registered from the outset.

Formal enterprises that started up unregistered witness 19.4 per cent higher average annual sales growth than enterprises starting up registered (i.e., 8.6 per cent compared with 7.2 per cent) and 34.7 per cent higher annual employment growth than enterprises registered at start-up (i.e., 6.6 per cent compared with 4.9 per cent). Moreover, the longer start-ups spend unregistered before registering, the better are their annual sales and employment growth rates. For each year a firm remains unregistered, annual sales growth rates are 0.149 percentage points higher and annual employment growth rates 0.177 percentage points higher than for registered start-ups, and the turning point after which it is no longer beneficial in terms of firm performance to remain unregistered is greater than 60 years for annual sales growth rates and 80 years for annual employment growth rates. Contrary to previous assertions, furthermore, no significant differences exist in future annual productivity growth rates of formal enterprises starting up registered and unregistered. The outcome was to provide a strong rationale for paying greater policy attention to formalising informal entrepreneurship.

Chapter 5 then concluded by showing how such findings on the positive impacts of starting up unregistered and remaining unregistered, which contest previous normative assumptions, provide a strong rationale for a more rigorous evaluation of the other normatively driven views regarding the advantages and disadvantages of informal entrepreneurship. Until now, many of the assumptions about its advantages and disadvantages have not been subjected to an evidence-based evaluation, such as that customers benefit from more affordable goods and services. Until these costs and benefits of informal entrepreneurship are evaluated, the overall net impact of informal entrepreneurship will not be known. Indeed such an evidence-based evaluation of each of its purported positive and negative features provides a major agenda for future research on informal entrepreneurship.

Having outlined the extent and nature of informal entrepreneurship, and discussed the impacts of starting up unregistered on subsequent firm performance, Chapter 6 turned its attention to explaining the cross-national variations in informal entrepreneurship that had been identified in Chapter 4. As Part I of the book highlighted, recent years have seen the emergence of an institutional theory approach which asserts that when formal institutional failures result in an asymmetry between the formal and informal institutions, informal entrepreneurship is more prevalent. This chapter, therefore, firstly evaluated whether there is a significant association between the prevalence of informal entrepreneurship and institutional asymmetry and, secondly, sought to identify the formal institutional failures that are associated with the greater prevalence of informal entrepreneurship.

Analysing WBES data from 142 countries collected between 2006 and 2014 on the extent to which formal firms identify that they are competing with unregistered or informal competitors, a multivariate regression analysis revealed not only the validity of the institutional asymmetry thesis, which asserts that the greater the institutional asymmetry, the higher are the levels of informal entrepreneurship, but also the formal institutional failures that are associated with the greater prevalence of informal entrepreneurship. This positively confirmed the modernisation and political economy explanations and negatively confirmed the tenets of the neo-liberal thesis. The finding is that the prevalence of informal entrepreneurship is greater when there is a lower level of economic development and lower quality of governance but also lower levels of state intervention. The likelihood of formal firms competing with unregistered or informal enterprises is higher in countries where GDP per capita is lower, there are higher levels of corruption, regulations are lower, the tax revenue-to-GDP ratio is lower and expenditure on the state is lower as a proportion of GDP.

Tackling Informal Sector Entrepreneurship

Having provided this understanding of the variations in the prevalence of informal entrepreneurship, the impacts of starting up unregistered and the range of formal institutional failures that lead to higher levels of informal entrepreneurship, Part III turned its attention to how to tackle entrepreneurship in the informal sector. To commence, Chapter 7 reviewed four hypothetical policy goals: do nothing, deregulate formal entrepreneurship, eradicate informal entrepreneurship or formalise informal entrepreneurship. Reviewing the range of advantages and disadvantages of each of these goals, this chapter revealed that formalising informal entrepreneurship is the most viable policy choice. Given this goal, Chapter 7 then concluded by outlining the policy approaches and measures available for formalising informal entrepreneurship.

On the one hand, and reviewed in-depth in Chapter 8, there is the hard direct policy approach that not only seeks to dissuade entrepreneurs from operating in the informal sector but also to incentivise and encourage them to operate in the formal sector. These hard direct policy measures therefore seek to directly increase the costs, and reduce the benefits of informality, and reduce the costs and increase the benefits of operating in the formal sector. In doing so, the intention is to tackle those formal institutional failures, such as the powerlessness of formal institutions, which result in the greater prevalence of informal entrepreneurship. Using these policy measures alone, however, does not tackle the full range of formal institutional failures that produce institutional asymmetry and thus the greater prevalence of informal entrepreneurship. They only tackle one aspect of the formal institutional failings that result in the prevalence of informal entrepreneurship, namely, the relative powerless of the enforcement regime.

On the other hand, therefore, and to tackle the other formal institutional failures that lead to institutional symmetry and the greater prevalence of informal entrepreneurship, a 'soft' indirect policy approach has been outlined and reviewed in Chapter 9. This approach tackles the other formal institutional failings, namely, the formal institutional resource misallocations and inefficiencies, voids and weaknesses, and instability and uncertainty. The policy measures in this approach are twofold. Firstly, and to reduce institutional asymmetry, a series of educational and awareness-raising initiatives are pursued to bring the norms, values and beliefs of entrepreneurs and citizens more into line with the codified laws and regulations. Indeed, across many countries, there has been a focus upon awareness-raising campaigns that have the objective of changing the norms, values and beliefs of entrepreneurs and citizens to align the formal and informal institutions. However, the likelihood of these campaigns bringing into symmetry the formal and informal institutions is small, unless the other formal institutional failures and imperfections are solved that have resulted in this institutional asymmetry, namely, the formal institutional resource misallocations and inefficiencies and the formal institutional voids and weaknesses.

Secondly, therefore, reform of the formal institutions was proposed in Chapter 9 to make them more palatable to entrepreneurs and citizens. These initiatives include not only a variety of process innovations across government that develop the perceived level of procedural and redistributive justice and fairness of government to reduce institutional symmetry but also the tackling of the various wider formal institutional failures which Part II revealed are significantly associated with greater institutional asymmetry, such as increasing the level of regulation, tax revenue as a percentage of GDP and the expense of government as a percentage of GDP.

These two broad policy approaches of pursuing hard direct and soft indirect policy measures are not either/or choices. They are not mutually exclusive. Given that each policy approach tackles a different set of formal institutional failures and imperfections, both are required to tackle informal entrepreneurship. In recent years, therefore, debate has occurred about how these should be combined and sequenced. On the one hand, a responsive regulation approach has been advocated that combines all these approaches but sequences them by starting with the soft policy measures, and if these do not have the desired effect, then hard incentives to encourage formalisation are used, and as a last resort when all else fails, the hard deterrents are employed (Braithwaite, 2002). On the other hand, a slippery slope approach has been advocated, which argues that compliance is greatest when both the power of authorities (achieved by using a hard direct policy approach and measures) and trust in authorities (achieved using a soft indirect policy approach and measures) is high (Kirchler *et al.*, 2008). If either the power of, or trust in, authorities is low, then governments will find themselves on a slippery slope, and informal entrepreneurship will prevail.

Which of these two ways of combining and sequencing these hard direct and soft indirect policy approaches and measures is most effective has not been resolved. More research is therefore required on which way of combining these policy approaches and measures is most effective in different contexts is now required.

However, to obtain a fuller understanding of how to combine and sequence the hard direct and soft indirect measures when tackling informal entrepreneurship, evaluations will be required of which individual policy measures work and which do not, albeit perhaps in conjunction with other measures. Currently few evaluations exist of the effectiveness of even individual policy measures, never mind their effectiveness when used in conjunction with other measures or in which contexts. There is therefore a considerable amount of research required before solutions for specific contexts can be firmly advocated. Hopefully, nevertheless, this book has started to detail the range of potential approaches and measures required to formalise informal entrepreneurship. What can be stated with certainty, however, is that hard direct measures which solely focus upon increasing the penalties and risks of detection are not going to result in a formalisation of informal entrepreneurship. There is a need for governments to be much wider ranging in terms of their thinking and policy proposals than has so far been the case.

In sum, if this book results in less normative and more evidence-based evaluations of the costs and benefits of informal entrepreneurship in different contexts, then it will have fulfilled one of its major intentions. If the outcome of this is then greater consideration of what should be done about informal entrepreneurship, along with a shift away from simply seeking to eradicate it by increasing the penalties and risks of detection, and towards using the full range of hard and soft policy measures available, then this book will have achieved its wider objective.

References

Baumol, W.J. (1990). Entrepreneurship: Productive, unproductive, and destructive. *Journal of Political Economy*, 98(5), pp. 893–921.

Baumol, W.J. and Blinder, A. (2008). *Macroeconomics: Principles and policy*. Cincinnati, OH: South-Western Publishing.

Braithwaite, J. (2002). *Restorative justice and responsive regulation*. New York: Oxford University Press.

Godfrey, P.C. (2011). Toward a theory of the informal economy. *Academy of Management Annals*, 5(1), pp. 231–277.

Godfrey, P.C. (2015). Introduction: Why the informal economy matters to management. In: P.C. Godfrey, Ed., *Management, society, and the informal economy*. London: Routledge, pp. 1–20.

Helmke, G. and Levitsky, S. (2004). Informal institutions and comparative politics: A research agenda. *Perspectives on Politics*, 2(6), pp. 725–740.

Kirchler, E., Hoelzl, E. and Wahl, I. (2008). Enforced versus voluntary tax compliance: The 'slippery slope' framework. *Journal of Economic Psychology*, 29, pp. 210–225.

Kistruck, G.M., Webb, J.W., Sutter, C.J. and Bailey, A.V.G. (2015). The double-edged sword of legitimacy in base-of-the-pyramid markets. *Journal of Business Venturing*, 30(3), pp. 436–451.

North, D.C. (1990). *Institutions, institutional change and economic performance*. Cambridge: Cambridge University Press.

Scott, W.R. (2008). *Institutions and organizations: Ideas and interests*. London: Sage.

Siqueira, A.C.O., Webb, J.W. and Bruton, G.D. (2016). Informal entrepreneurship and industry conditions. *Entrepreneurship Theory and Practice*, 40(1), pp. 177–200.

Webb, J.W., Tihanyi, L., Ireland, R.D. and Sirmon, D.G. (2009). You say illegal, I say legitimate: Entrepreneurship in the informal economy. *Academy of Management Review*, 34(3), pp. 492–510.

Welter, F., Smallbone, D. and Pobol, A. (2015). Entrepreneurial activity in the informal economy: A missing piece of the jigsaw puzzle. *Entrepreneurship and Regional Development*, 27(5/6), pp. 292–306.

Index

For Product Safety Concerns and Information please contact our EU
representative GPSR@taylorandfrancis.com
Taylor & Francis Verlag GmbH, Kaufingerstraße 24, 80331 München, Germany

www.ingramcontent.com/pod-product-compliance
Ingram Content Group UK Ltd.
Pitfield, Milton Keynes, MK11 3LW, UK
UKHW020939180425
457613UK00019B/471